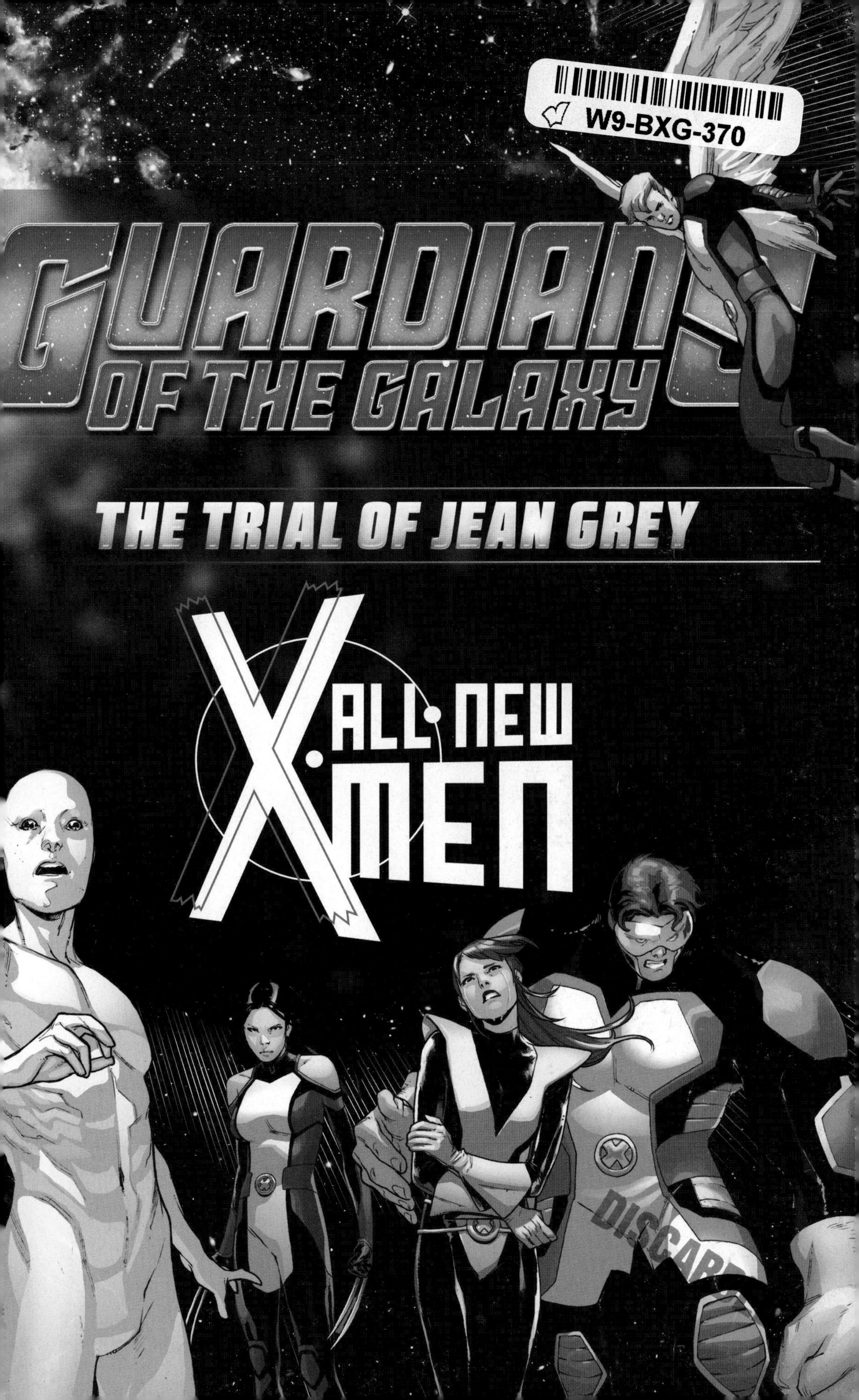

GUARDIANS OF THE GALAXY
THE TRIAL OF JEAN GREY
ALL-NEW X-MEN

GUARDIANS OF THE GALAXY/ALL-NEW X-MEN: THE TRIAL OF JEAN GREY. Contains material originally published in magazine form as GUARDIANS OF THE GALAXY #11-13 and ALL-NEW X-MEN #22-24 printing 2015. ISBN# 978-0-7851-6609-2. Published by MARVEL WORLDWIDE, INC., a subsidiary of MARVEL ENTERTAINMENT, LLC. OFFICE OF PUBLICATION: 135 West 50th Street, New York, NY 10020. Copy © 2014 and 2015 Marvel Characters, Inc. All rights reserved. All characters featured in this issue and the distinctive names and likenesses thereof, and all related indicia are trademarks of Marvel Chara Inc. No similarity between any of the names, characters, persons, and/or institutions in this magazine with those of any living or dead person or institution is intended, and any such similarity which may e purely coincidental. **Printed in the U.S.A.** ALAN FINE, EVP - Office of the President, Marvel Worldwide, Inc. and EVP & CMO Marvel Characters B.V.; DAN BUCKLEY, Publisher & President - Print, Animation & Divisions; JOE QUESADA, Chief Creative Officer; TOM BREVOORT, SVP of Publishing; DAVID BOGART, SVP of Operations & Procurement, Publishing; C.B. CEBULSKI, SVP of Creator & Content Development; GABRIEL, SVP Print, Sales & Marketing; JIM O'KEEFE, VP of Operations & Logistics; DAN CARR, Executive Director of Publishing Technology; SUSAN CRESPI, Editorial Operations Manager; ALEX MORALES, Publ Operations Manager; STAN LEE, Chairman Emeritus. For information regarding advertising in Marvel Comics or on Marvel.com, please contact Niza Disla, Director of Marvel Partnerships, at ndisla@marvel For Marvel subscription inquiries, please call 800-217-9158. **3**

10 9 8 7 6 5 4 3 2 1

TAR-LORD GAMORA ROCKET RACCOON GROOT DRAX ANGELA

GUARDIANS OF THE GALAXY / ALL-NEW X-MEN

THE TRIAL OF JEAN GREY

WRITER: **BRIAN MICHAEL BENDIS**

GUARDIANS OF THE GALAXY #11-13

ARTISTS: **SARA PICHELLI** WITH **STUART IMMONEN** (#12) & **DAVID MARQUEZ** (#13)
ADDITIONAL INKS, #12: **WADE VON GRAWBADGER** COLORIST: **JUSTIN PONSOR**
LETTERER: **VC'S CORY PETIT** COVER ART: **SARA PICHELLI & JUSTIN PONSOR**
EDITORS: **ELLIE PYLE** & **STEPHEN WACKER**

ALL-NEW X-MEN #22-24

PENCILER: **STUART IMMONEN** INKER: **WADE VON GRAWBADGER**
COLORIST: **MARTE GRACIA** LETTERER: **VC'S CORY PETIT**
COVER ART: **STUART IMMONEN, WADE VON GRAWBADGER & MARTE GRACIA**
ASSISTANT EDITOR: **XANDER JAROWEY** ASSOCIATE EDITOR: **JORDAN D. WHITE** EDITOR: **NICK LOWE**

X-MEN CREATED BY **STAN LEE** AND **JACK KIRBY**

COLLECTION EDITOR: **JENNIFER GRÜNWALD** ASSISTANT EDITOR: **SARAH BRUNSTAD**
ASSOCIATE MANAGING EDITOR: **ALEX STARBUCK** EDITOR, SPECIAL PROJECTS: **MARK D. BEAZLEY**
NIOR EDITOR, SPECIAL PROJECTS: **JEFF YOUNGQUIST** SVP PRINT, SALES & MARKETING: **DAVID GABRIEL**

EDITOR IN CHIEF: **AXEL ALONSO** CHIEF CREATIVE OFFICER: **JOE QUESADA**
PUBLISHER: **DAN BUCKLEY** EXECUTIVE PRODUCER: **ALAN FINE**

PREVIOUSLY IN GUARDIANS OF THE GALAXY...

PETER QUILL'S ESTRANGED FATHER, THE KING OF SPARTAX, TRIED TO CAPTURE THE GUARDIANS FOR DISOBEYING HIS NEW RULE THAT NO ALIEN HAND MAY TOUCH THE PLANET EARTH. IN RETURN, PETER SHAMED HIM WITH SOME COLORFUL PUBLIC DEFIANCE.

THE HUNTER/WARRIOR ANGELA HAS COME TO THIS GALAXY BECAUSE OF A TIME-SPACE CONTINUUM ACCIDENT. SHE IS TRYING TO FIGURE OUT HER PLACE IN THE GALAXY.

THANOS' ARMY CAME VERY CLOSE TO TAKING THE PLANET EARTH, BUT THE GUARDIANS HELPED SAVE THE PLANET. THE MAD TITAN HAS DISAPPEARED.

PREVIOUSLY IN ALL-NEW X-MEN...

THE ORIGINAL X-MEN WERE BROUGHT TO THE PRESENT TO HELP SHOW THE PRESENT-DAY X-MEN HOW FAR THEY HAVE STRAYED FROM XAVIER'S DREAM. AFTER LEARNING OF THEIR FUTURE, THE ORIGINAL X-MEN FOUND THEMSELVES IN CONFLICT WITH ONE ANOTHER AS THEY TRIED TO COME TO GRIPS WITH WHAT THEIR DESTINY WILL BRING. THIS ESPECIALLY AFFECTED JEAN GREY AND SCOTT SUMMERS AS THEY LEARNED OF THEIR FUTURE TOGETHER AND JEAN'S SUBSEQUENT DEATHS.

ALTHOUGH THEY HAVE ATTEMPTED TO RETURN TO THEIR OWN TIME, THEY DISCOVERED THAT THEY ARE, IN FACT, STUCK IN THE PRESENT. RECENTLY MOVING FROM WOLVERINE'S JEAN GREY SCHOOL TO PRESENT-DAY CYCLOPS' NEW XAVIER SCHOOL, THEY HAVE BEEN JOINED BY THE NEWLY RESCUED X-23. YET, THIS NEW HOME MAY NOT BE AS SAFE AND SECURE AS THEY HAVE BEEN LED TO BELIEVE.

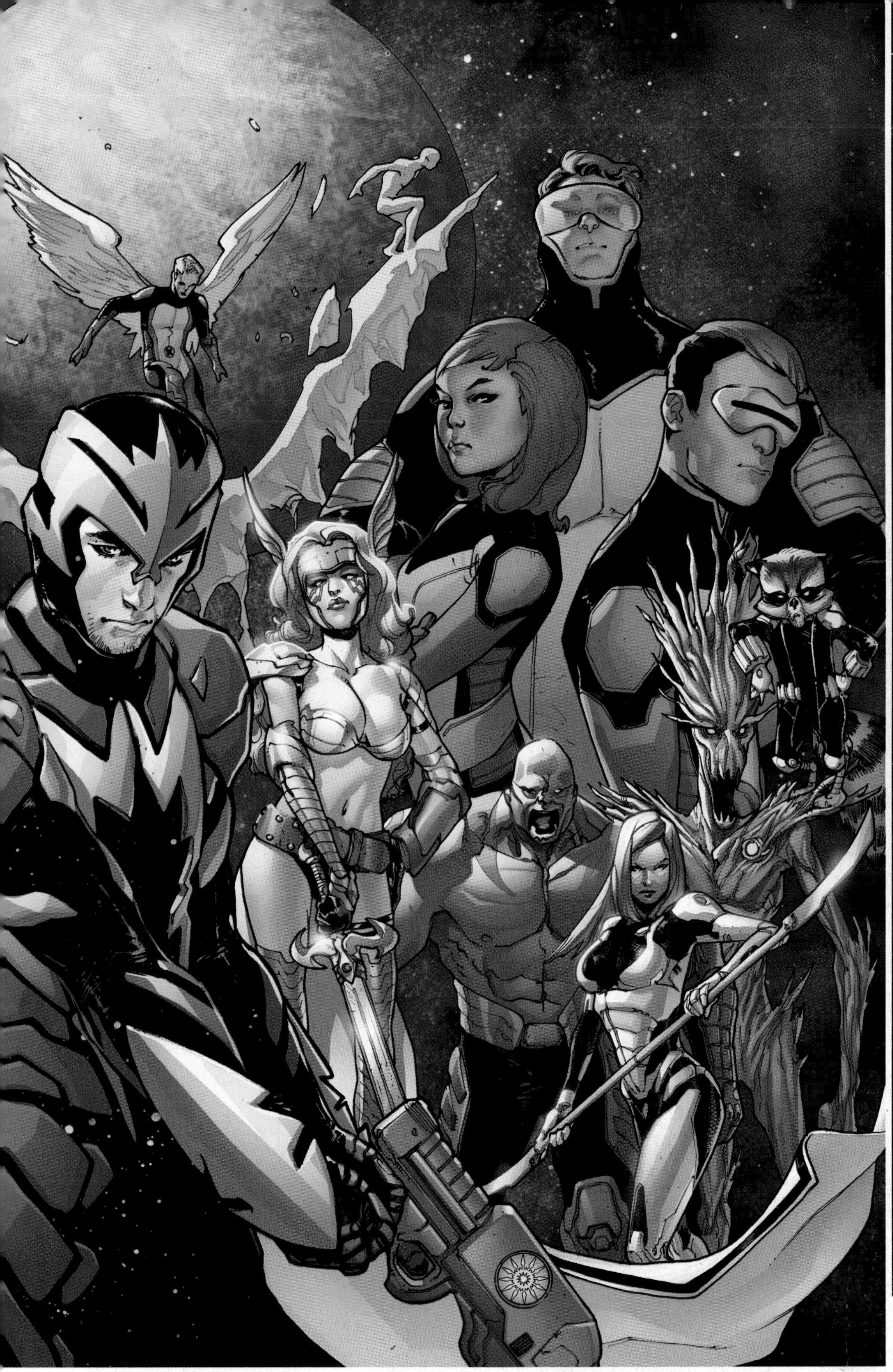

GUARDIANS OF THE GALAXY 11

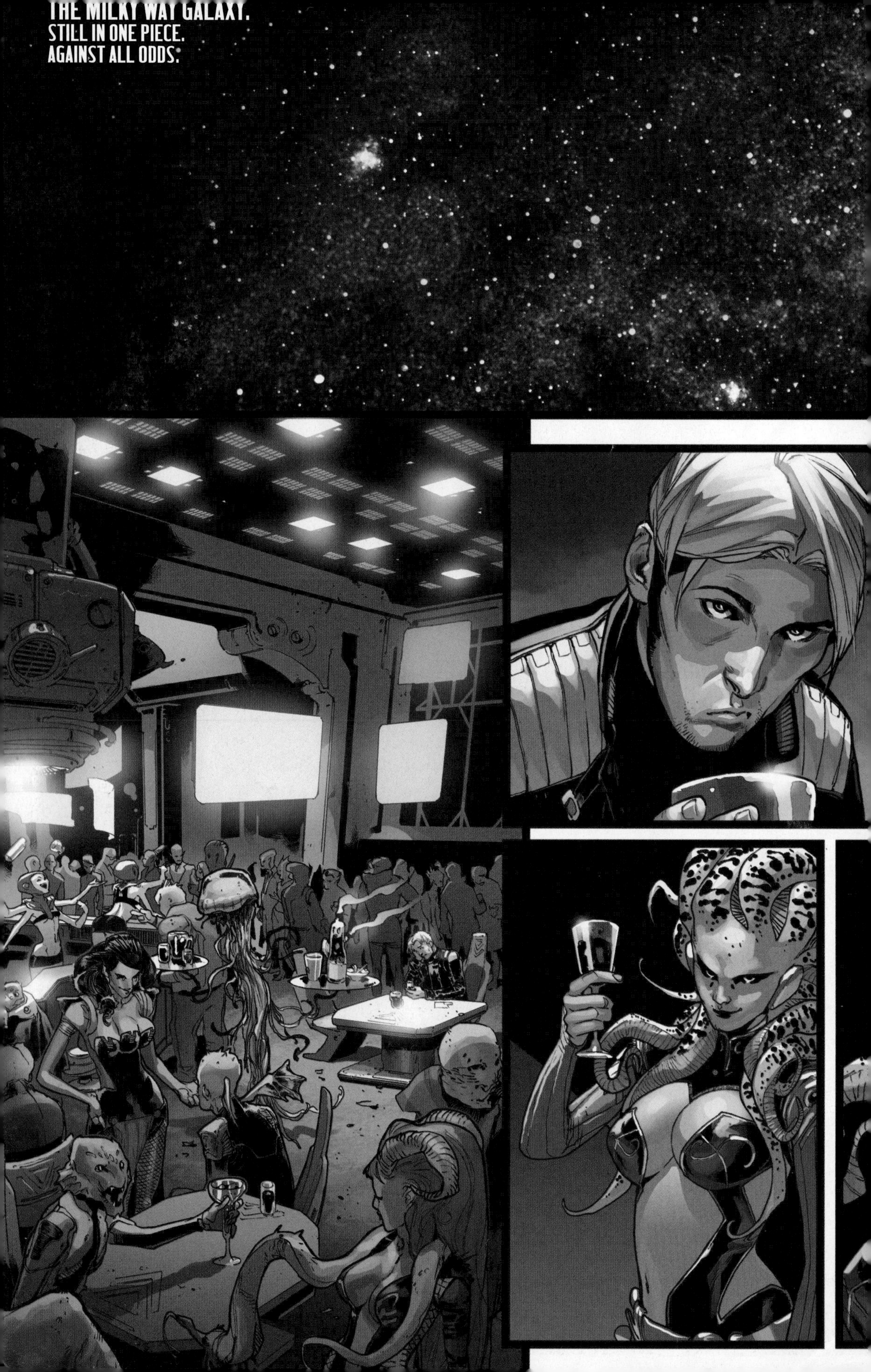
THE MILKY WAY GALAXY.
STILL IN ONE PIECE.
AGAINST ALL ODDS.

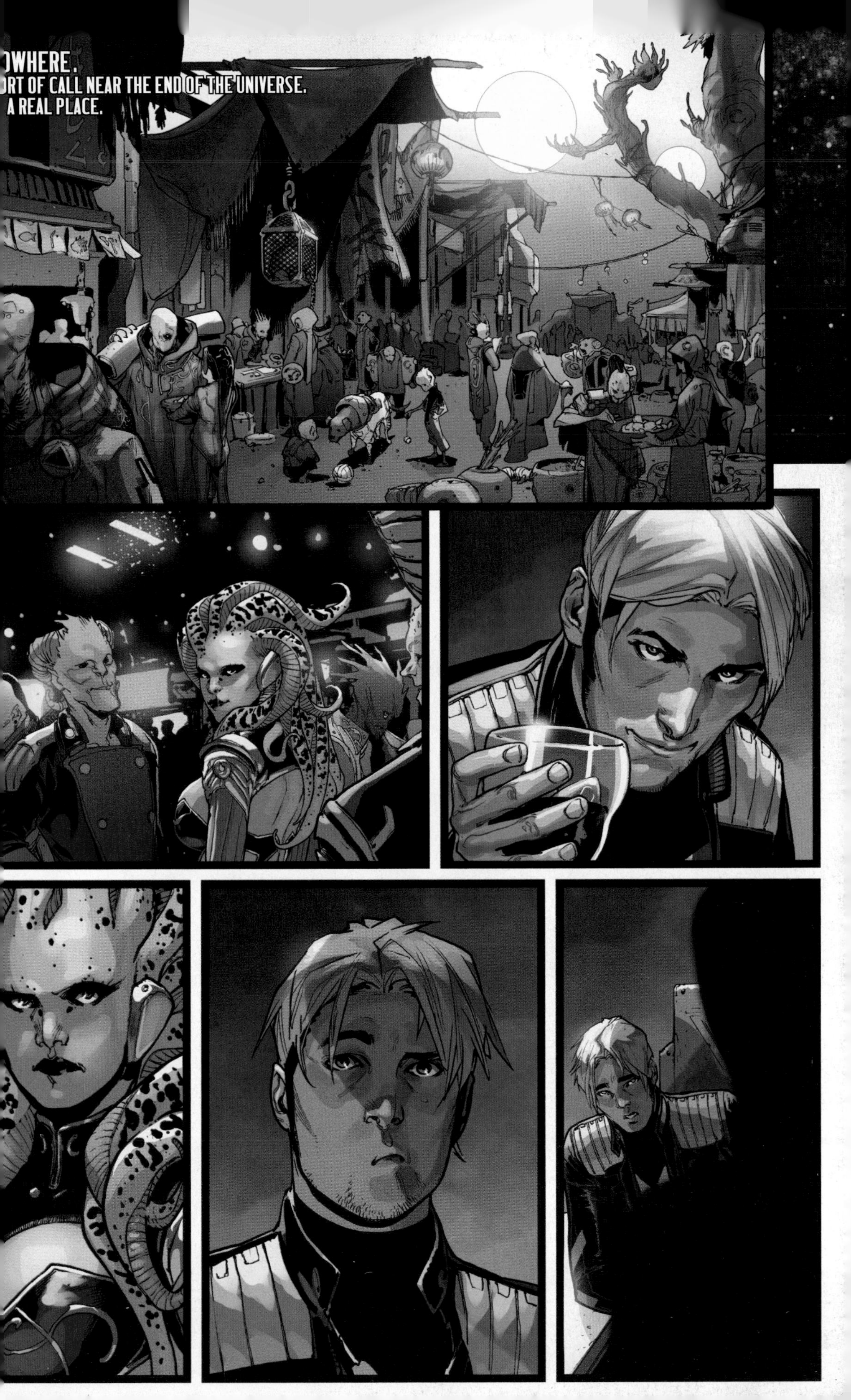

OWHERE.
ORT OF CALL NEAR THE END OF THE UNIVERSE.
A REAL PLACE.

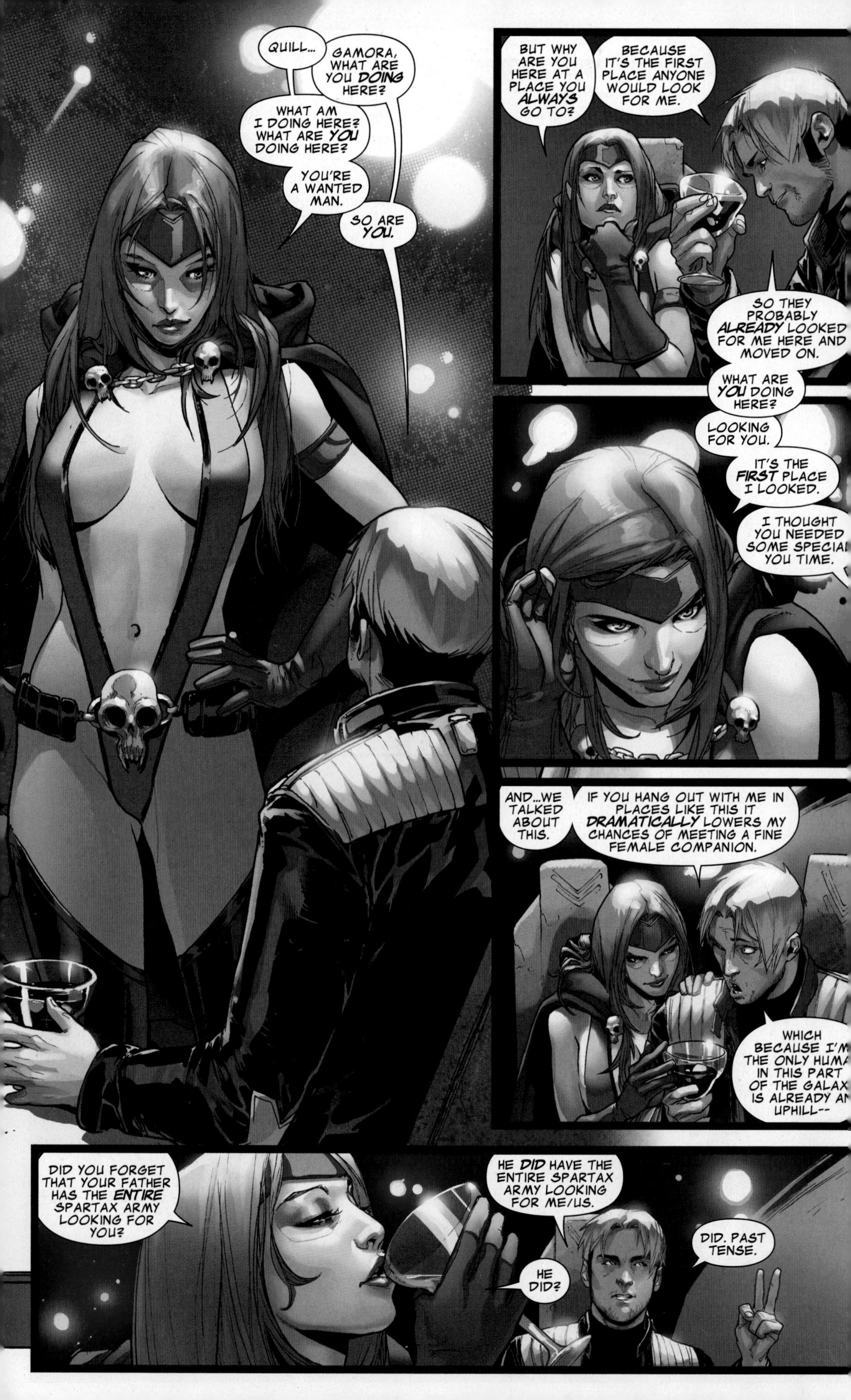
QUILL...
GAMORA, WHAT ARE YOU DOING HERE?
WHAT AM I DOING HERE? WHAT ARE YOU DOING HERE?
YOU'RE A WANTED MAN.
SO ARE YOU.
BUT WHY ARE YOU HERE AT A PLACE YOU ALWAYS GO TO?
BECAUSE IT'S THE FIRST PLACE ANYONE WOULD LOOK FOR ME.
SO THEY PROBABLY ALREADY LOOKED FOR ME HERE AND MOVED ON.
WHAT ARE YOU DOING HERE?
LOOKING FOR YOU.
IT'S THE FIRST PLACE I LOOKED.
I THOUGHT YOU NEEDED SOME SPECIA
YOU TIME.
AND...WE TALKED ABOUT THIS.
IF YOU HANG OUT WITH ME IN PLACES LIKE THIS IT DRAMATICALLY LOWERS MY CHANCES OF MEETING A FINE FEMALE COMPANION.
WHICH BECAUSE I'M THE ONLY HUMA IN THIS PART OF THE GALAX IS ALREADY AN UPHILL--
DID YOU FORGET THAT YOUR FATHER HAS THE ENTIRE SPARTAX ARMY LOOKING FOR YOU?
HE DID HAVE THE ENTIRE SPARTAX ARMY LOOKING FOR ME/US.
HE DID?
DID. PAST TENSE.

HE *DID* HAVE THE ENTIRE SPARTAX ARMY LOOKING FOR ME AND *NOW* HE HAS THE ENTIRE SPARTAX ARMY LOOKING FOR *THANOS.*

HE DIDN'T FORGET ABOUT YOU.

I *AM* HARD TO FORGET.

SO WHAT'S THE PLAN?

PLAN?

WHAT ARE WE GOING TO DO NEXT?

WHAT ARE WE GOING TO DO NEXT?

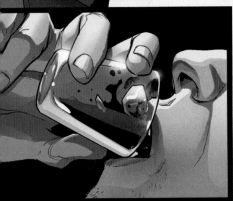

FIRST *YOU* ARE GOING TO LOOK DOWN AT YOUR BELLY BUTTON...

AND YOU'RE GOING TO SEE THAT MY ONE-OF-A-KIND ELEMENTAL GUN IS POINTED RIGHT AT IT.

THEN YOU ARE GOING TO TELL ME WHO YOU *REALLY* ARE.

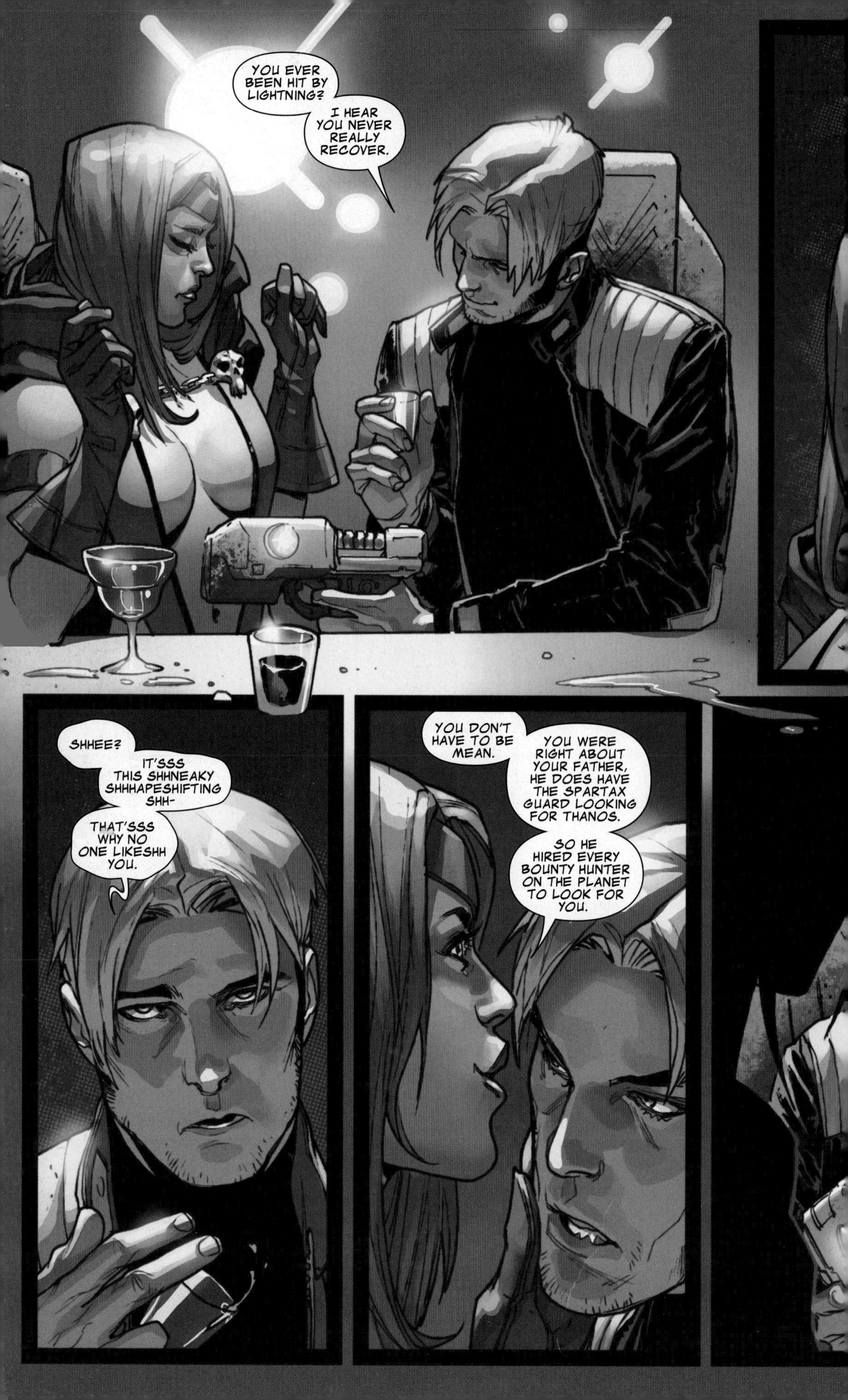
YOU EVER BEEN HIT BY LIGHTNING?
I HEAR YOU NEVER REALLY RECOVER.
SHHEE?
IT'SSS THIS SHHNEAKY SHHHAPESHIFTING SHH-
THAT'SSS WHY NO ONE LIKESHH YOU.
YOU DON'T HAVE TO BE MEAN.
YOU WERE RIGHT ABOUT YOUR FATHER, HE DOES HAVE THE SPARTAX GUARD LOOKING FOR THANOS.
SO HE HIRED EVERY BOUNTY HUNTER ON THE PLANET TO LOOK FOR YOU.

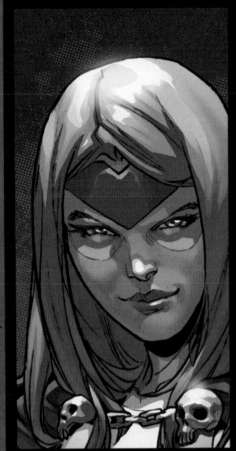

AAWWW, %#$@&*#!

YOU'RE A SKRULL, AREN'T YOU?

BOUNTY HUNTER SSHHHKRULL BOUNTY HUNTER.

SLAM

AND THE DRINK THE BARTENDER SERVED YOU-- WELL, I THINK YOU'RE FIGURING IT OUT.

"SO, HOW IS EVERYBODY DOING?"

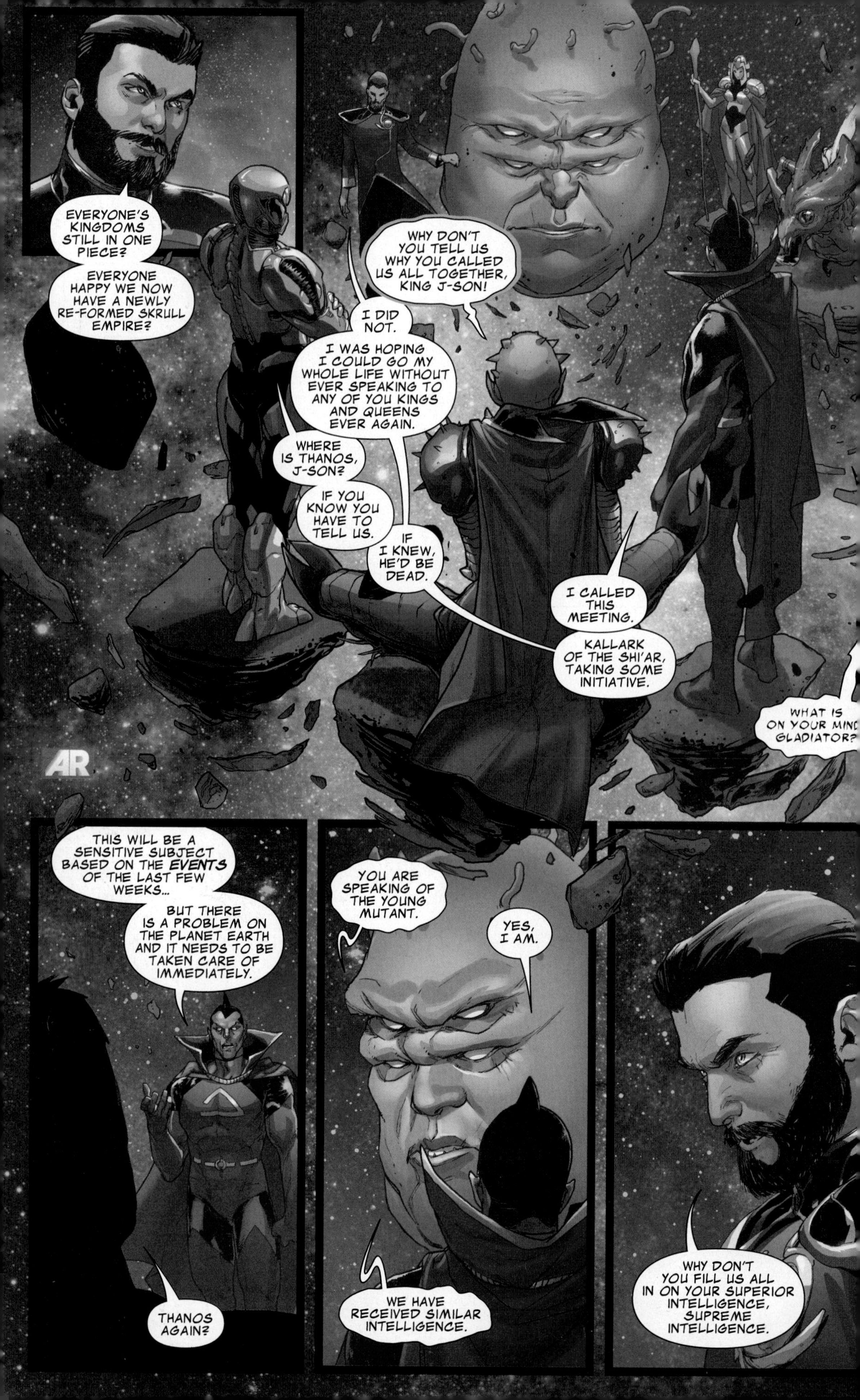
EVERYONE'S KINGDOMS STILL IN ONE PIECE?
EVERYONE HAPPY WE NOW HAVE A NEWLY RE-FORMED SKRULL EMPIRE?
WHY DON'T YOU TELL US WHY YOU CALLED US ALL TOGETHER, KING J-SON!
I DID NOT.
I WAS HOPING I COULD GO MY WHOLE LIFE WITHOUT EVER SPEAKING TO ANY OF YOU KINGS AND QUEENS EVER AGAIN.
WHERE IS THANOS, J-SON?
IF YOU KNOW YOU HAVE TO TELL US.
IF I KNEW, HE'D BE DEAD.
I CALLED THIS MEETING.
KALLARK OF THE SHI'AR, TAKING SOME INITIATIVE.
WHAT IS ON YOUR MIND GLADIATOR?
THIS WILL BE A SENSITIVE SUBJECT BASED ON THE *EVENTS* OF THE LAST FEW WEEKS...
BUT THERE IS A PROBLEM ON THE PLANET EARTH AND IT NEEDS TO BE TAKEN CARE OF IMMEDIATELY.
THANOS AGAIN?
YOU ARE SPEAKING OF THE YOUNG MUTANT.
YES, I AM.
WE HAVE RECEIVED SIMILAR INTELLIGENCE.
WHY DON'T YOU FILL US ALL IN ON YOUR SUPERIOR INTELLIGENCE, SUPREME INTELLIGENCE.

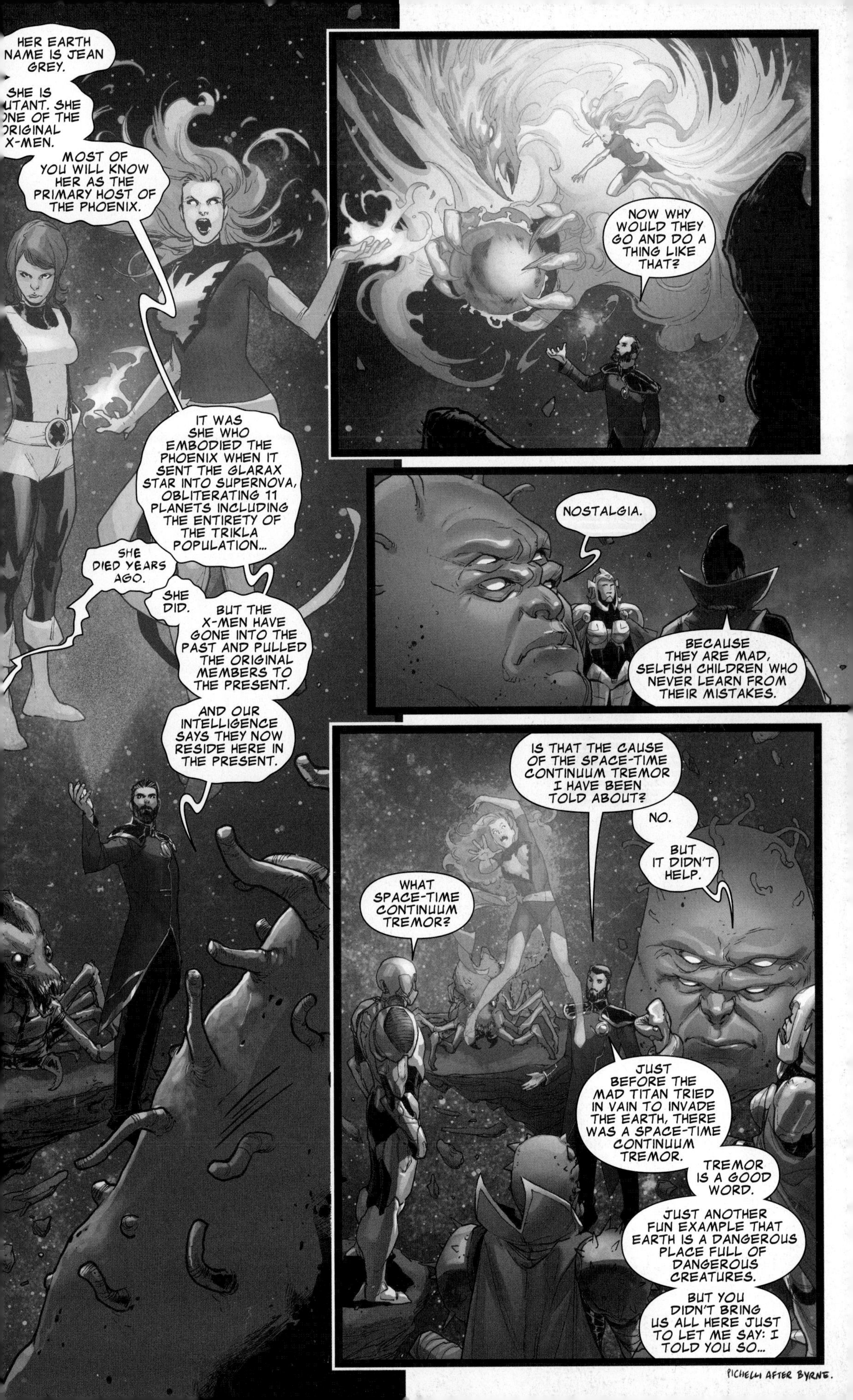
HER EARTH NAME IS JEAN GREY.
SHE IS UTANT. SHE ONE OF THE ORIGINAL X-MEN.
MOST OF YOU WILL KNOW HER AS THE PRIMARY HOST OF THE PHOENIX.
NOW WHY WOULD THEY GO AND DO A THING LIKE THAT?
IT WAS SHE WHO EMBODIED THE PHOENIX WHEN IT SENT THE GLARAX STAR INTO SUPERNOVA, OBLITERATING 11 PLANETS INCLUDING THE ENTIRETY OF THE TRIKLA POPULATION...
NOSTALGIA.
BECAUSE THEY ARE MAD, SELFISH CHILDREN WHO NEVER LEARN FROM THEIR MISTAKES.
SHE DIED YEARS AGO.
SHE DID.
BUT THE X-MEN HAVE GONE INTO THE PAST AND PULLED THE ORIGINAL MEMBERS TO THE PRESENT.
AND OUR INTELLIGENCE SAYS THEY NOW RESIDE HERE IN THE PRESENT.
IS THAT THE CAUSE OF THE SPACE-TIME CONTINUUM TREMOR I HAVE BEEN TOLD ABOUT?
NO.
BUT IT DIDN'T HELP.
WHAT SPACE-TIME CONTINUUM TREMOR?
JUST BEFORE THE MAD TITAN TRIED IN VAIN TO INVADE THE EARTH, THERE WAS A SPACE-TIME CONTINUUM TREMOR.
TREMOR IS A GOOD WORD.
JUST ANOTHER FUN EXAMPLE THAT EARTH IS A DANGEROUS PLACE FULL OF DANGEROUS CREATURES.
BUT YOU DIDN'T BRING US ALL HERE JUST TO LET ME SAY: I TOLD YOU SO...
PICHELLI AFTER BYRNE.

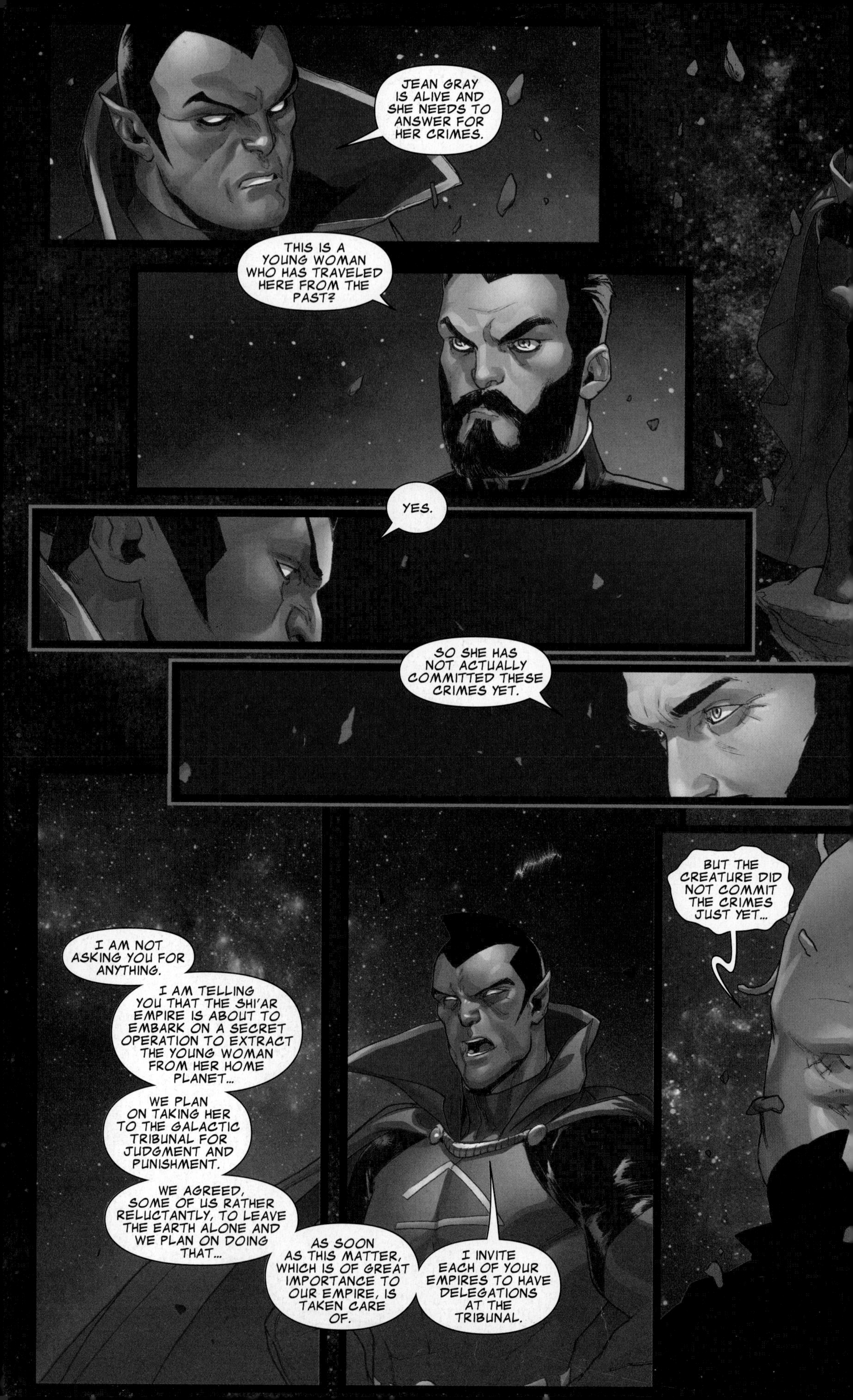
JEAN GRAY IS ALIVE AND SHE NEEDS TO ANSWER FOR HER CRIMES.
THIS IS A YOUNG WOMAN WHO HAS TRAVELED HERE FROM THE PAST?
YES.
SO SHE HAS NOT ACTUALLY COMMITTED THESE CRIMES YET.
I AM NOT ASKING YOU FOR ANYTHING.
I AM TELLING YOU THAT THE SHI'AR EMPIRE IS ABOUT TO EMBARK ON A SECRET OPERATION TO EXTRACT THE YOUNG WOMAN FROM HER HOME PLANET...
WE PLAN ON TAKING HER TO THE GALACTIC TRIBUNAL FOR JUDGMENT AND PUNISHMENT.
WE AGREED, SOME OF US RATHER RELUCTANTLY, TO LEAVE THE EARTH ALONE AND WE PLAN ON DOING THAT...
AS SOON AS THIS MATTER, WHICH IS OF GREAT IMPORTANCE TO OUR EMPIRE, IS TAKEN CARE OF.
I INVITE EACH OF YOUR EMPIRES TO HAVE DELEGATIONS AT THE TRIBUNAL.
BUT THE CREATURE DID NOT COMMIT THE CRIMES JUST YET...

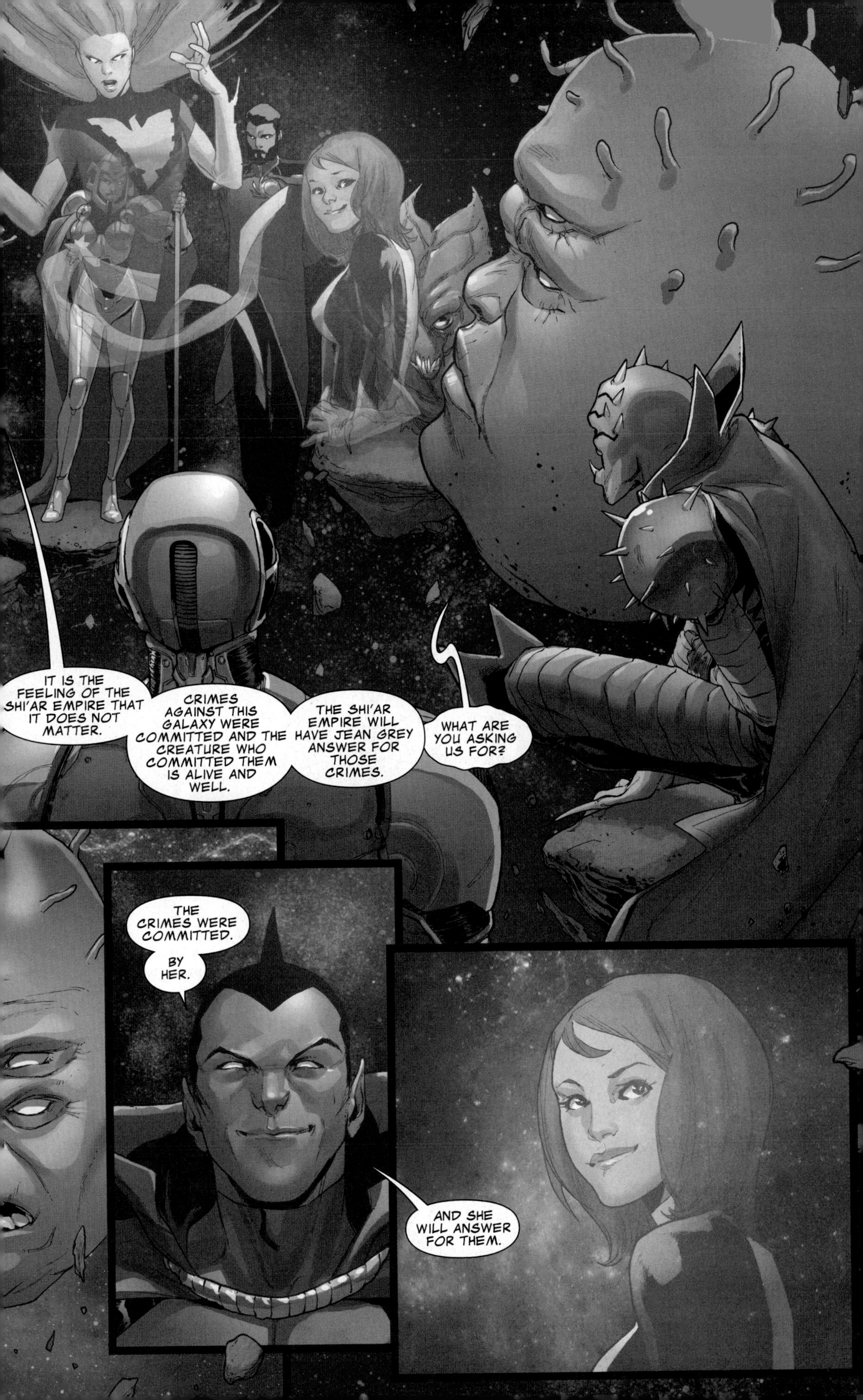
IT IS THE FEELING OF THE SHI'AR EMPIRE THAT IT DOES NOT MATTER.
CRIMES AGAINST THIS GALAXY WERE COMMITTED AND THE CREATURE WHO COMMITTED THEM IS ALIVE AND WELL.
THE SHI'AR EMPIRE WILL HAVE JEAN GREY ANSWER FOR THOSE CRIMES.
WHAT ARE YOU ASKING US FOR?
THE CRIMES WERE COMMITTED.
BY HER.
AND SHE WILL ANSWER FOR THEM.

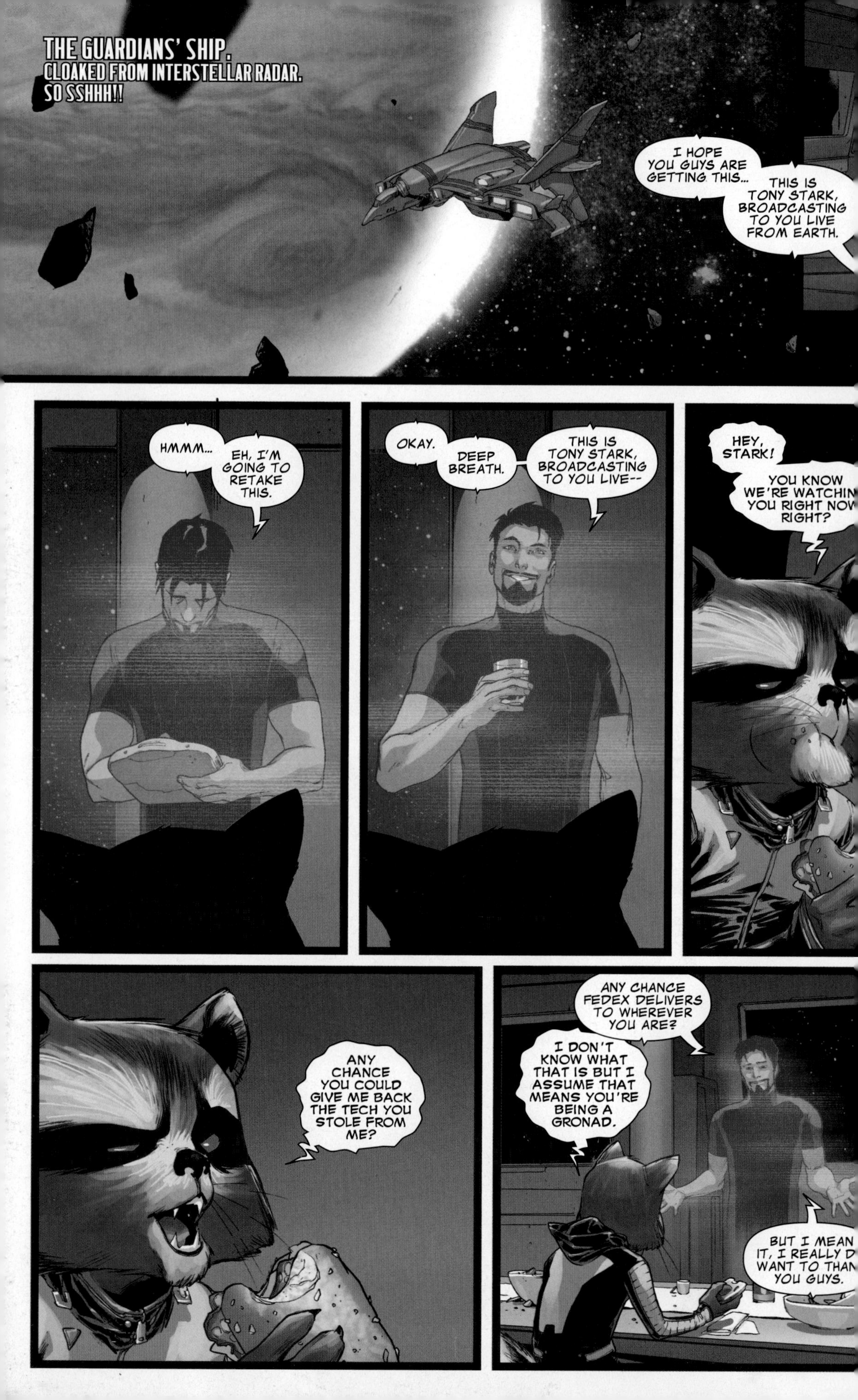
THE GUARDIANS' SHIP.
CLOAKED FROM INTERSTELLAR RADAR.
SO SSHHH!!
I HOPE YOU GUYS ARE GETTING THIS...
THIS IS TONY STARK, BROADCASTING TO YOU LIVE FROM EARTH.
HMMM...
EH, I'M GOING TO RETAKE THIS.
OKAY.
DEEP BREATH.
THIS IS TONY STARK, BROADCASTING TO YOU LIVE--
HEY, STARK!
YOU KNOW WE'RE WATCHIN YOU RIGHT NOW RIGHT?
ANY CHANCE YOU COULD GIVE ME BACK THE TECH YOU STOLE FROM ME?
ANY CHANCE FEDEX DELIVERS TO WHEREVER YOU ARE?
I DON'T KNOW WHAT THAT IS BUT I ASSUME THAT MEANS YOU'RE BEING A GRONAD.
BUT I MEAN IT, I REALLY D WANT TO THAN YOU GUYS.

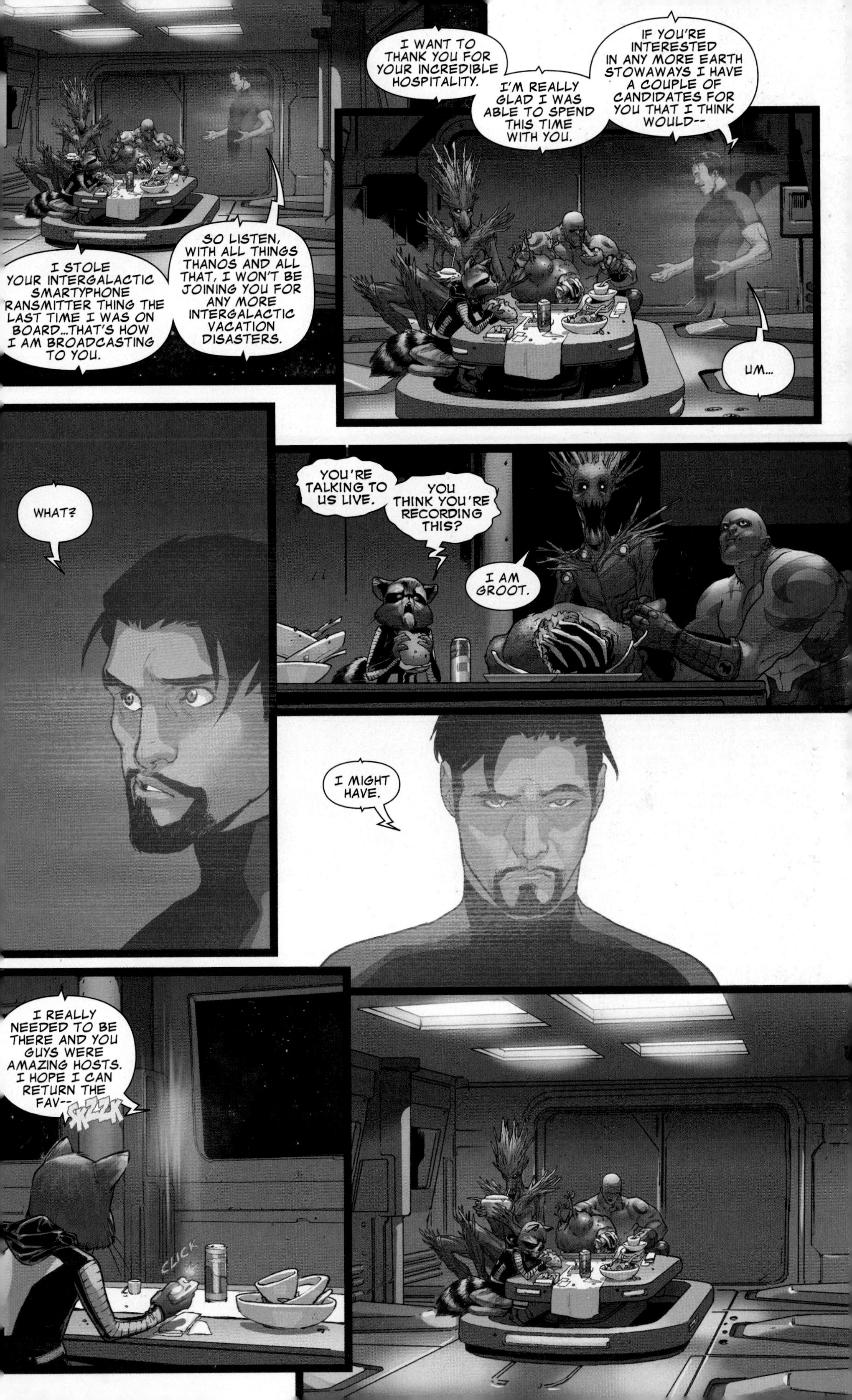
I STOLE YOUR INTERGALACTIC SMARTYPHONE RANSMITTER THING THE LAST TIME I WAS ON BOARD...THAT'S HOW I AM BROADCASTING TO YOU.
SO LISTEN, WITH ALL THINGS THANOS AND ALL THAT, I WON'T BE JOINING YOU FOR ANY MORE INTERGALACTIC VACATION DISASTERS.
I WANT TO THANK YOU FOR YOUR INCREDIBLE HOSPITALITY.
I'M REALLY GLAD I WAS ABLE TO SPEND THIS TIME WITH YOU.
IF YOU'RE INTERESTED IN ANY MORE EARTH STOWAWAYS I HAVE A COUPLE OF CANDIDATES FOR YOU THAT I THINK WOULD--
UM...
WHAT?
YOU'RE TALKING TO US LIVE.
YOU THINK YOU'RE RECORDING THIS?
I AM GROOT.
I MIGHT HAVE.
I REALLY NEEDED TO BE THERE AND YOU GUYS WERE AMAZING HOSTS. I HOPE I CAN RETURN THE FAV--
SKZZK
CLICK

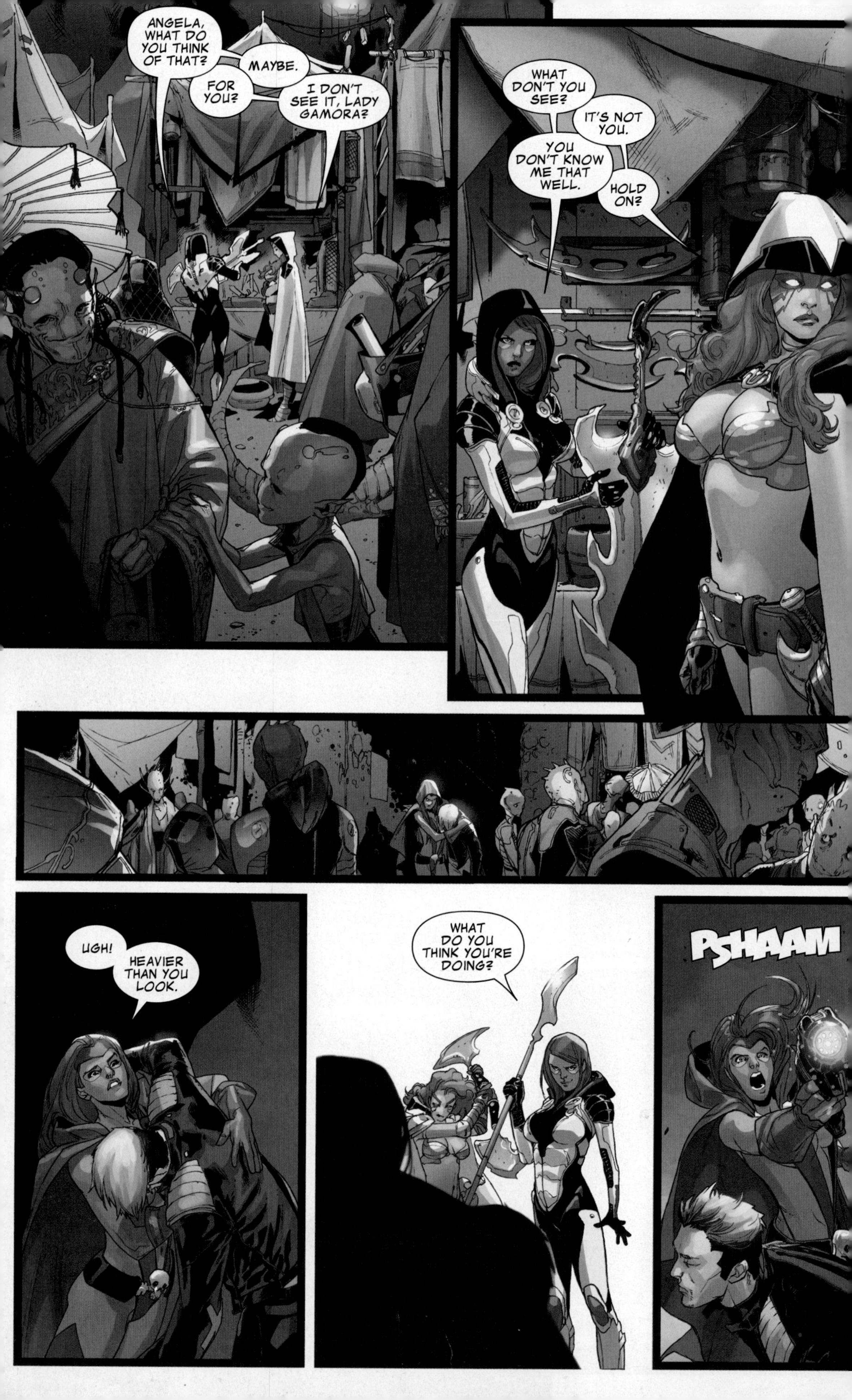
ANGELA, WHAT DO YOU THINK OF THAT?
MAYBE.
FOR YOU?
I DON'T SEE IT, LADY GAMORA?
WHAT DON'T YOU SEE?
IT'S NOT YOU.
YOU DON'T KNOW ME THAT WELL.
HOLD ON?
UGH!
HEAVIER THAN YOU LOOK.
WHAT DO YOU THINK YOU'RE DOING?
PSHAAM

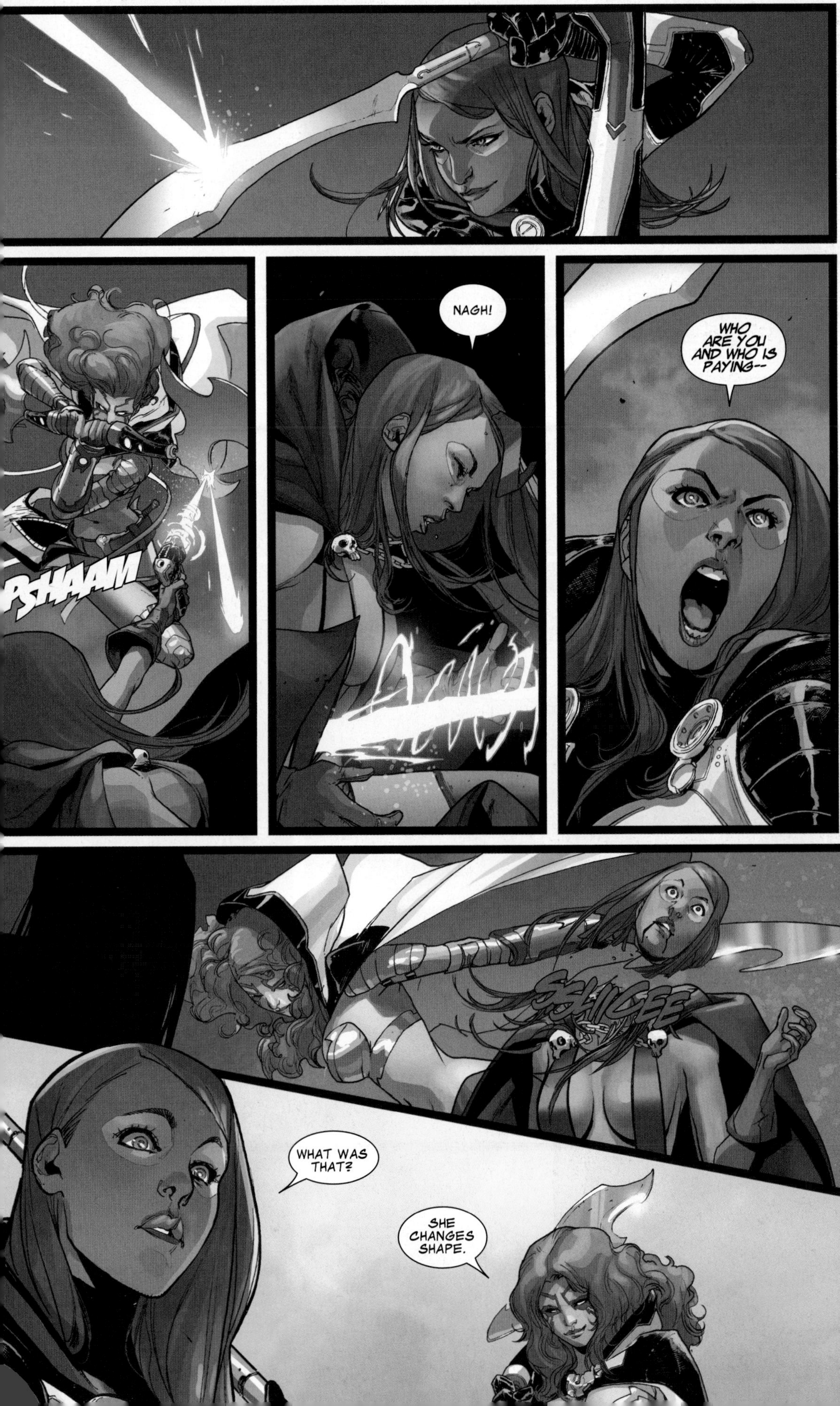
PSHAAM
NAGH!
WHO ARE YOU AND WHO IS PAYING--
SSLICEE
WHAT WAS THAT?
SHE CHANGES SHAPE.

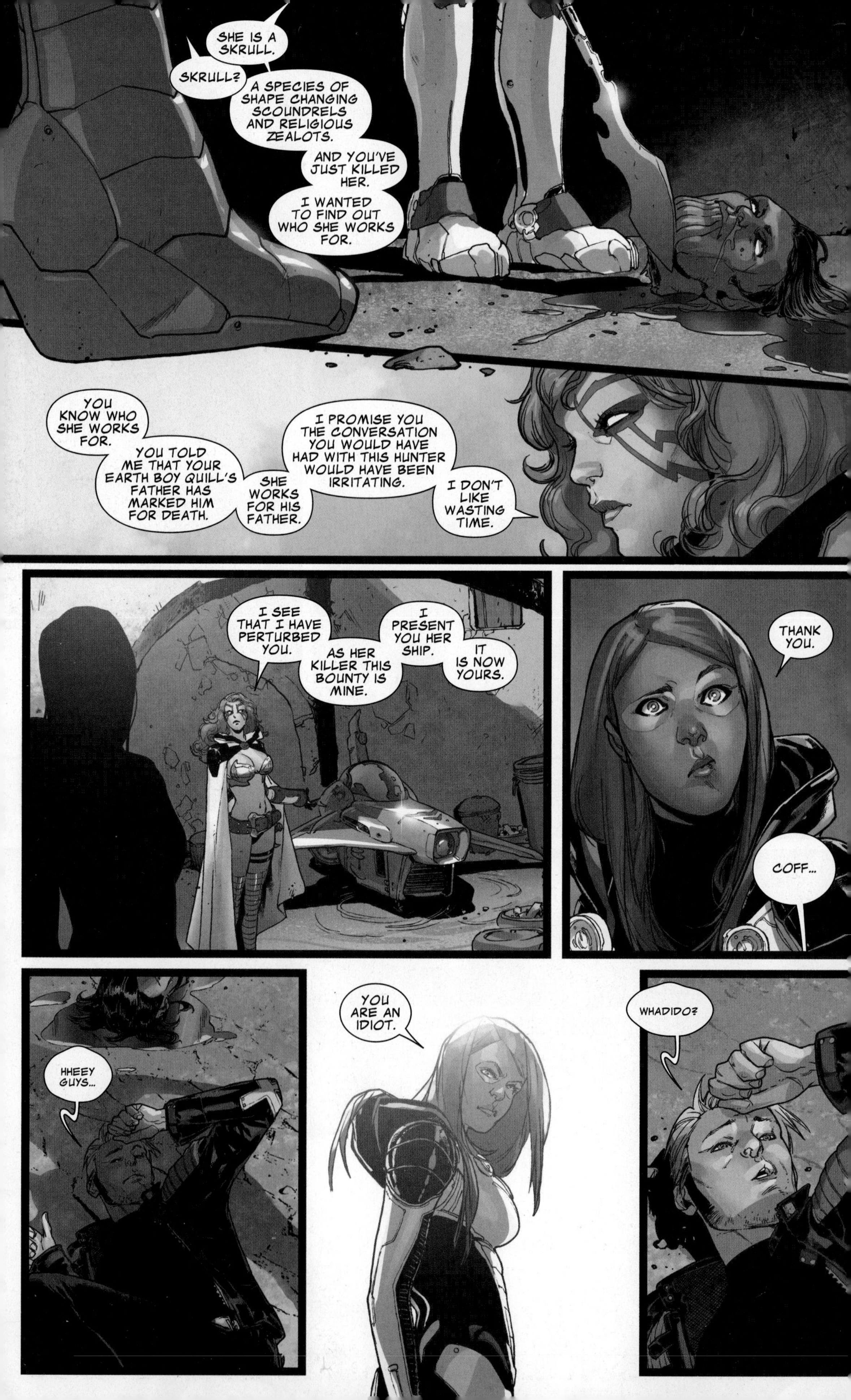

SHE IS A SKRULL.
SKRULL?
A SPECIES OF SHAPE CHANGING SCOUNDRELS AND RELIGIOUS ZEALOTS.
AND YOU'VE JUST KILLED HER.
I WANTED TO FIND OUT WHO SHE WORKS FOR.
YOU KNOW WHO SHE WORKS FOR.
YOU TOLD ME THAT YOUR EARTH BOY QUILL'S FATHER HAS MARKED HIM FOR DEATH.
SHE WORKS FOR HIS FATHER.
I PROMISE YOU THE CONVERSATION YOU WOULD HAVE HAD WITH THIS HUNTER WOULD HAVE BEEN IRRITATING.
I DON'T LIKE WASTING TIME.
I SEE THAT I HAVE PERTURBED YOU.
AS HER KILLER THIS BOUNTY IS MINE.
I PRESENT YOU HER SHIP.
IT IS NOW YOURS.
THANK YOU.
COFF...
HHEEY GUYS...
YOU ARE AN IDIOT.
WHADIDO?

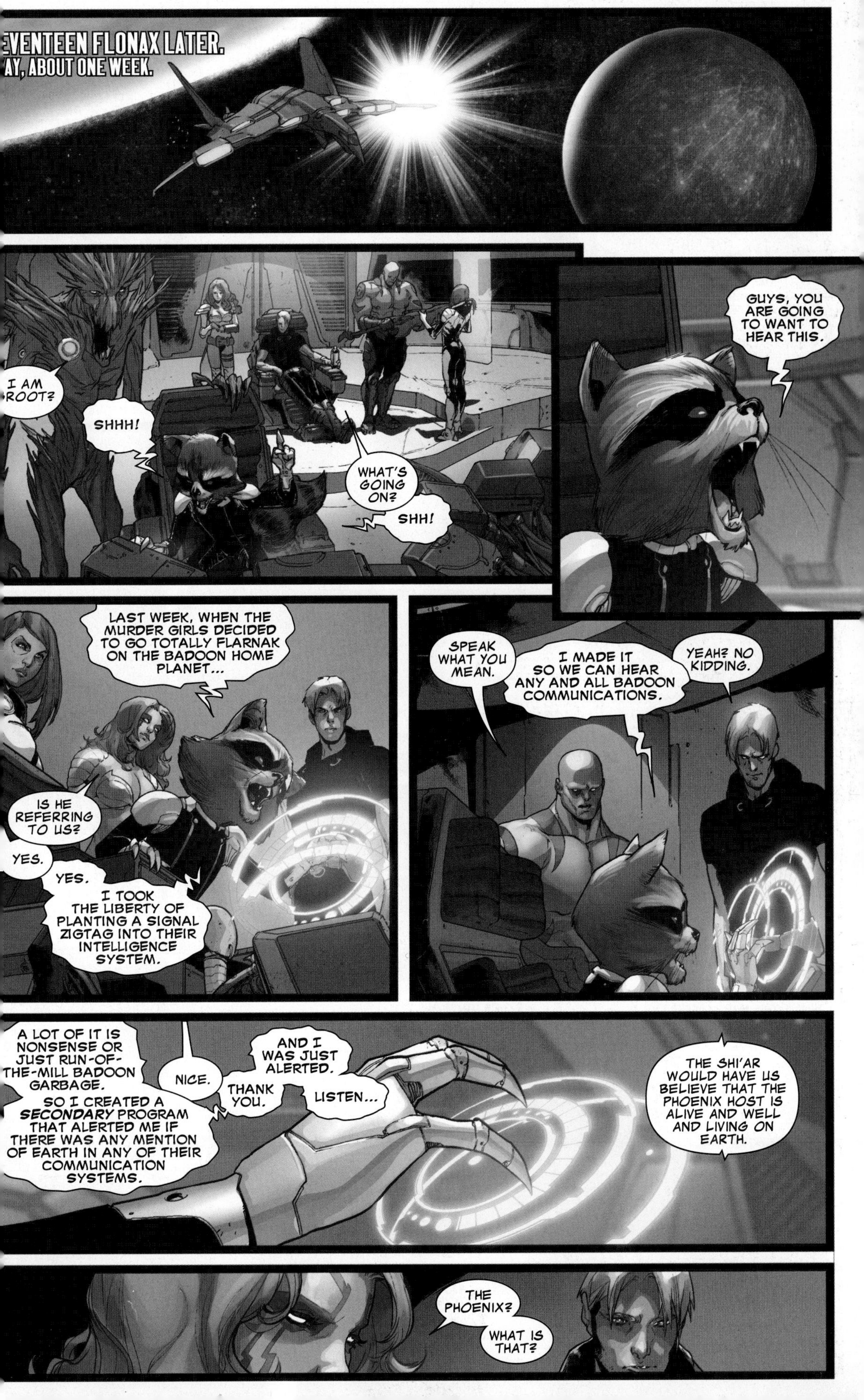

EVENTEEN FLONAX LATER.
AY, ABOUT ONE WEEK.
I AM ROOT?
SHHH!
WHAT'S GOING ON?
SHH!
GUYS, YOU ARE GOING TO WANT TO HEAR THIS.
LAST WEEK, WHEN THE MURDER GIRLS DECIDED TO GO TOTALLY FLARNAK ON THE BADOON HOME PLANET...
IS HE REFERRING TO US?
YES.
YES.
I TOOK THE LIBERTY OF PLANTING A SIGNAL ZIGTAG INTO THEIR INTELLIGENCE SYSTEM.
SPEAK WHAT YOU MEAN.
I MADE IT SO WE CAN HEAR ANY AND ALL BADOON COMMUNICATIONS.
YEAH? NO KIDDING.
A LOT OF IT IS NONSENSE OR JUST RUN-OF-THE-MILL BADOON GARBAGE.
NICE.
SO I CREATED A SECONDARY PROGRAM THAT ALERTED ME IF THERE WAS ANY MENTION OF EARTH IN ANY OF THEIR COMMUNICATION SYSTEMS.
THANK YOU.
AND I WAS JUST ALERTED.
LISTEN...
THE SHI'AR WOULD HAVE US BELIEVE THAT THE PHOENIX HOST IS ALIVE AND WELL AND LIVING ON EARTH.
THE PHOENIX?
WHAT IS THAT?

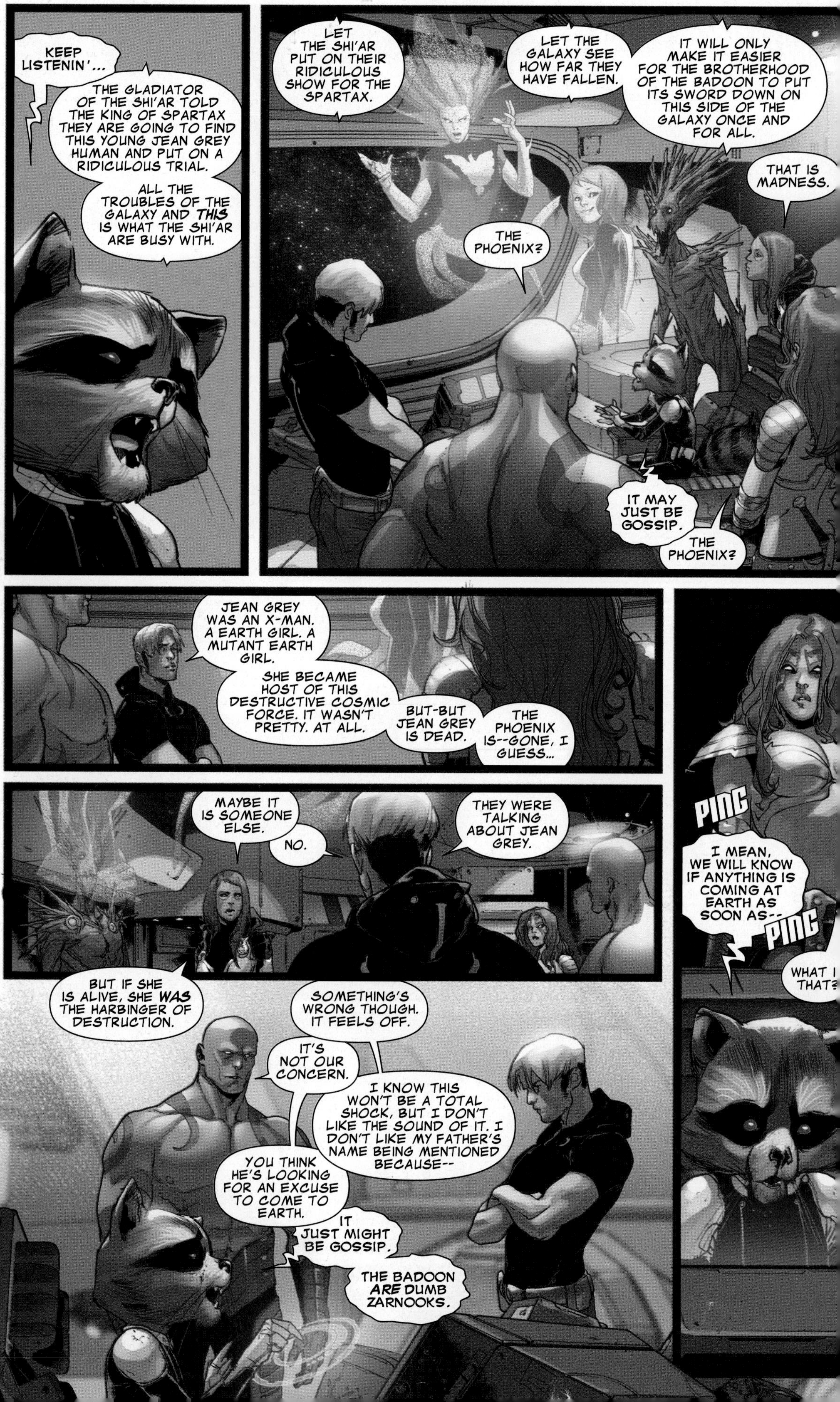
KEEP LISTENIN'...
THE GLADIATOR OF THE SHI'AR TOLD THE KING OF SPARTAX THEY ARE GOING TO FIND THIS YOUNG JEAN GREY HUMAN AND PUT ON A RIDICULOUS TRIAL.
ALL THE TROUBLES OF THE GALAXY AND THIS IS WHAT THE SHI'AR ARE BUSY WITH.
LET THE SHI'AR PUT ON THEIR RIDICULOUS SHOW FOR THE SPARTAX.
LET THE GALAXY SEE HOW FAR THEY HAVE FALLEN.
IT WILL ONLY MAKE IT EASIER FOR THE BROTHERHOOD OF THE BADOON TO PUT ITS SWORD DOWN ON THIS SIDE OF THE GALAXY ONCE AND FOR ALL.
THAT IS MADNESS.
THE PHOENIX?
IT MAY JUST BE GOSSIP.
THE PHOENIX?
JEAN GREY WAS AN X-MAN. A EARTH GIRL. A MUTANT EARTH GIRL.
SHE BECAME HOST OF THIS DESTRUCTIVE COSMIC FORCE. IT WASN'T PRETTY. AT ALL.
BUT-BUT JEAN GREY IS DEAD.
THE PHOENIX IS--GONE, I GUESS...
MAYBE IT IS SOMEONE ELSE.
NO.
THEY WERE TALKING ABOUT JEAN GREY.
BUT IF SHE IS ALIVE, SHE WAS THE HARBINGER OF DESTRUCTION.
SOMETHING'S WRONG THOUGH. IT FEELS OFF.
IT'S NOT OUR CONCERN.
I KNOW THIS WON'T BE A TOTAL SHOCK, BUT I DON'T LIKE THE SOUND OF IT. I DON'T LIKE MY FATHER'S NAME BEING MENTIONED BECAUSE--
YOU THINK HE'S LOOKING FOR AN EXCUSE TO COME TO EARTH.
IT JUST MIGHT BE GOSSIP.
THE BADOON ARE DUMB ZARNOOKS.
PING
I MEAN, WE WILL KNOW IF ANYTHING IS COMING AT EARTH AS SOON AS--
PING
WHAT I THAT?

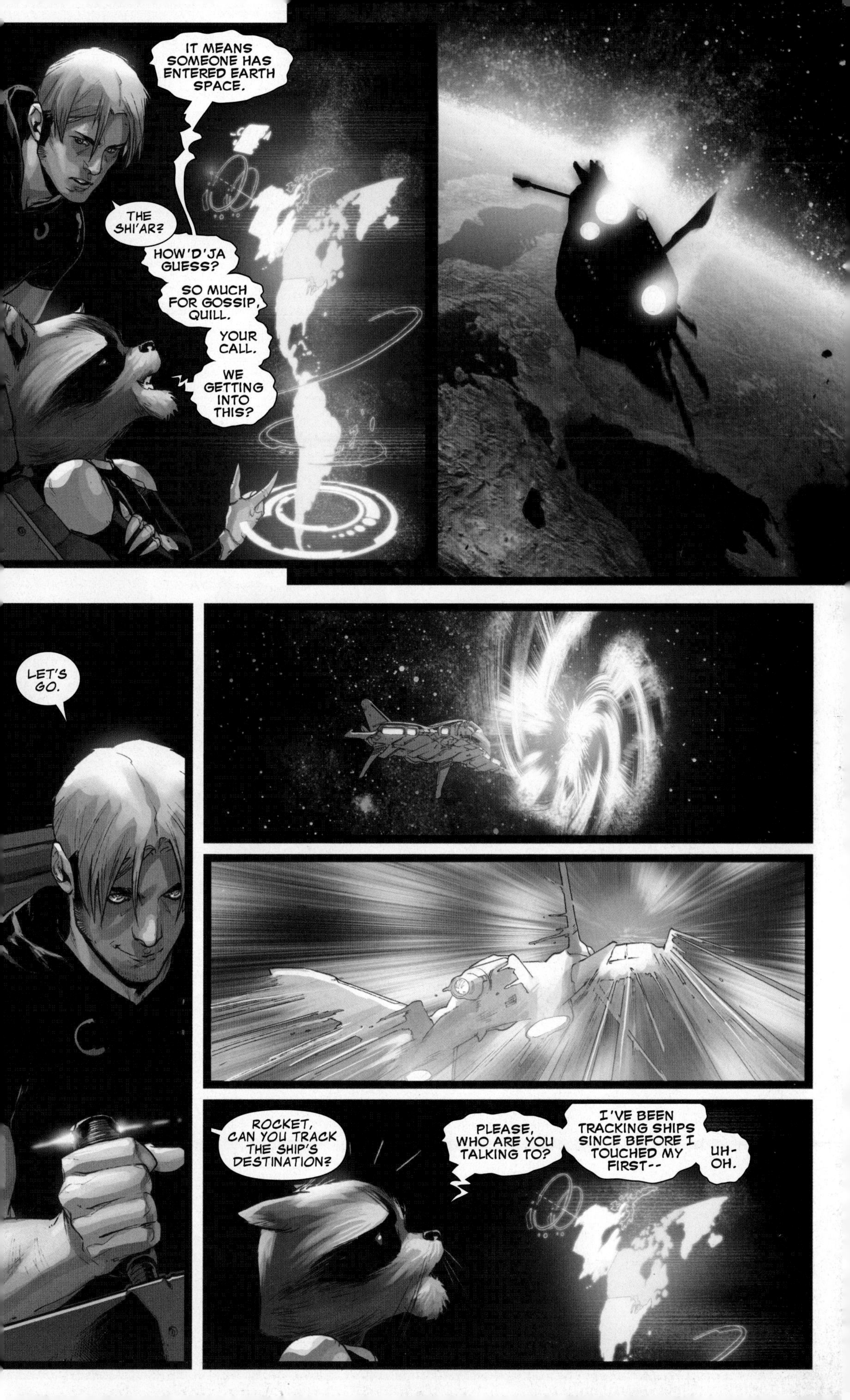
IT MEANS SOMEONE HAS ENTERED EARTH SPACE.
THE SHI'AR?
HOW'D'JA GUESS?
SO MUCH FOR GOSSIP, QUILL.
YOUR CALL.
WE GETTING INTO THIS?
LET'S GO.
ROCKET, CAN YOU TRACK THE SHIP'S DESTINATION?
PLEASE, WHO ARE YOU TALKING TO?
I'VE BEEN TRACKING SHIPS SINCE BEFORE I TOUCHED MY FIRST--
UH-OH.

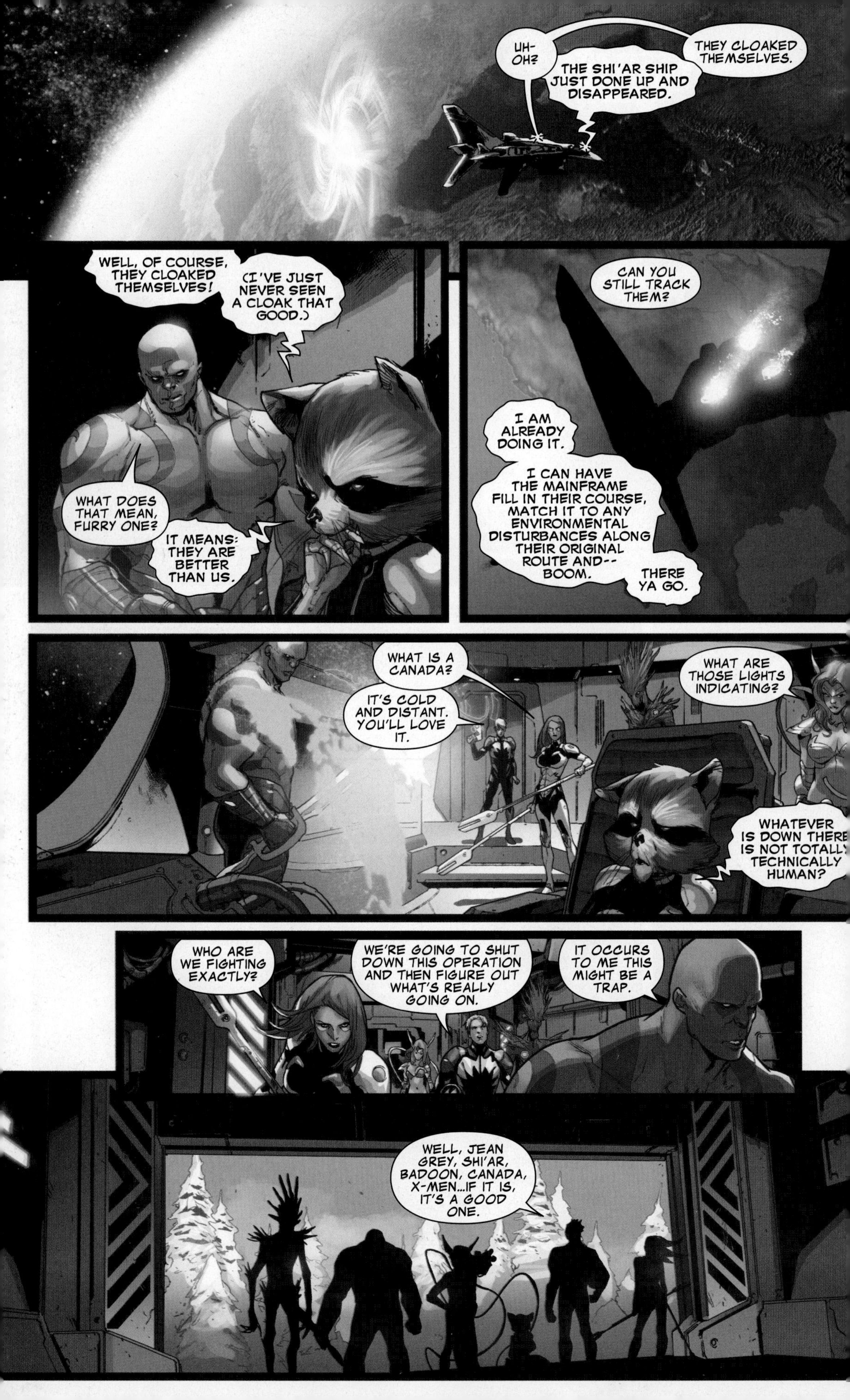
UH-OH?
THE SHI'AR SHIP JUST DONE UP AND DISAPPEARED.
THEY CLOAKED THEMSELVES.
WELL, OF COURSE, THEY CLOAKED THEMSELVES!
(I'VE JUST NEVER SEEN A CLOAK THAT GOOD.)
WHAT DOES THAT MEAN, FURRY ONE?
IT MEANS: THEY ARE BETTER THAN US.
CAN YOU STILL TRACK THEM?
I AM ALREADY DOING IT.
I CAN HAVE THE MAINFRAME FILL IN THEIR COURSE, MATCH IT TO ANY ENVIRONMENTAL DISTURBANCES ALONG THEIR ORIGINAL ROUTE AND-- BOOM.
THERE YA GO.
WHAT IS A CANADA?
IT'S COLD AND DISTANT. YOU'LL LOVE IT.
WHAT ARE THOSE LIGHTS INDICATING?
WHATEVER IS DOWN THERE IS NOT TOTALLY TECHNICALLY HUMAN?
WHO ARE WE FIGHTING EXACTLY?
WE'RE GOING TO SHUT DOWN THIS OPERATION AND THEN FIGURE OUT WHAT'S REALLY GOING ON.
IT OCCURS TO ME THIS MIGHT BE A TRAP.
WELL, JEAN GREY, SHI'AR, BADOON, CANADA, X-MEN...IF IT IS, IT'S A GOOD ONE.

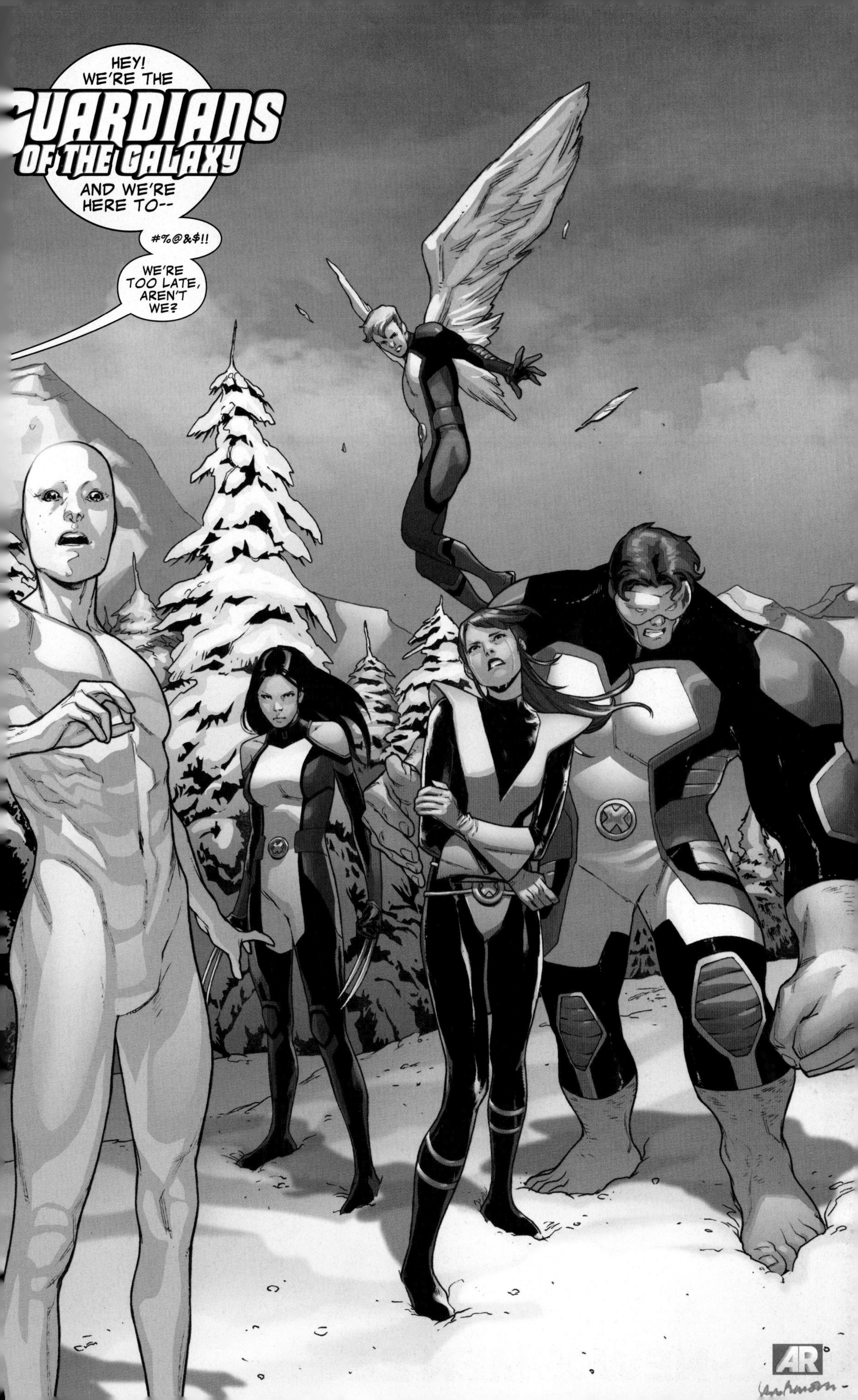
HEY! WE'RE THE GUARDIANS OF THE GALAXY AND WE'RE HERE TO--
#%@&$!!
WE'RE TOO LATE, AREN'T WE?

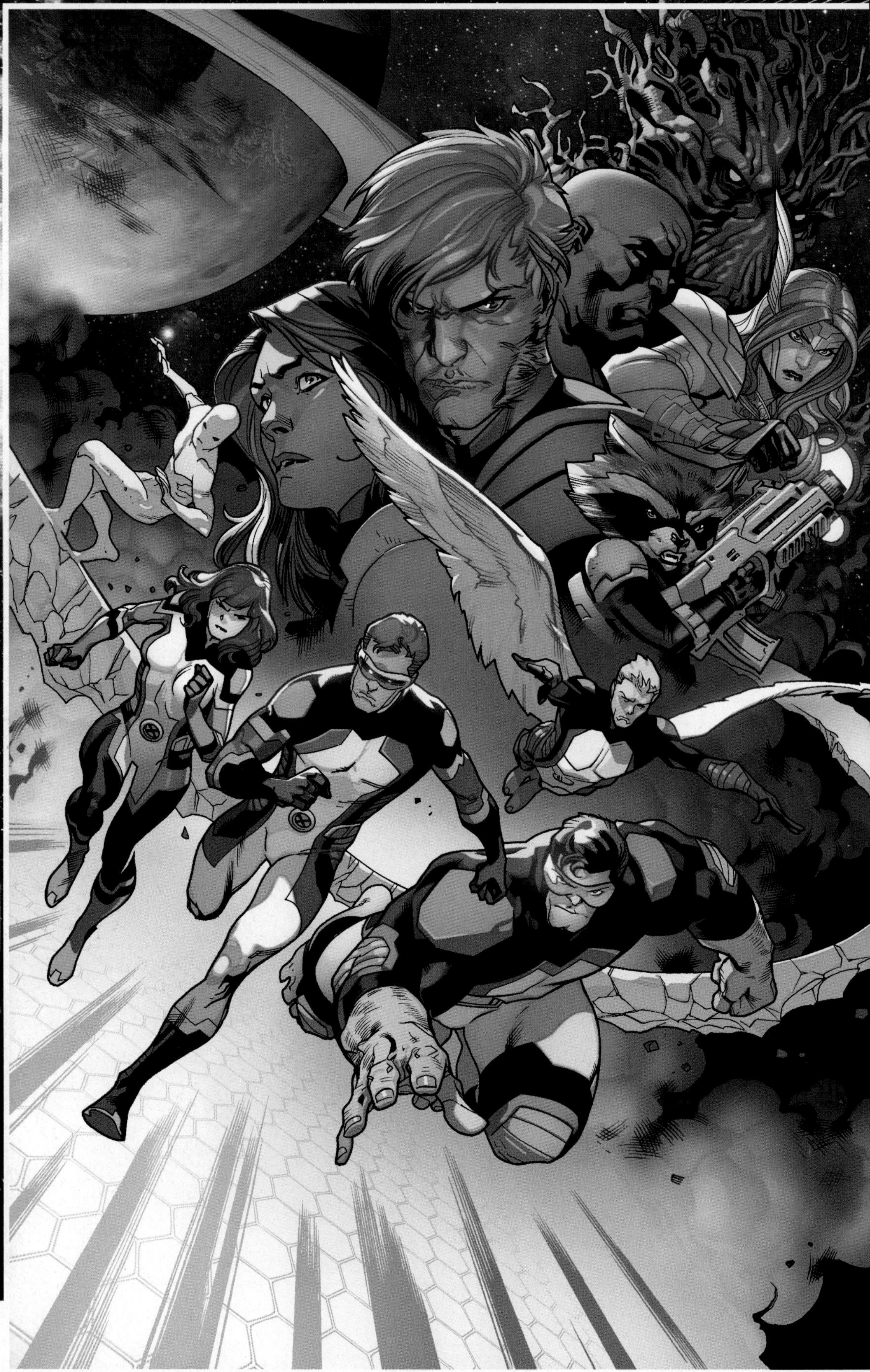

ALL-NEW X-MEN 22

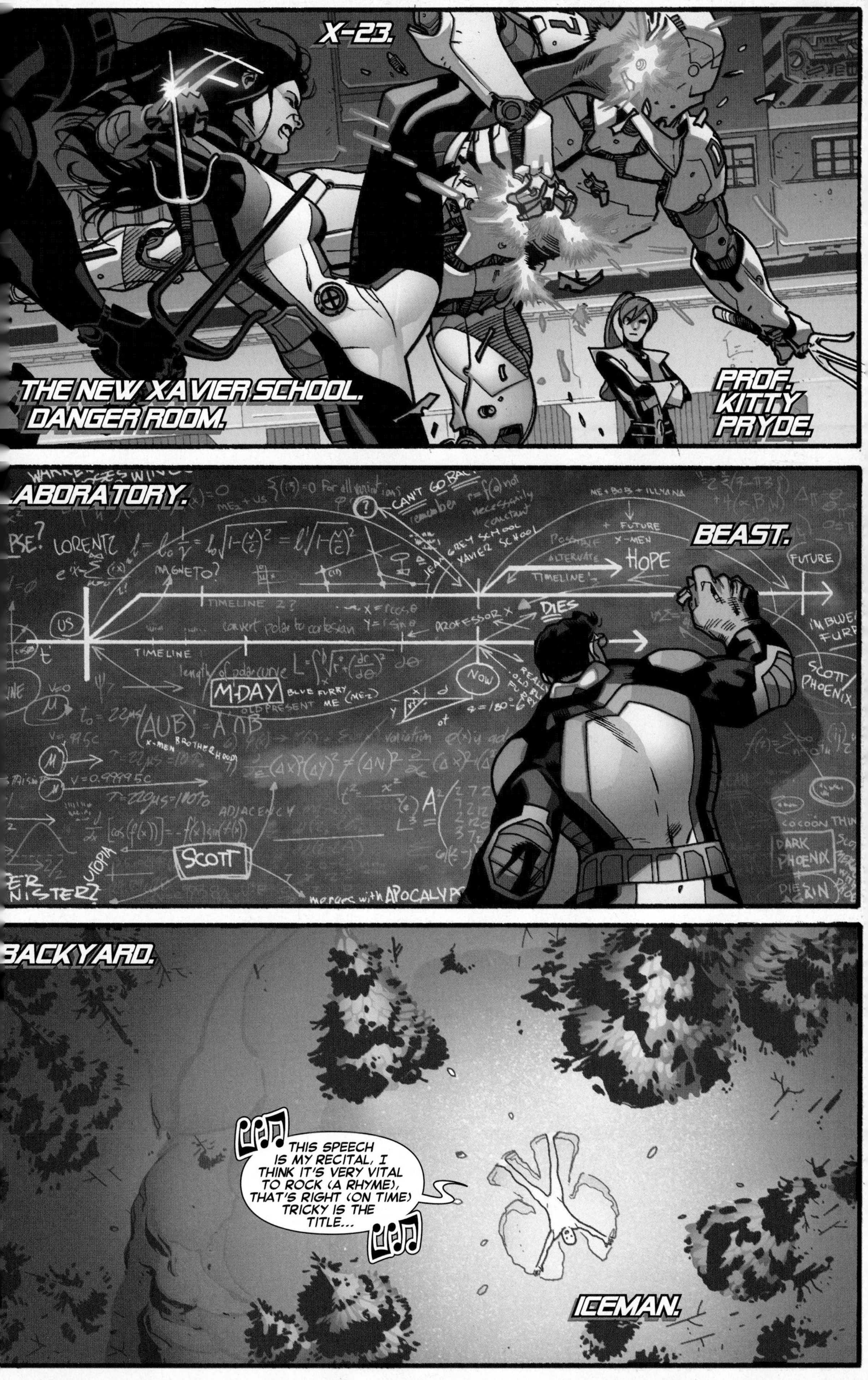
X-23.
THE NEW XAVIER SCHOOL. DANGER ROOM.
PROF. KITTY PRYDE.
ABORATORY.
BEAST.
BACKYARD.
THIS SPEECH IS MY RECITAL, I THINK IT'S VERY VITAL TO ROCK (A RHYME), THAT'S RIGHT (ON TIME) TRICKY IS THE TITLE...
ICEMAN.

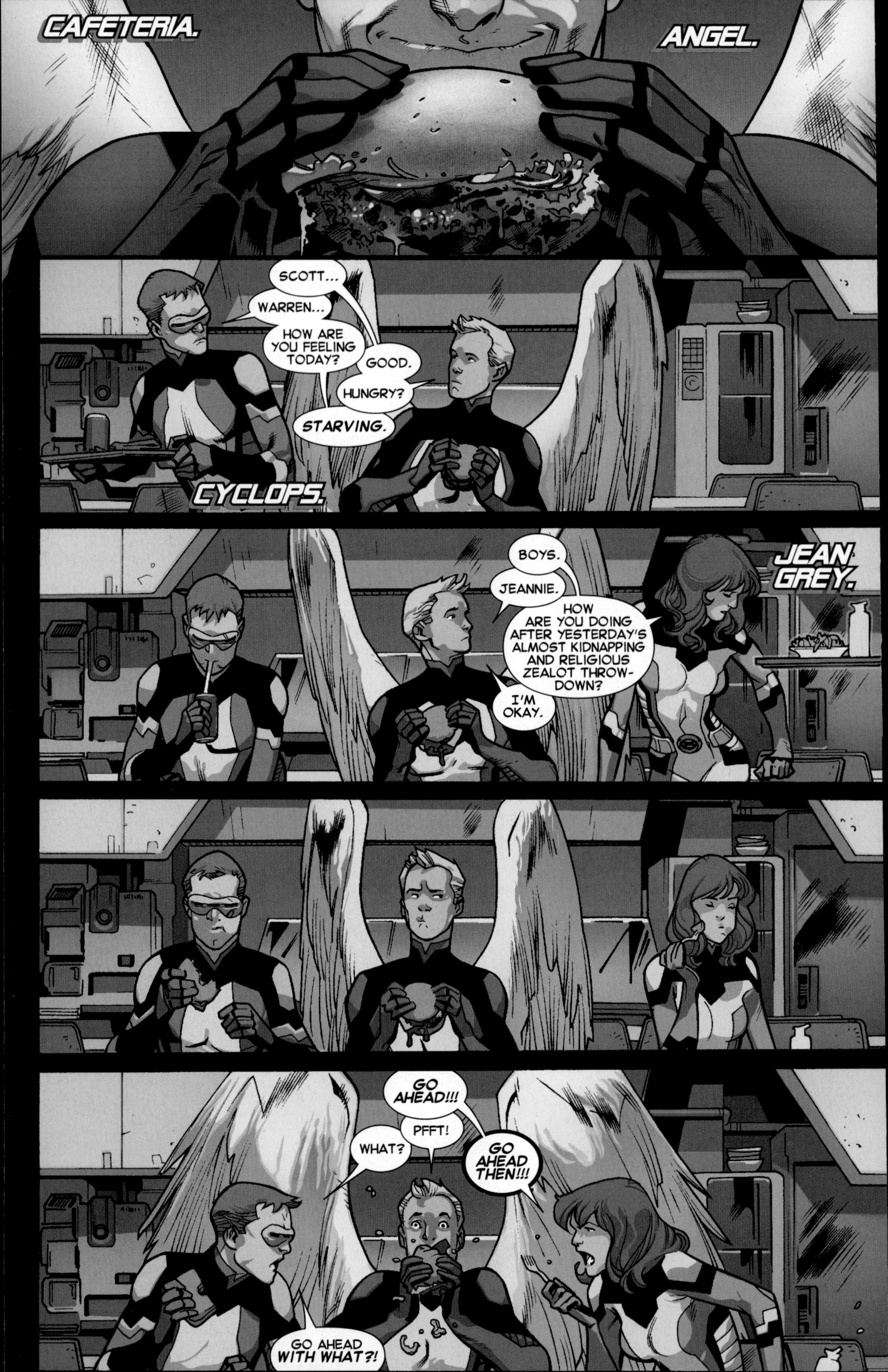
CAFETERIA.
ANGEL.
SCOTT...
WARREN...
HOW ARE YOU FEELING TODAY?
GOOD.
HUNGRY?
STARVING.
CYCLOPS.
BOYS.
JEANNIE.
JEAN GREY.
HOW ARE YOU DOING AFTER YESTERDAY'S ALMOST KIDNAPPING AND RELIGIOUS ZEALOT THROW-DOWN?
I'M OKAY.
GO AHEAD!!!
PFFT!
WHAT?
GO AHEAD THEN!!!
GO AHEAD WITH WHAT?!

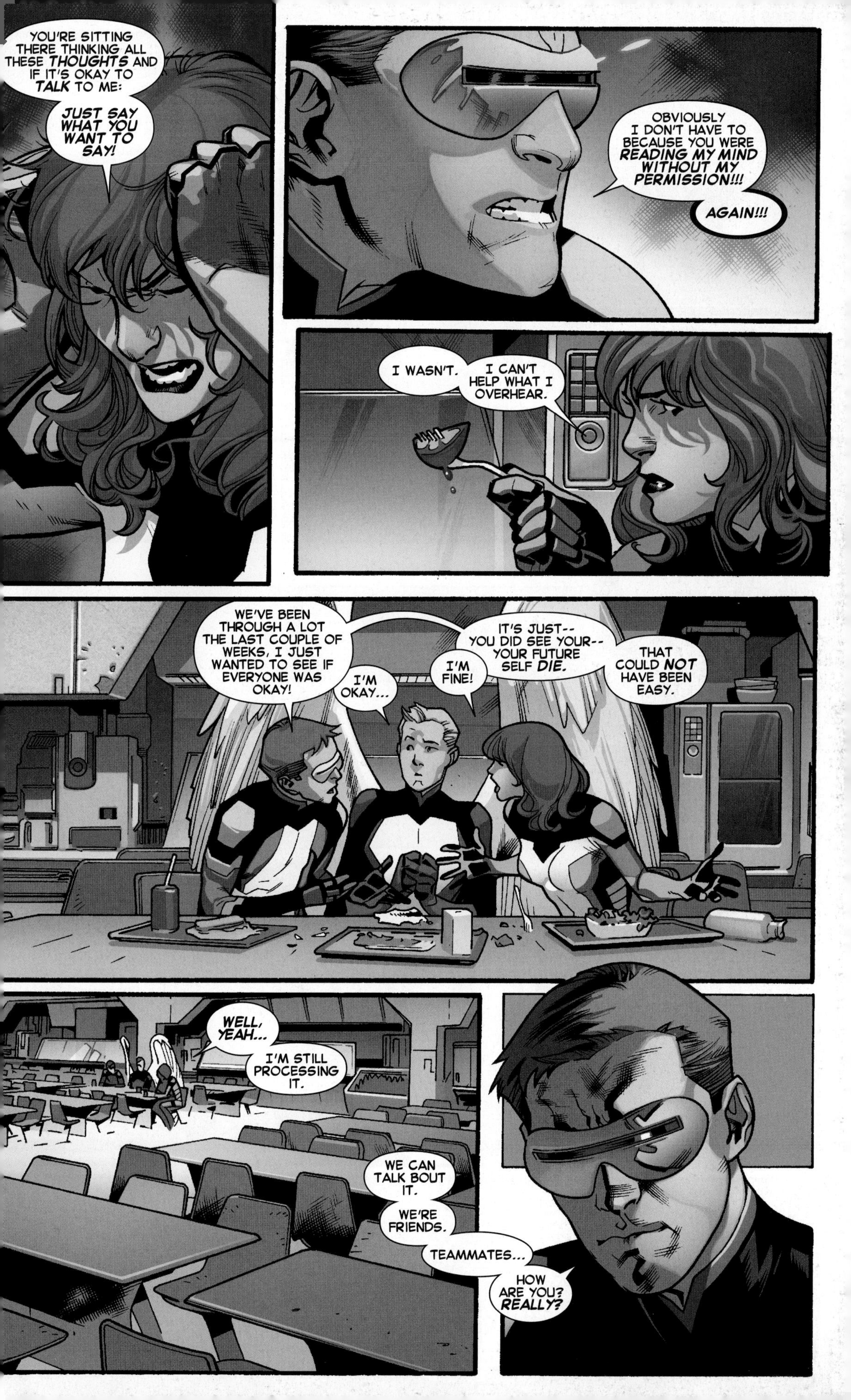

YOU'RE SITTING THERE THINKING ALL THESE *THOUGHTS* AND IF IT'S OKAY TO *TALK* TO ME:
JUST SAY WHAT YOU WANT TO SAY!
OBVIOUSLY I DON'T HAVE TO BECAUSE YOU WERE *READING MY MIND WITHOUT MY PERMISSION!!!*
AGAIN!!!
I WASN'T.
I CAN'T HELP WHAT I OVERHEAR.
WE'VE BEEN THROUGH A LOT THE LAST COUPLE OF WEEKS, I JUST WANTED TO SEE IF EVERYONE WAS OKAY!
I'M OKAY...
I'M FINE!
IT'S JUST-- YOU DID SEE YOUR-- YOUR FUTURE SELF *DIE.*
THAT COULD *NOT* HAVE BEEN EASY.
WELL, YEAH...
I'M STILL PROCESSING IT.
WE CAN TALK BOUT IT.
WE'RE FRIENDS.
TEAMMATES...
HOW ARE YOU? *REALLY?*

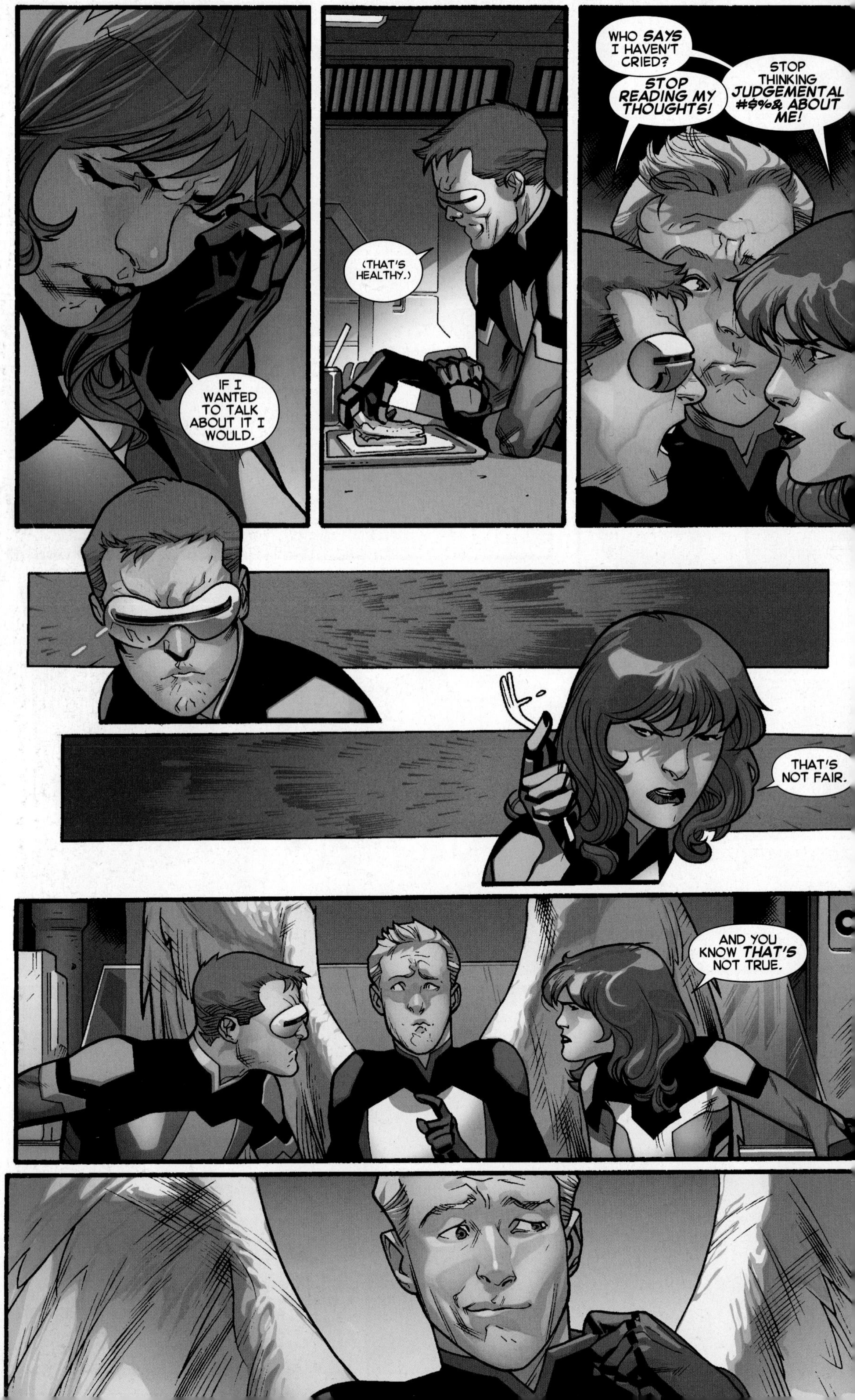
IF I WANTED TO TALK ABOUT IT I WOULD.
(THAT'S HEALTHY.)
WHO SAYS I HAVEN'T CRIED?
STOP READING MY THOUGHTS!
STOP THINKING JUDGEMENTAL #$%& ABOUT ME!
THAT'S NOT FAIR.
AND YOU KNOW THAT'S NOT TRUE.

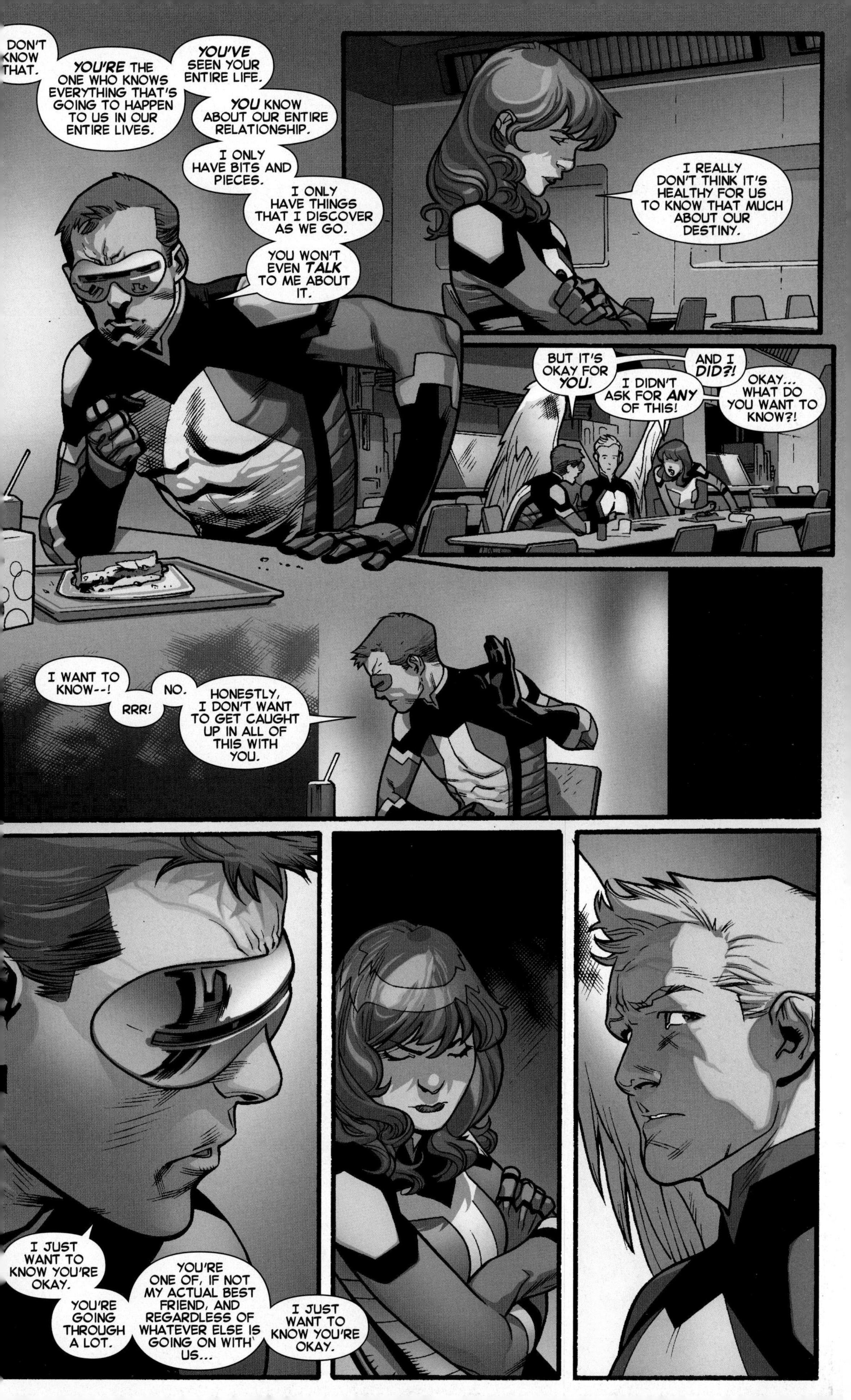
DON'T KNOW THAT.
YOU'RE THE ONE WHO KNOWS EVERYTHING THAT'S GOING TO HAPPEN TO US IN OUR ENTIRE LIVES.
YOU'VE SEEN YOUR ENTIRE LIFE.
YOU KNOW ABOUT OUR ENTIRE RELATIONSHIP.
I ONLY HAVE BITS AND PIECES.
I ONLY HAVE THINGS THAT I DISCOVER AS WE GO.
YOU WON'T EVEN TALK TO ME ABOUT IT.
I REALLY DON'T THINK IT'S HEALTHY FOR US TO KNOW THAT MUCH ABOUT OUR DESTINY.
BUT IT'S OKAY FOR YOU.
AND I DID?!
I DIDN'T ASK FOR ANY OF THIS!
OKAY... WHAT DO YOU WANT TO KNOW?!
I WANT TO KNOW--!
RRR!
NO.
HONESTLY, I DON'T WANT TO GET CAUGHT UP IN ALL OF THIS WITH YOU.
I JUST WANT TO KNOW YOU'RE OKAY.
YOU'RE GOING THROUGH A LOT.
YOU'RE ONE OF, IF NOT MY ACTUAL BEST FRIEND, AND REGARDLESS OF WHATEVER ELSE IS GOING ON WITH US...
I JUST WANT TO KNOW YOU'RE OKAY.

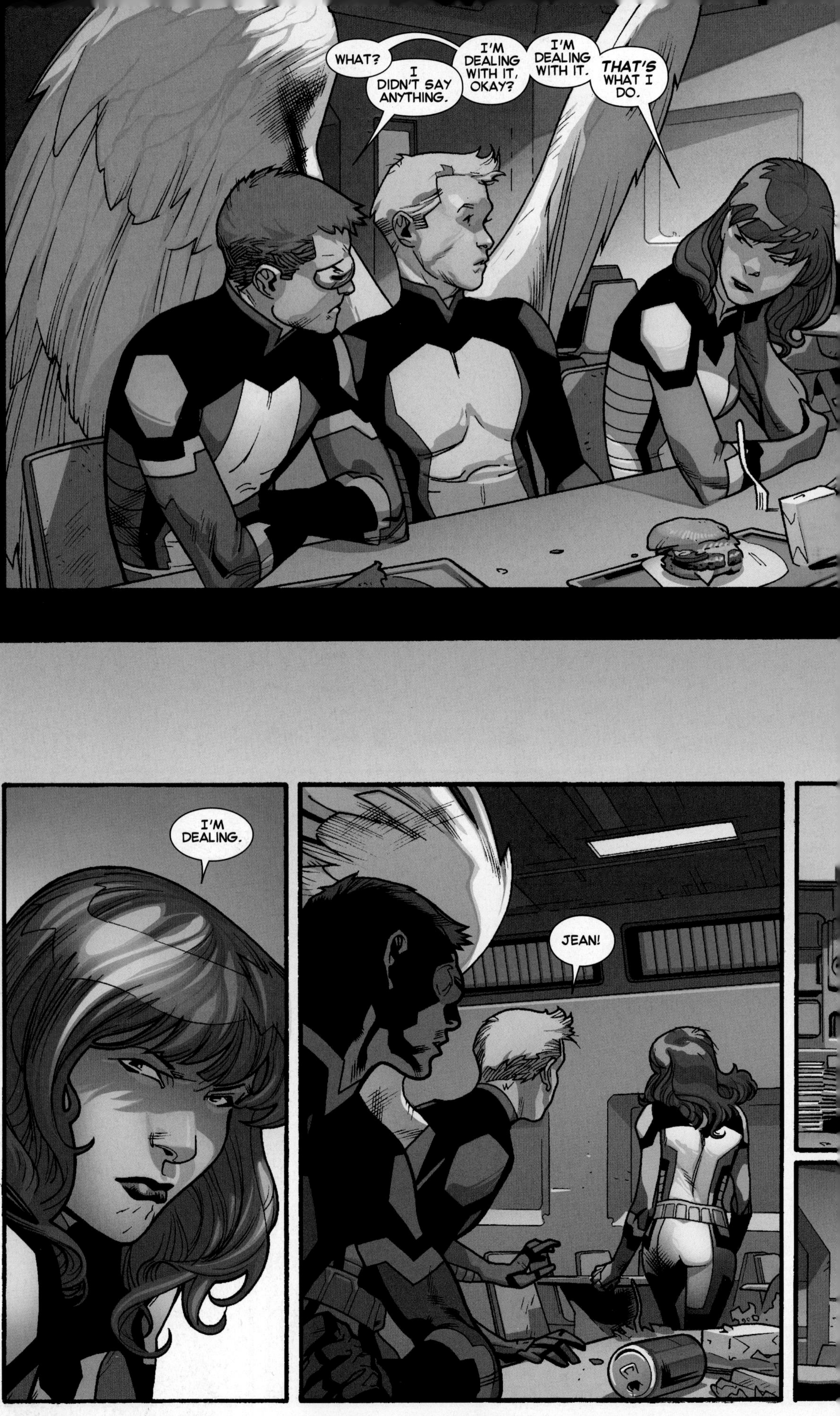
WHAT?
I DIDN'T SAY ANYTHING.
I'M DEALING WITH IT, OKAY?
I'M DEALING WITH IT.
THAT'S WHAT I DO.
I'M DEALING.
JEAN!

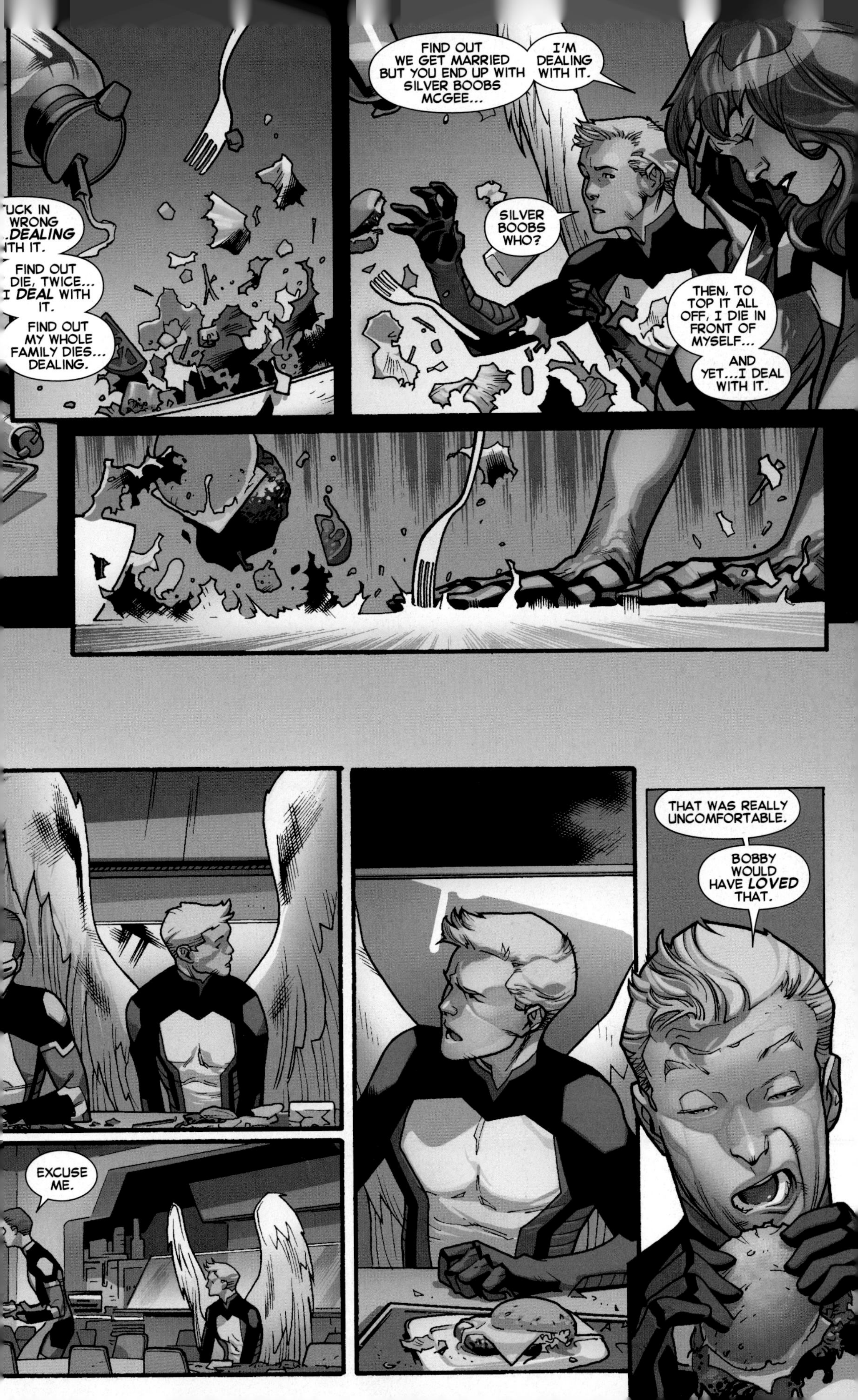
UCK IN WRONG ...DEALING ITH IT.
FIND OUT DIE, TWICE... I DEAL WITH IT.
FIND OUT MY WHOLE FAMILY DIES... DEALING.
FIND OUT WE GET MARRIED BUT YOU END UP WITH SILVER BOOBS MCGEE...
I'M DEALING WITH IT.
SILVER BOOBS WHO?
THEN, TO TOP IT ALL OFF, I DIE IN FRONT OF MYSELF...
AND YET...I DEAL WITH IT.
EXCUSE ME.
THAT WAS REALLY UNCOMFORTABLE.
BOBBY WOULD HAVE LOVED THAT.

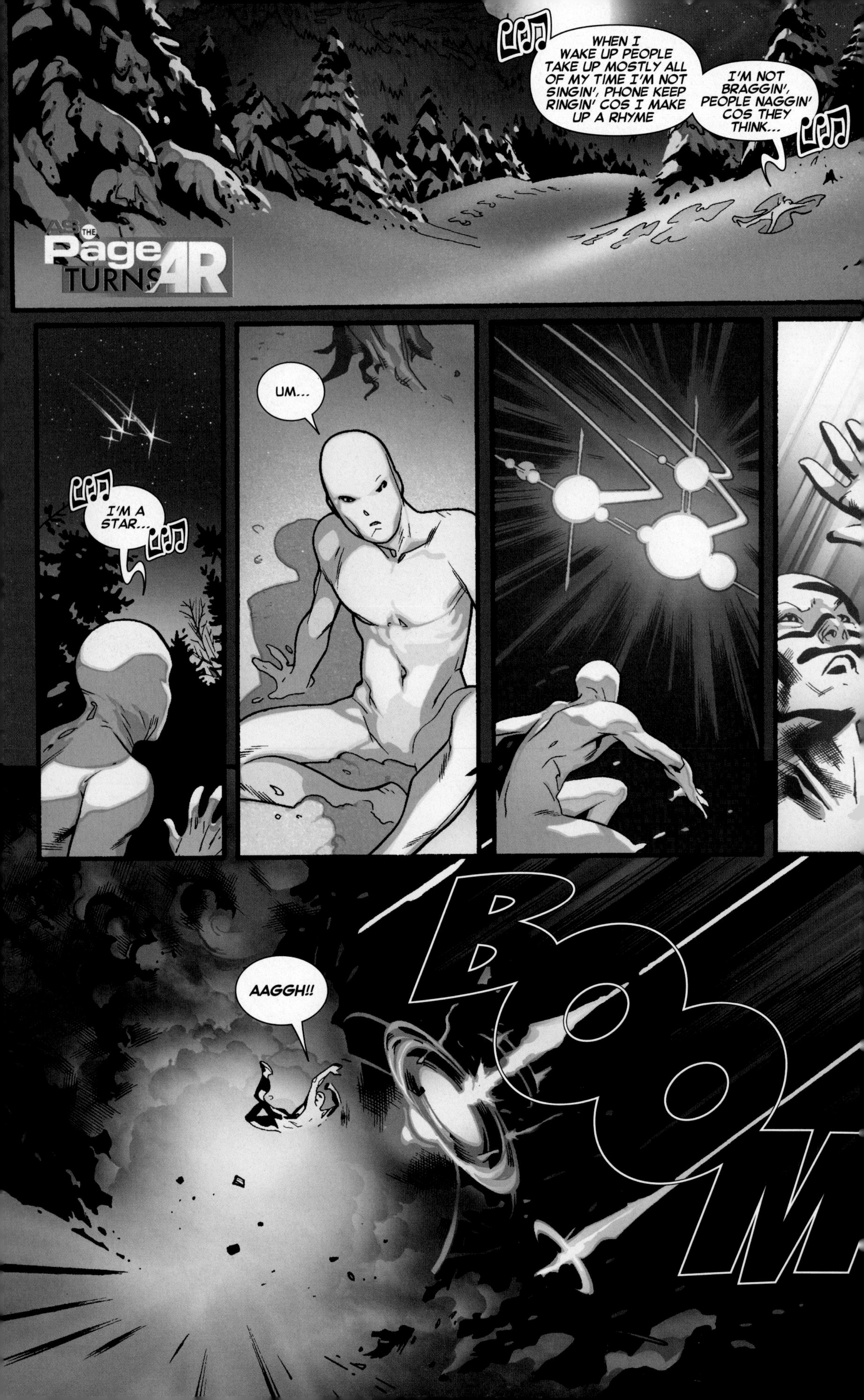
WHEN I WAKE UP PEOPLE TAKE UP MOSTLY ALL OF MY TIME I'M NOT SINGIN', PHONE KEEP RINGIN' COS I MAKE UP A RHYME
I'M NOT BRAGGIN', PEOPLE NAGGIN' COS THEY THINK...
AS THE Page TURNS AR
I'M A STAR...
UM...
AAGGH!!
BOOM

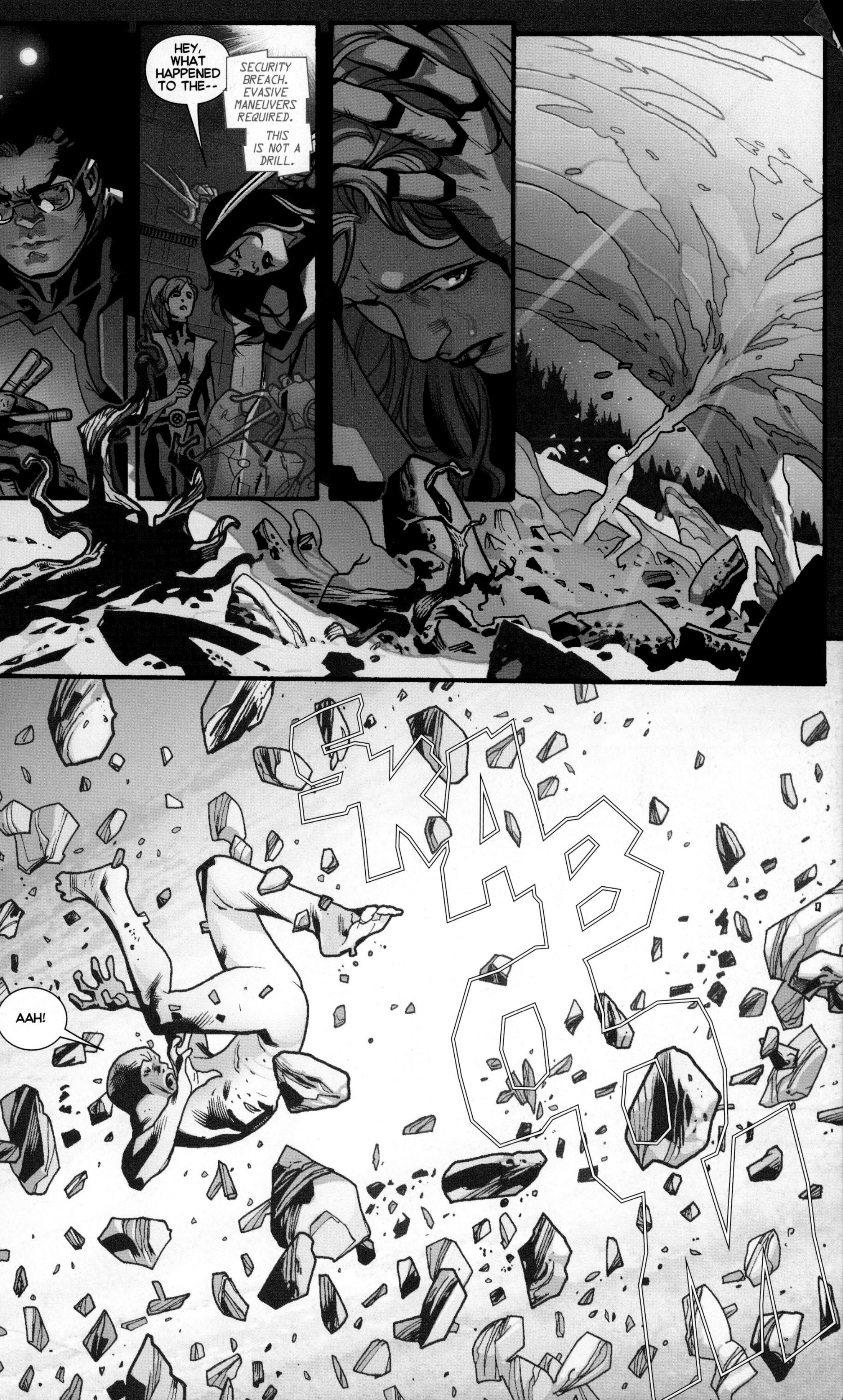
HEY, WHAT HAPPENED TO THE--
SECURITY BREACH. EVASIVE MANEUVERS REQUIRED.
THIS IS NOT A DRILL.
KA-BOOM
AAH!

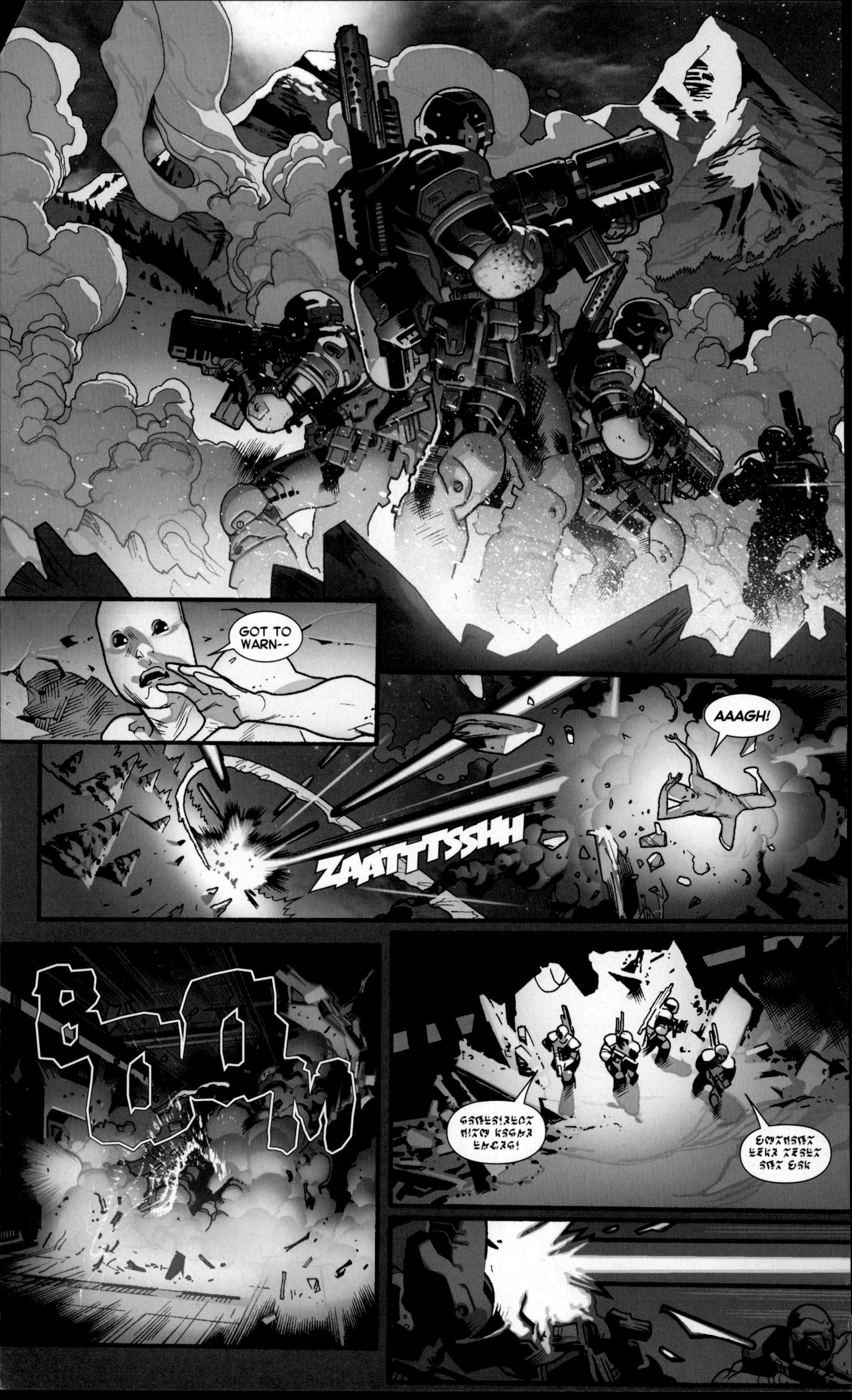
GOT TO WARN--
AAAGH!
ZAATTTSSHH
BOOM

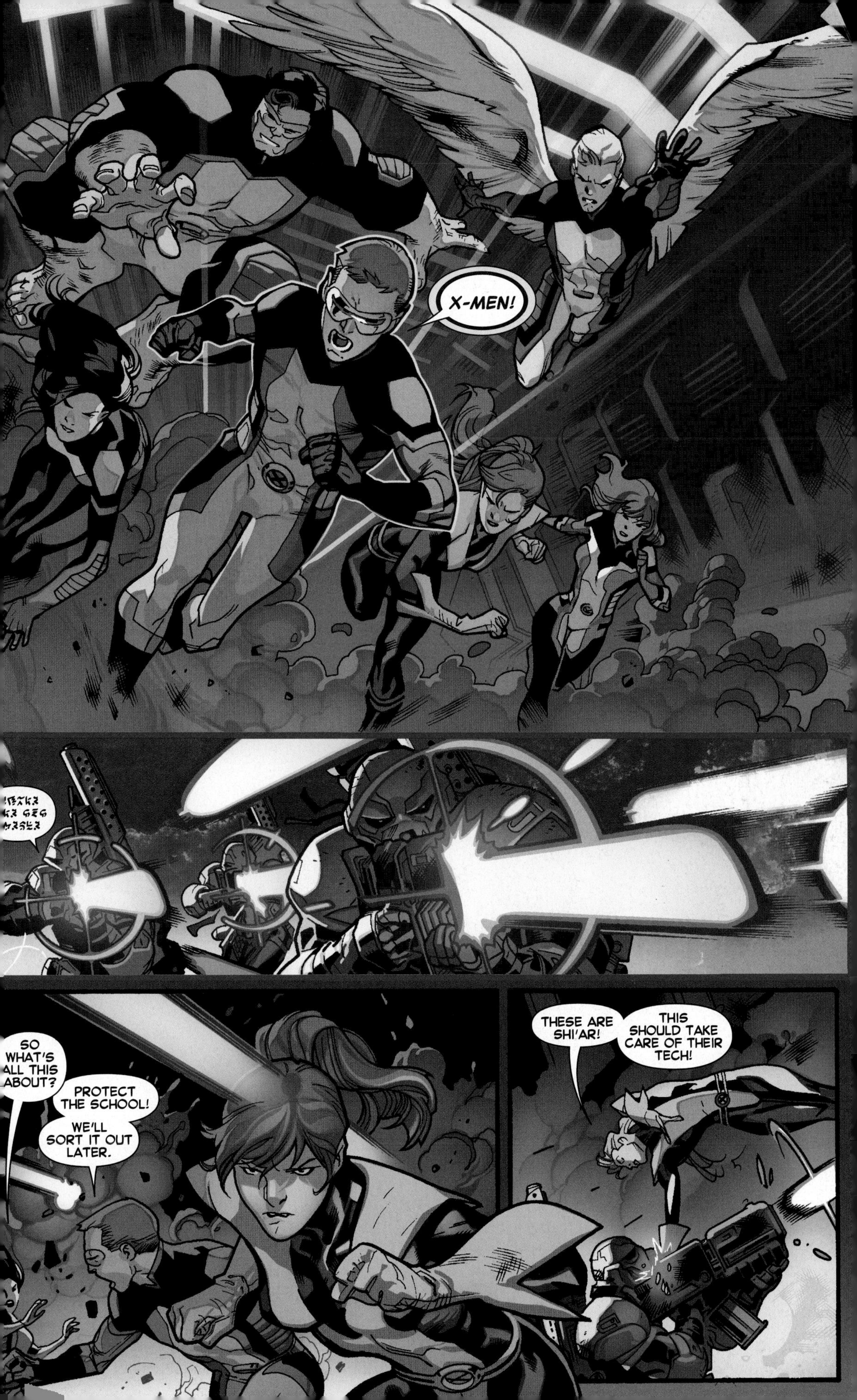
X-MEN!
SO WHAT'S ALL THIS ABOUT?
PROTECT THE SCHOOL!
WE'LL SORT IT OUT LATER.
THESE ARE SHI'AR!
THIS SHOULD TAKE CARE OF THEIR TECH!

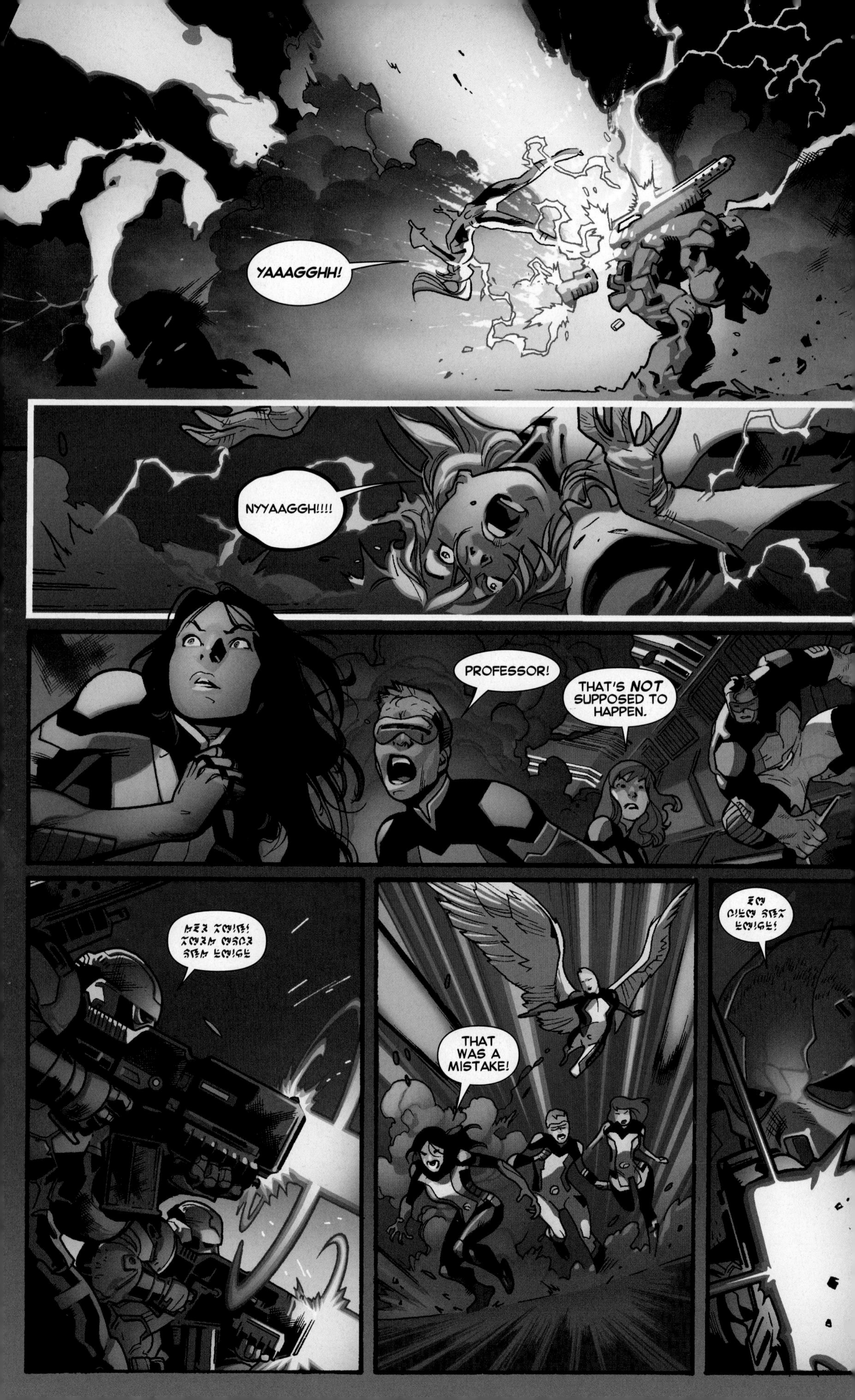
YAAAGGHH!
NYYAAGGH!!!!
PROFESSOR!
THAT'S NOT SUPPOSED TO HAPPEN.
THAT WAS A MISTAKE!

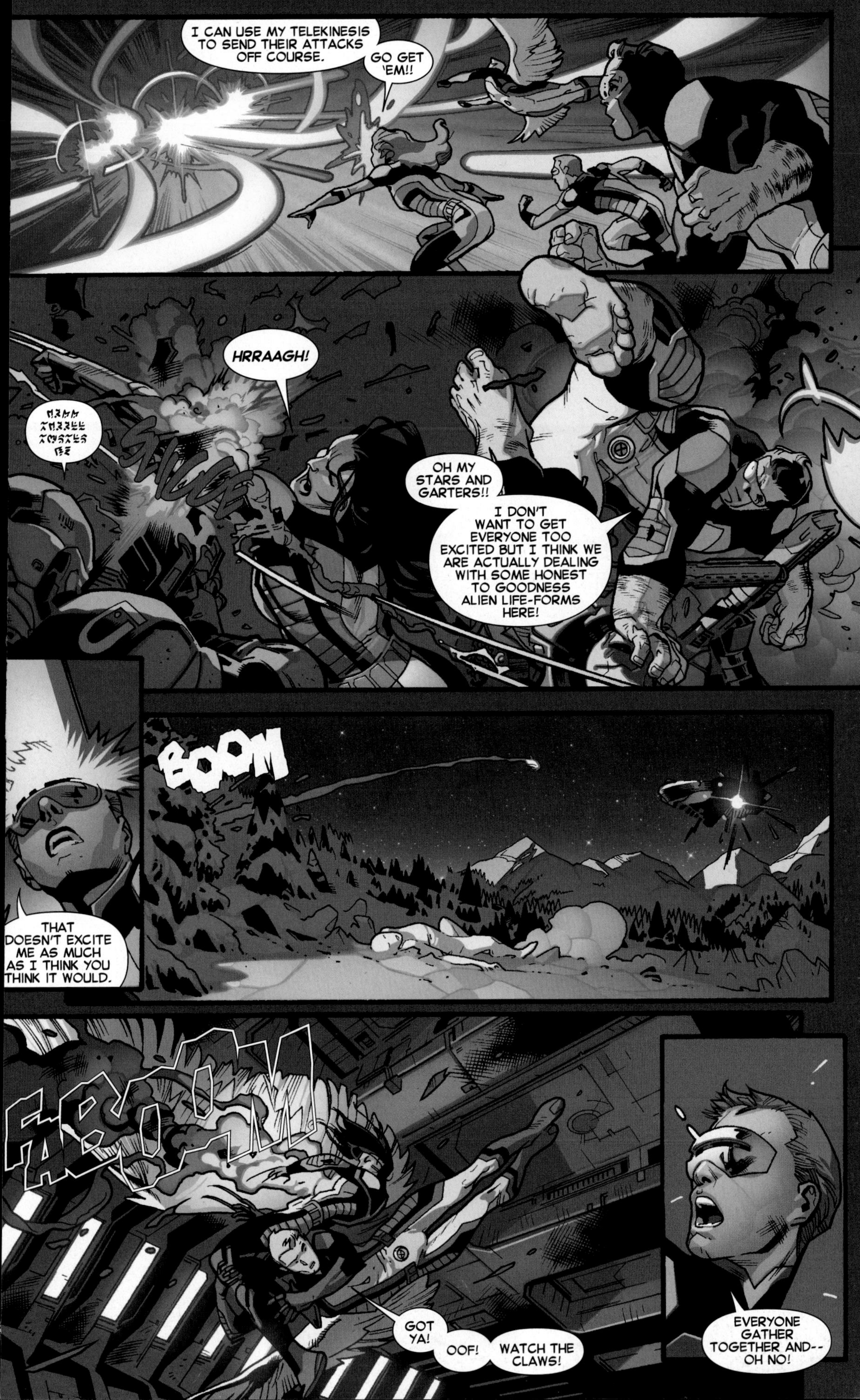
I CAN USE MY TELEKINESIS TO SEND THEIR ATTACKS OFF COURSE.
GO GET 'EM!!
HRRAAGH!
OH MY STARS AND GARTERS!!
I DON'T WANT TO GET EVERYONE TOO EXCITED BUT I THINK WE ARE ACTUALLY DEALING WITH SOME HONEST TO GOODNESS ALIEN LIFE-FORMS HERE!
THAT DOESN'T EXCITE ME AS MUCH AS I THINK YOU THINK IT WOULD.
BOOM
GOT YA!
OOF!
WATCH THE CLAWS!
EVERYONE GATHER TOGETHER AND-- OH NO!

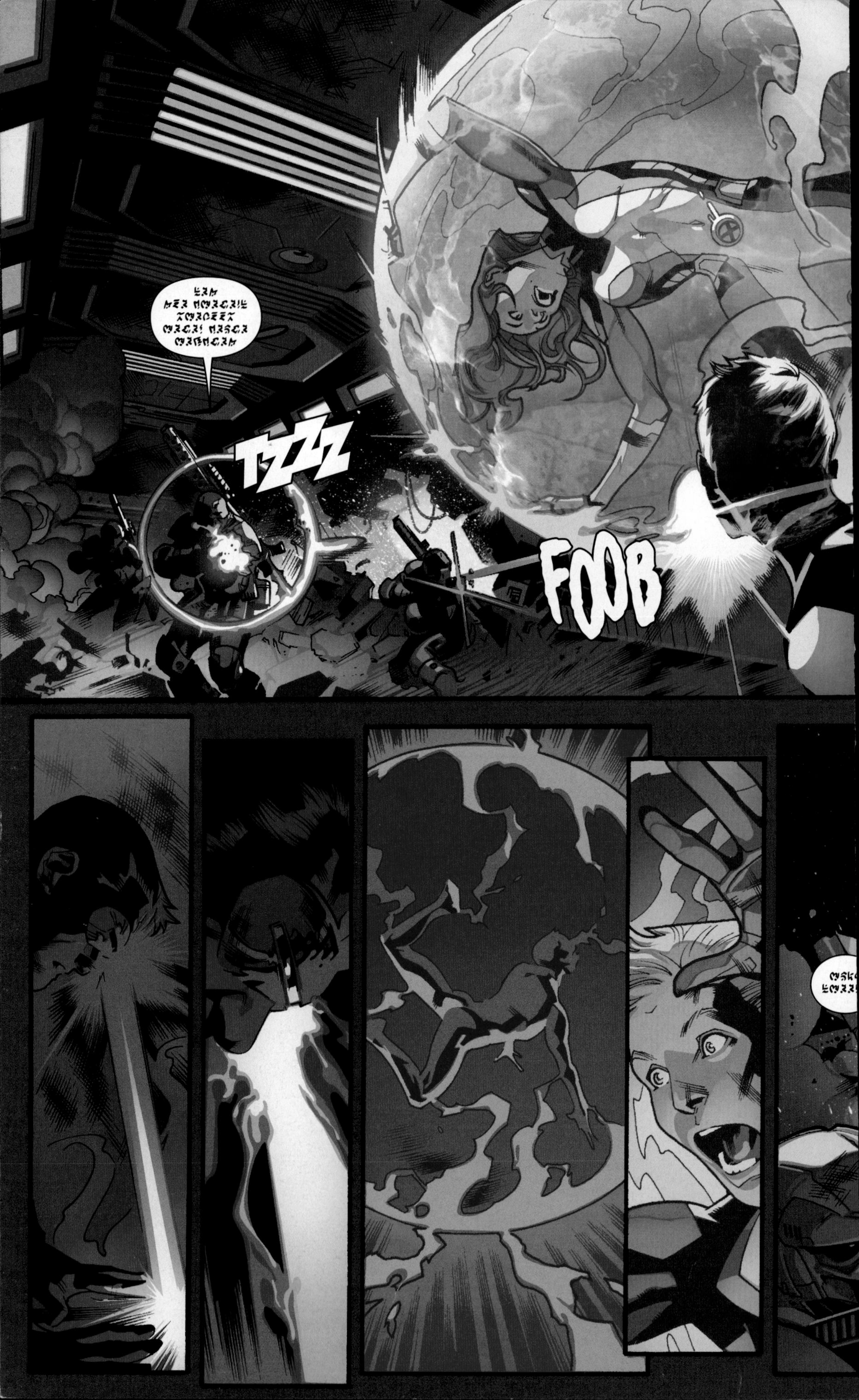
TZZZ
FOOB

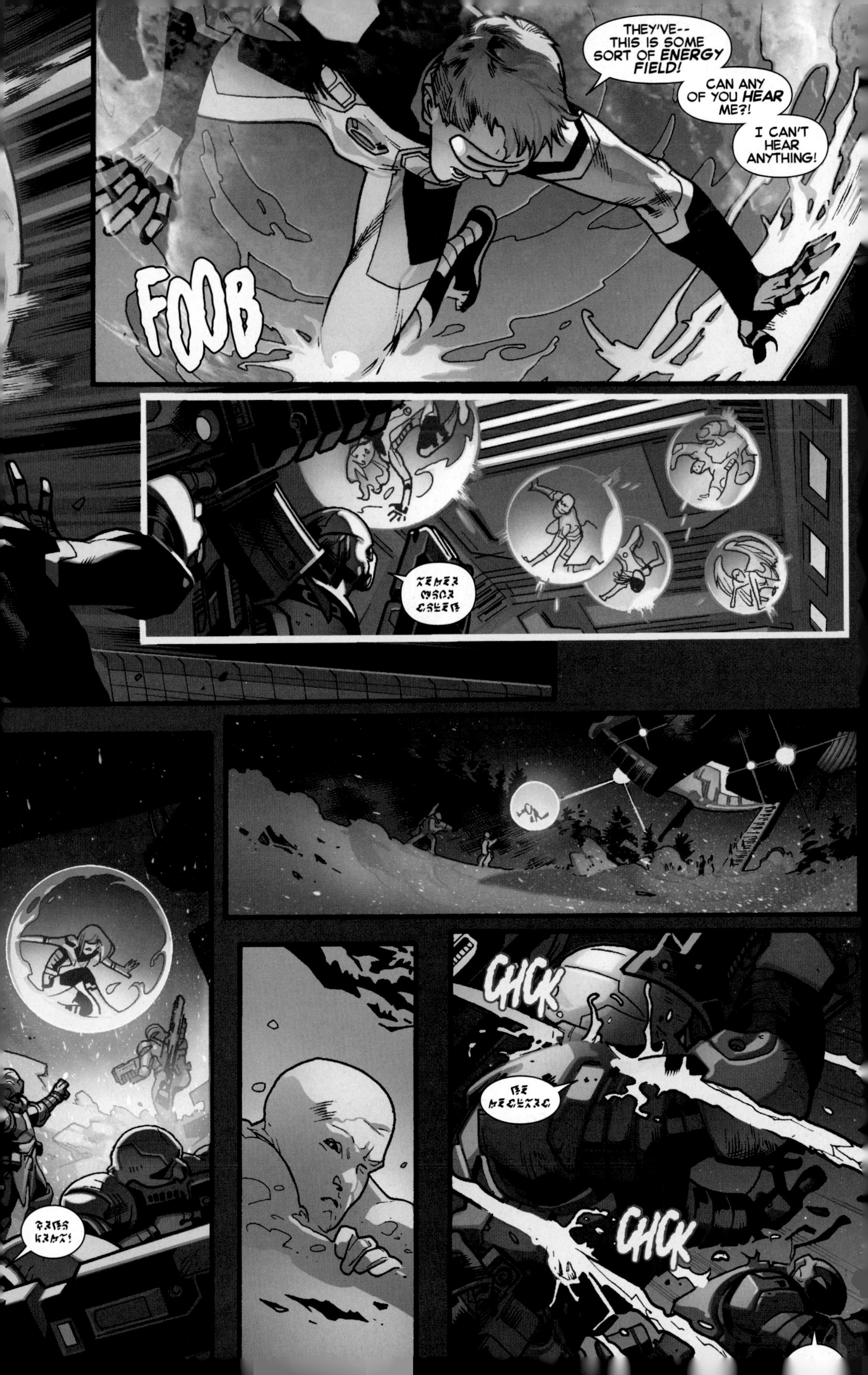
THEY'VE-- THIS IS SOME SORT OF ENERGY FIELD!
CAN ANY OF YOU HEAR ME?!
I CAN'T HEAR ANYTHING!
FOOB
CHCK
CHCK

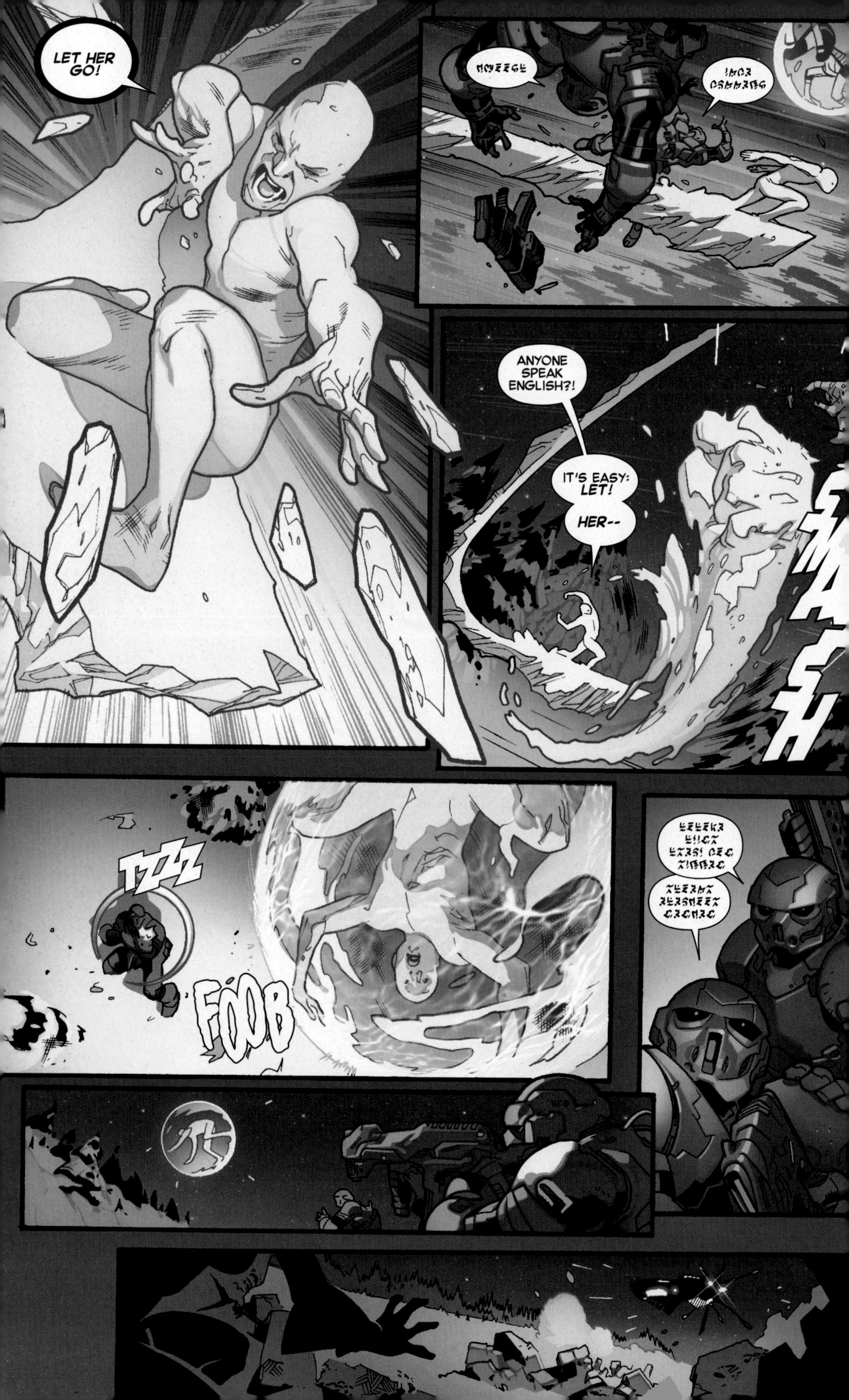
LET HER GO!
ANYONE SPEAK ENGLISH?!
IT'S EASY: LET!
HER--
SMASH
TZZZ
FOOB

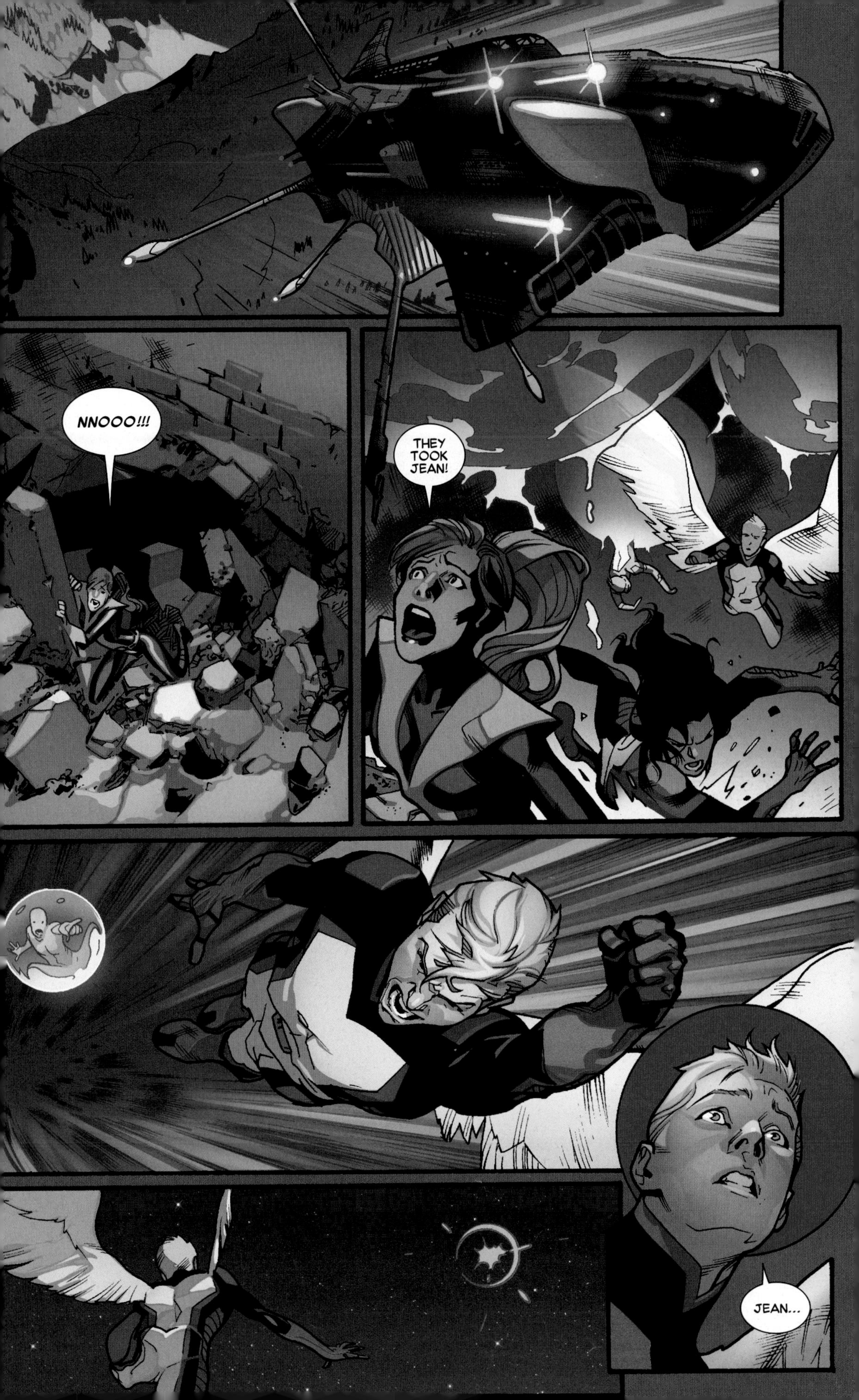
NNOOO!!!
THEY TOOK JEAN!
JEAN...

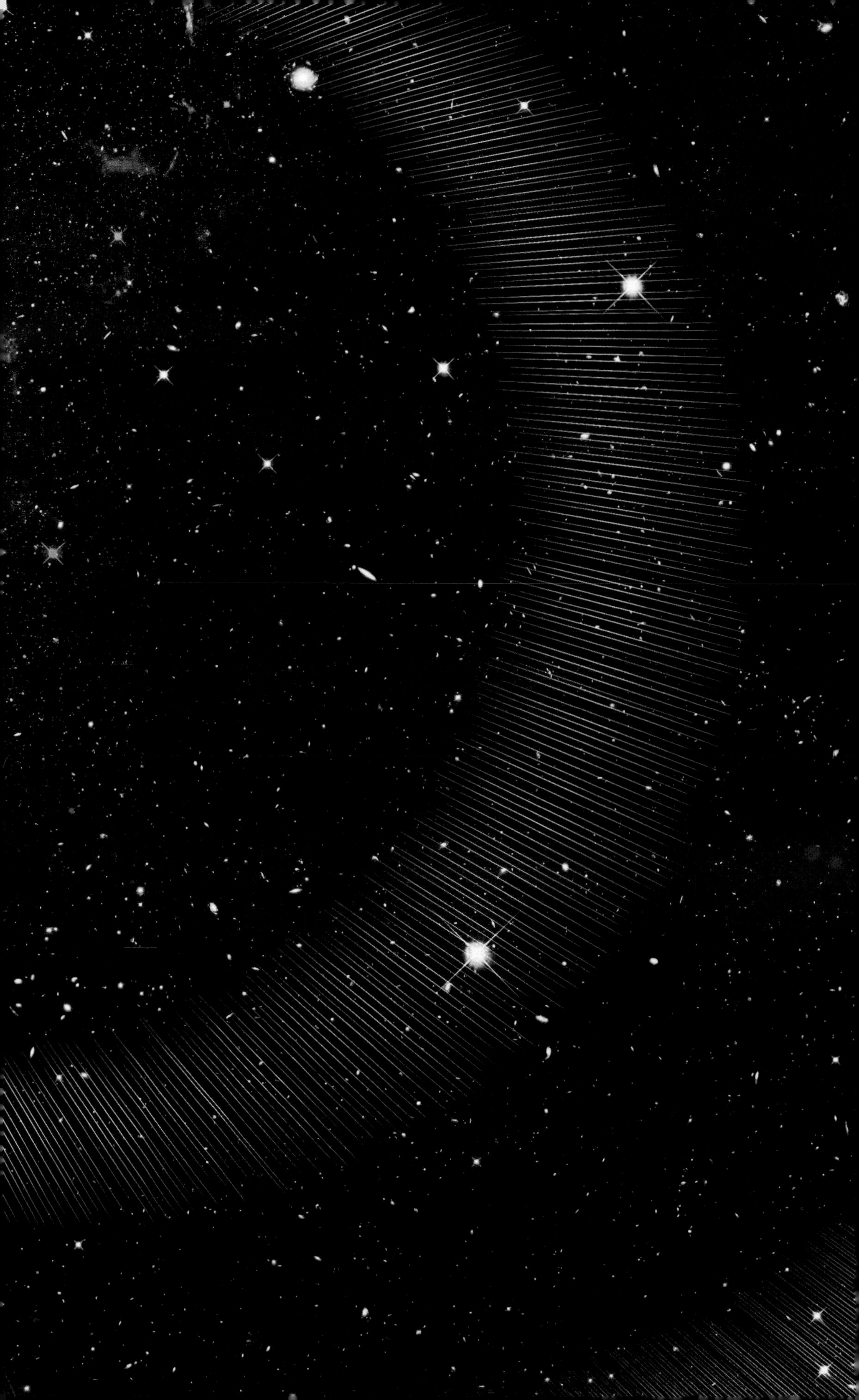

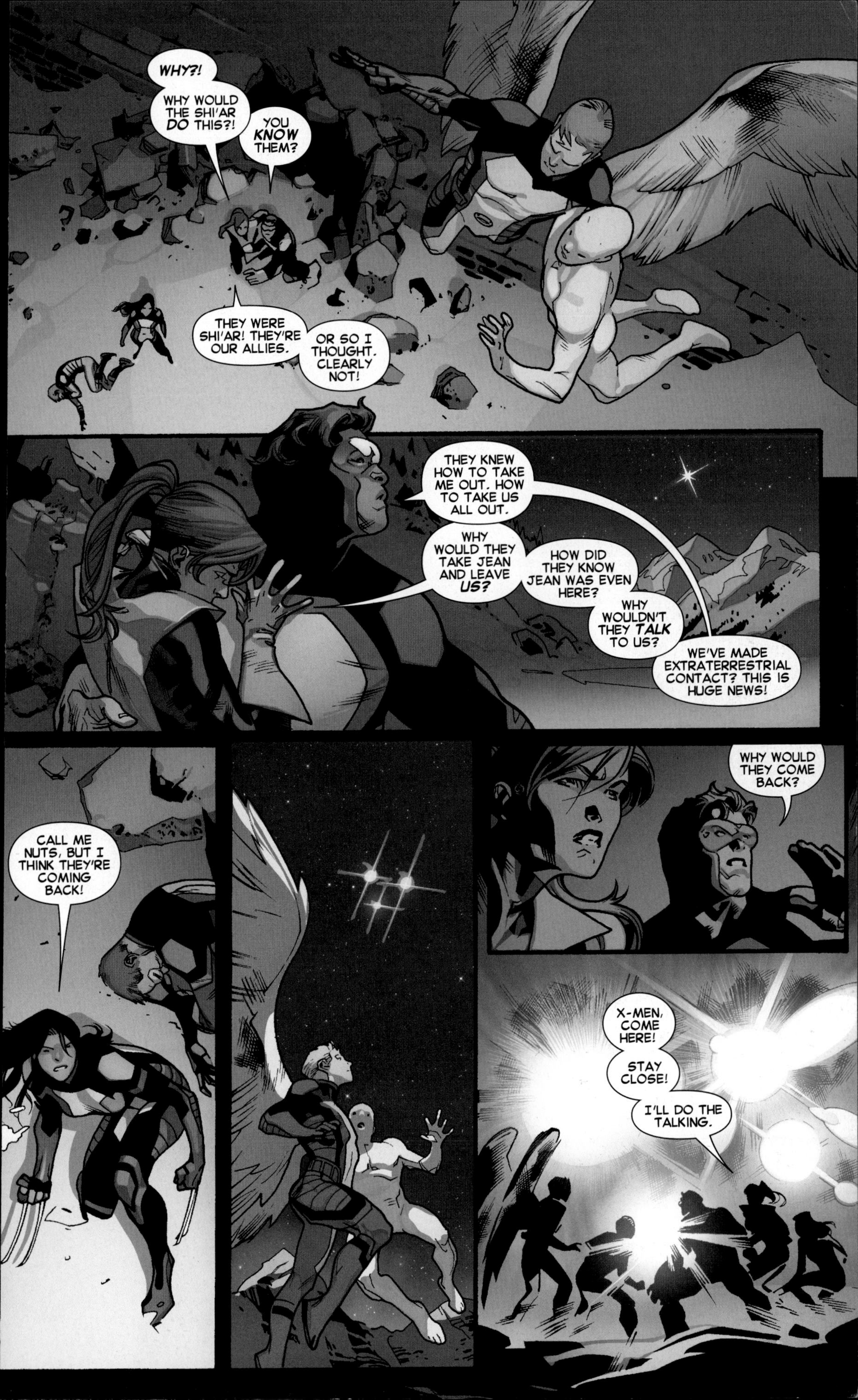
WHY?!
WHY WOULD THE SHI'AR DO THIS?!
YOU KNOW THEM?
THEY WERE SHI'AR! THEY'RE OUR ALLIES.
OR SO I THOUGHT. CLEARLY NOT!
THEY KNEW HOW TO TAKE ME OUT. HOW TO TAKE US ALL OUT.
WHY WOULD THEY TAKE JEAN AND LEAVE US?
HOW DID THEY KNOW JEAN WAS EVEN HERE?
WHY WOULDN'T THEY TALK TO US?
WE'VE MADE EXTRATERRESTRIAL CONTACT? THIS IS HUGE NEWS!
CALL ME NUTS, BUT I THINK THEY'RE COMING BACK!
WHY WOULD THEY COME BACK?
X-MEN, COME HERE!
STAY CLOSE!
I'LL DO THE TALKING.

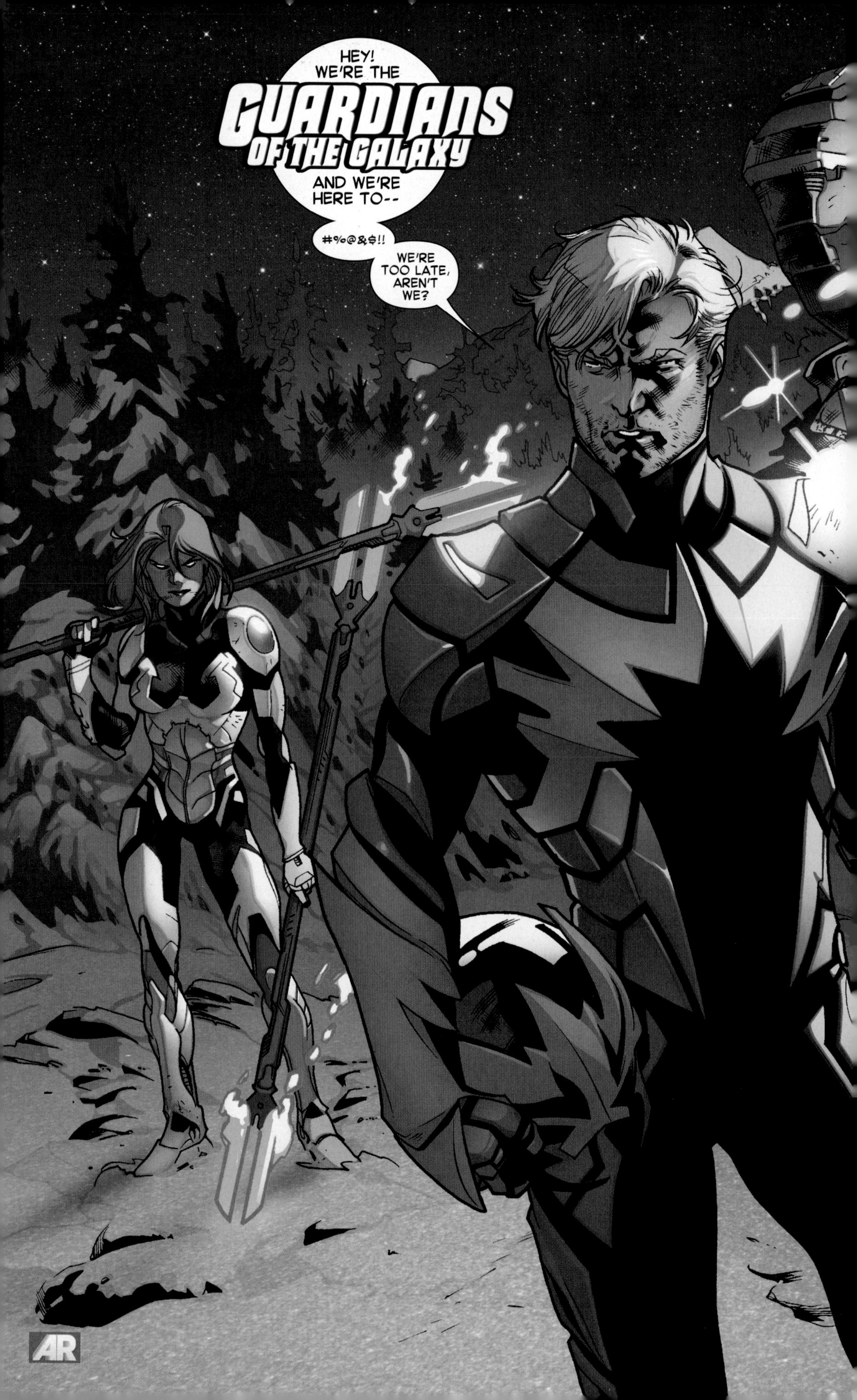
HEY! WE'RE THE GUARDIANS OF THE GALAXY AND WE'RE HERE TO--
#%@&$!!
WE'RE TOO LATE, AREN'T WE?

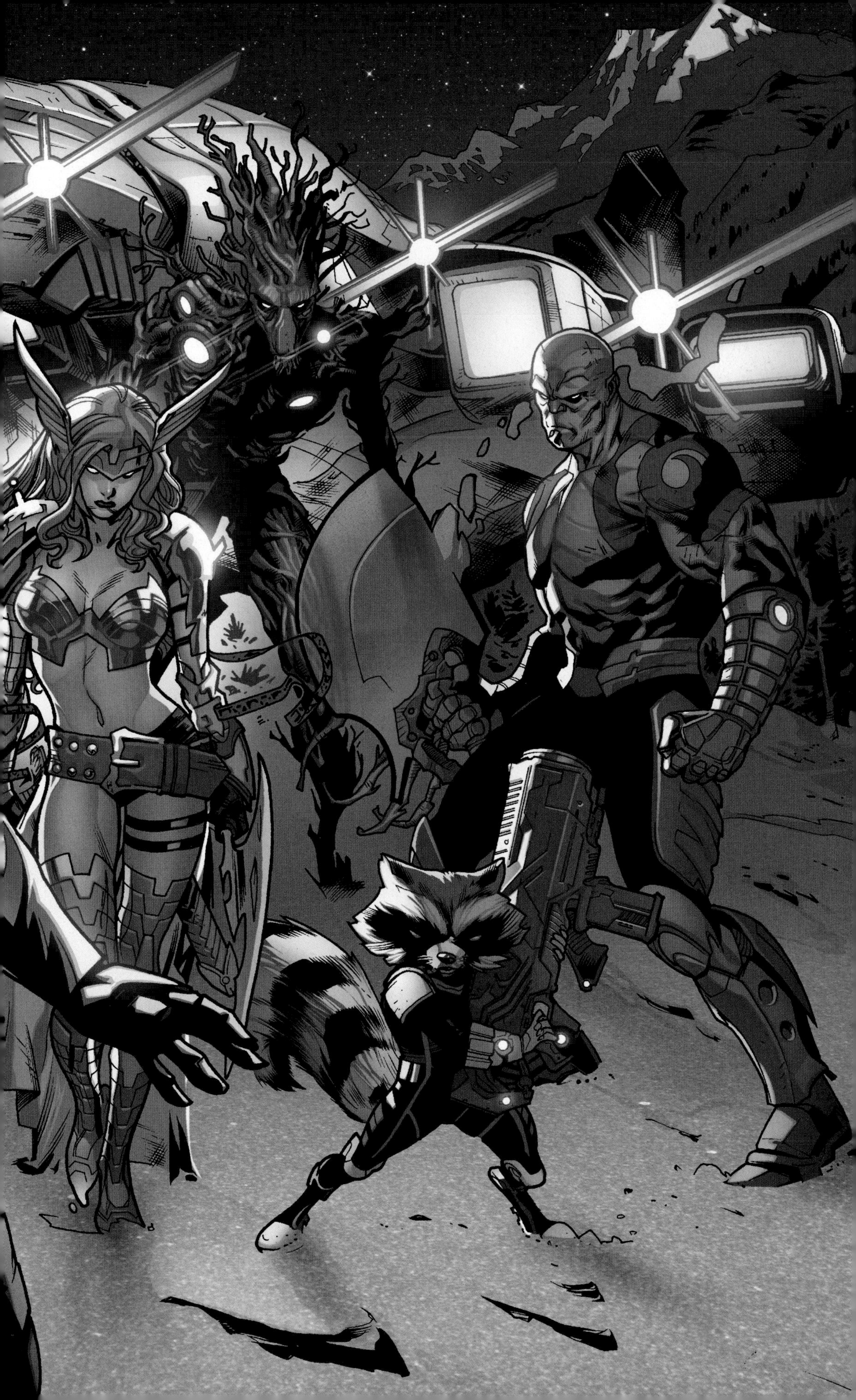

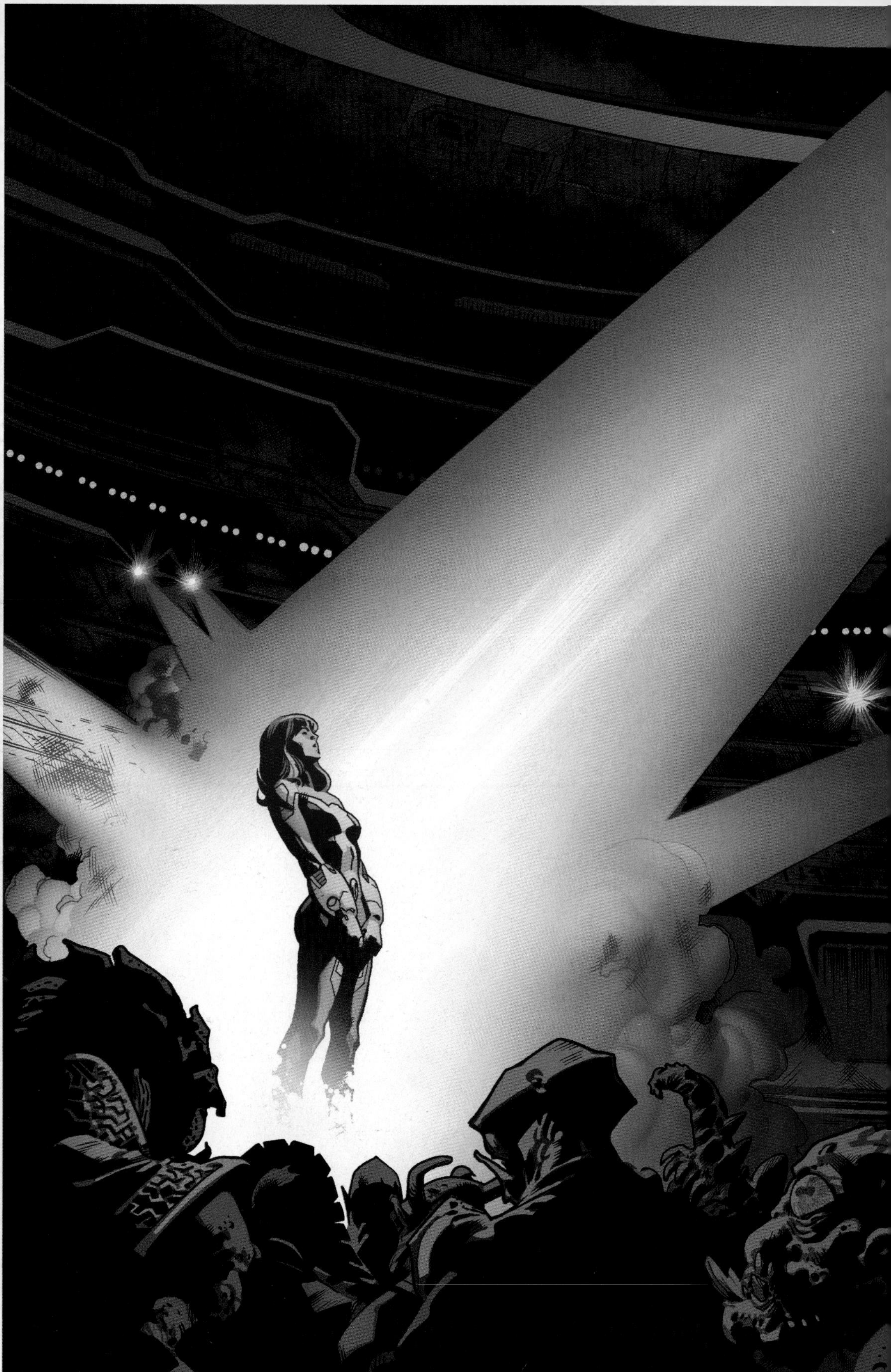

ALL-NEW X-MEN 23

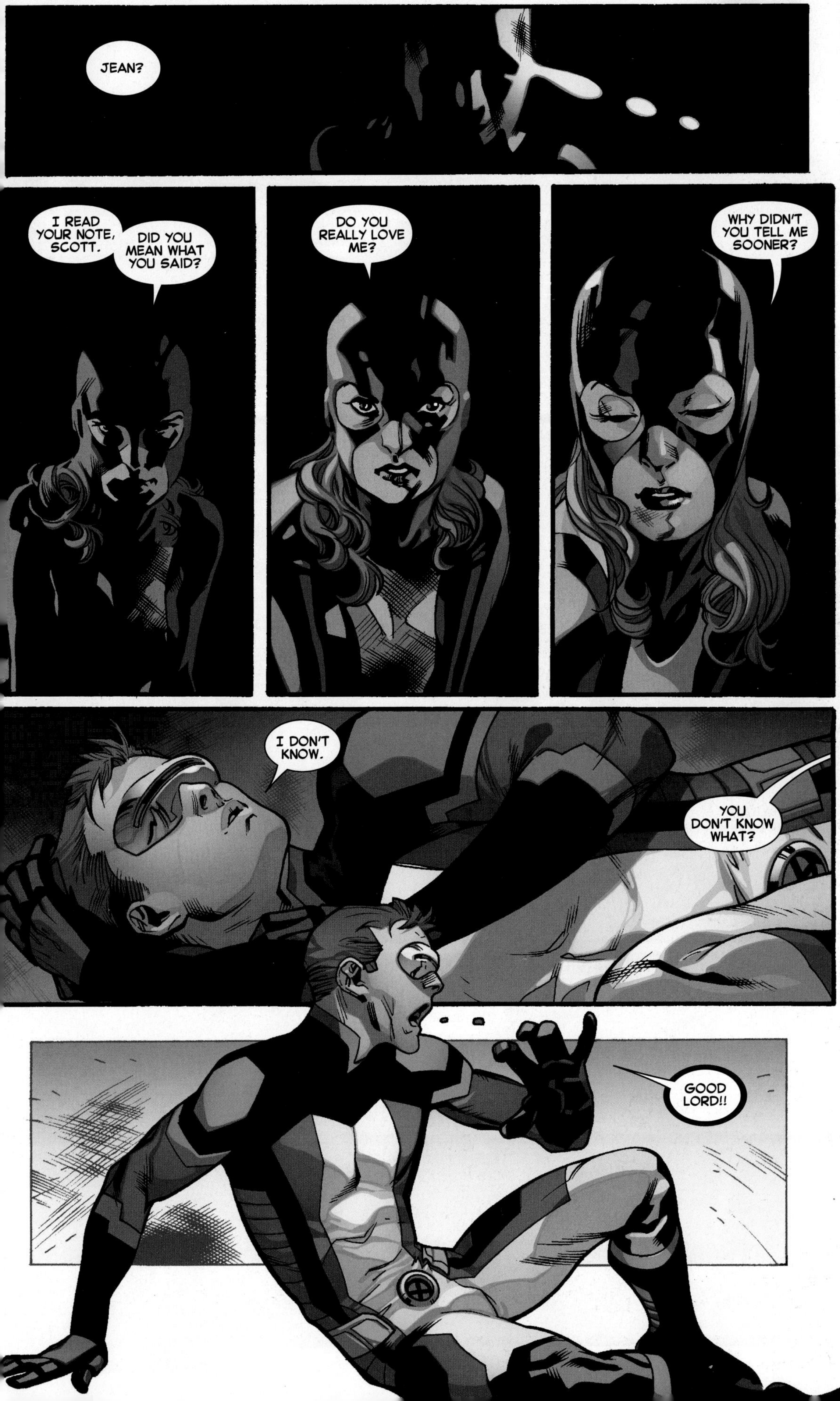
JEAN?
I READ YOUR NOTE, SCOTT.
DID YOU MEAN WHAT YOU SAID?
DO YOU REALLY LOVE ME?
WHY DIDN'T YOU TELL ME SOONER?
I DON'T KNOW.
YOU DON'T KNOW WHAT?
GOOD LORD!!

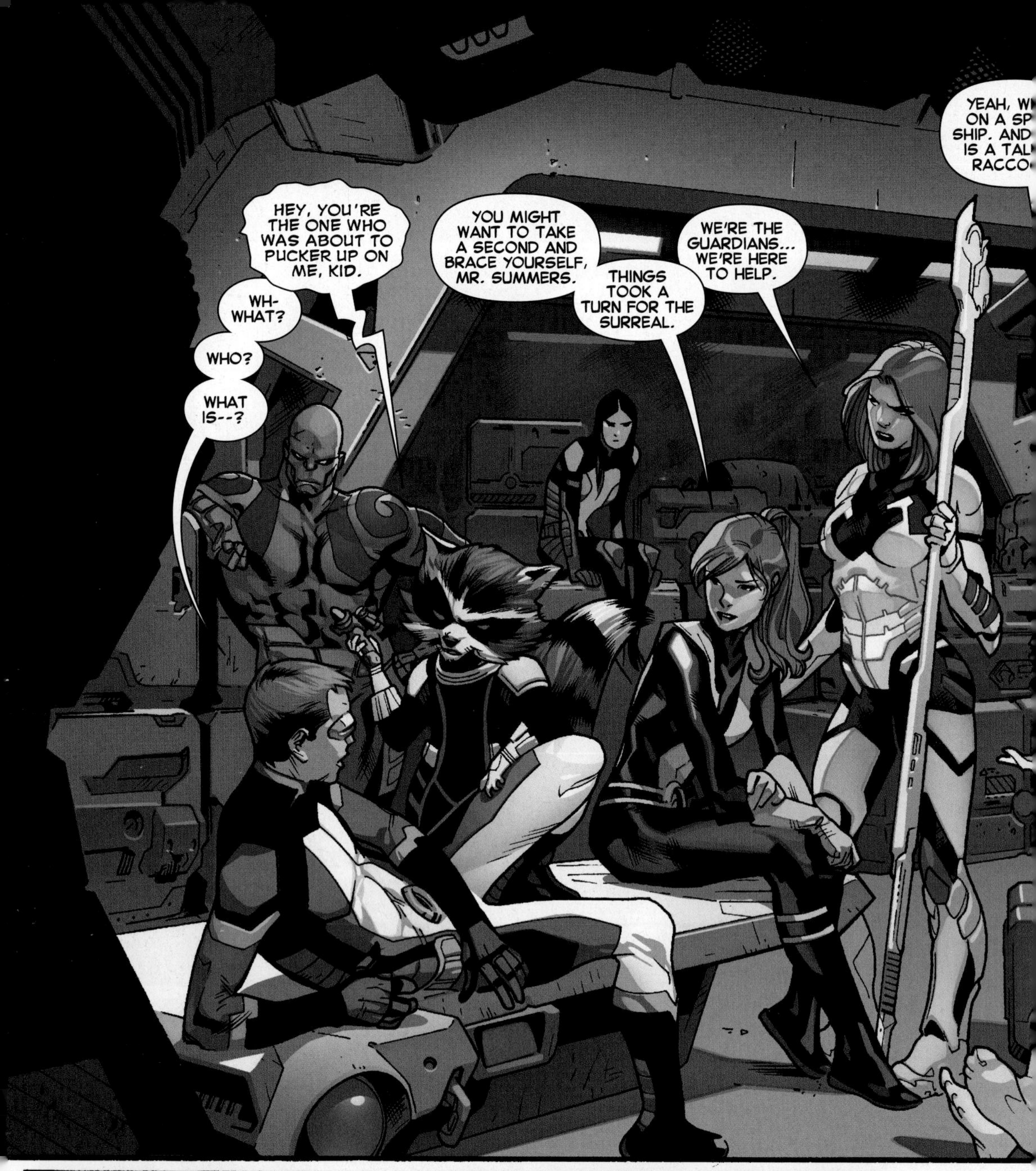
HEY, YOU'RE THE ONE WHO WAS ABOUT TO PUCKER UP ON ME, KID.
WH-WHAT?
WHO?
WHAT IS--?
YOU MIGHT WANT TO TAKE A SECOND AND BRACE YOURSELF, MR. SUMMERS.
THINGS TOOK A TURN FOR THE SURREAL.
WE'RE THE GUARDIANS... WE'RE HERE TO HELP.
YEAH, W
ON A SP
SHIP. AND
IS A TAL
RACCO

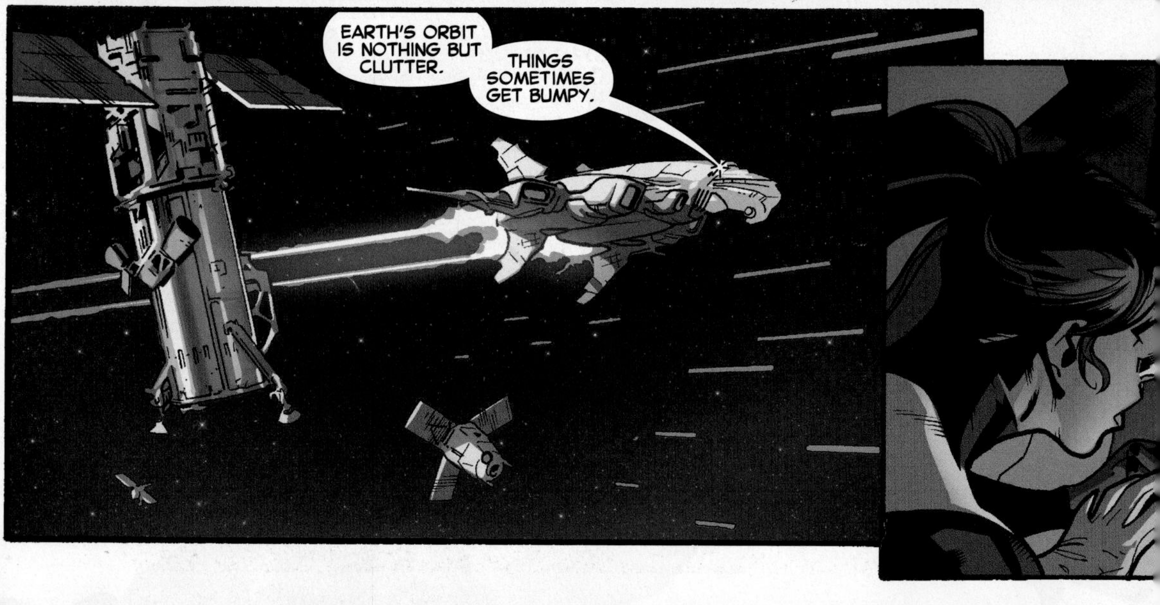
EARTH'S ORBIT IS NOTHING BUT CLUTTER.
THINGS SOMETIMES GET BUMPY.

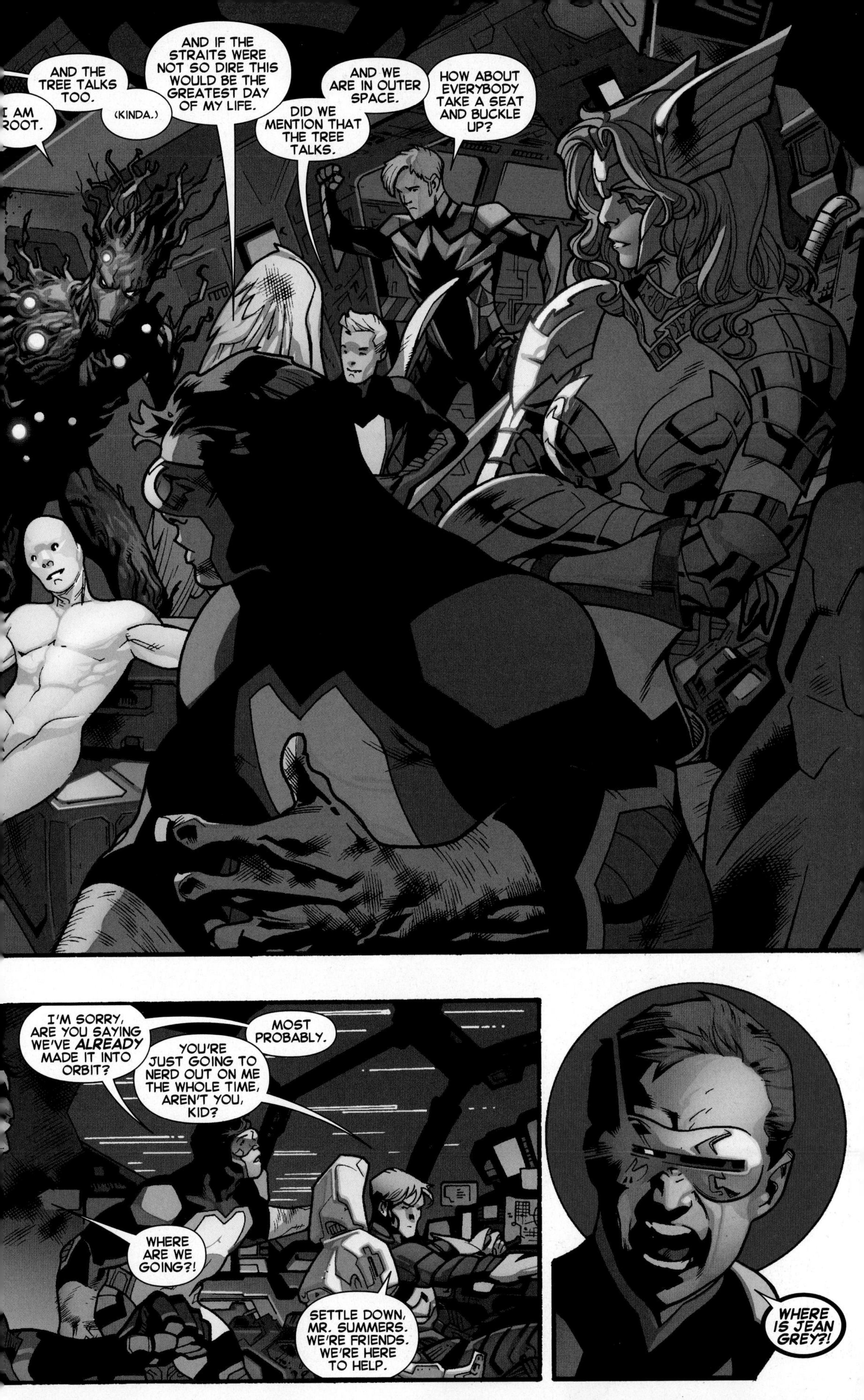

I AM ROOT.
AND THE TREE TALKS TOO.
(KINDA.)
AND IF THE STRAITS WERE NOT SO DIRE THIS WOULD BE THE GREATEST DAY OF MY LIFE.
AND WE ARE IN OUTER SPACE.
DID WE MENTION THAT THE TREE TALKS.
HOW ABOUT EVERYBODY TAKE A SEAT AND BUCKLE UP?
I'M SORRY, ARE YOU SAYING WE'VE *ALREADY* MADE IT INTO ORBIT?
MOST PROBABLY.
YOU'RE JUST GOING TO NERD OUT ON ME THE WHOLE TIME, AREN'T YOU, KID?
WHERE ARE WE GOING?!
SETTLE DOWN, MR. SUMMERS. WE'RE FRIENDS. WE'RE HERE TO HELP.
WHERE IS JEAN GREY?!

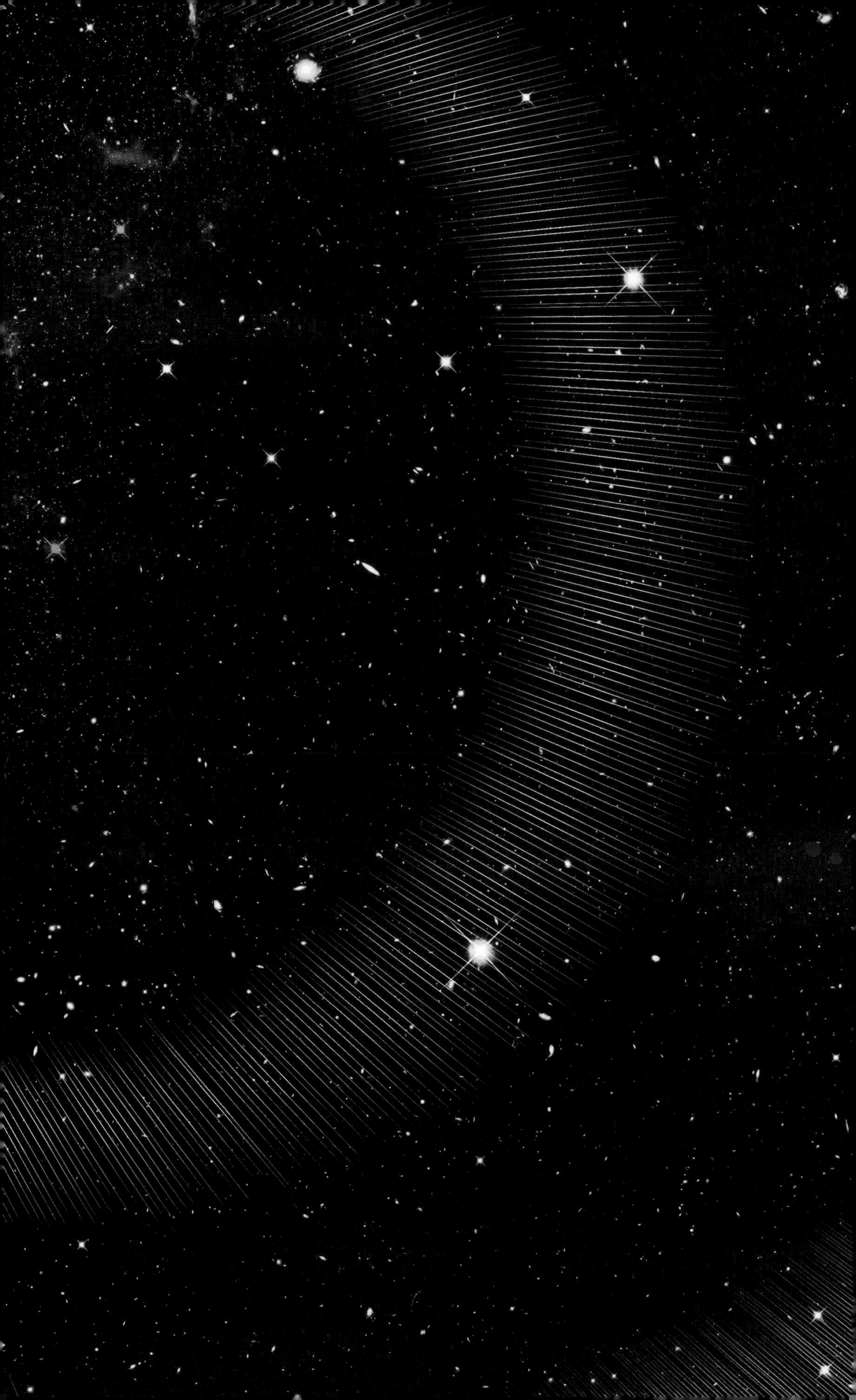

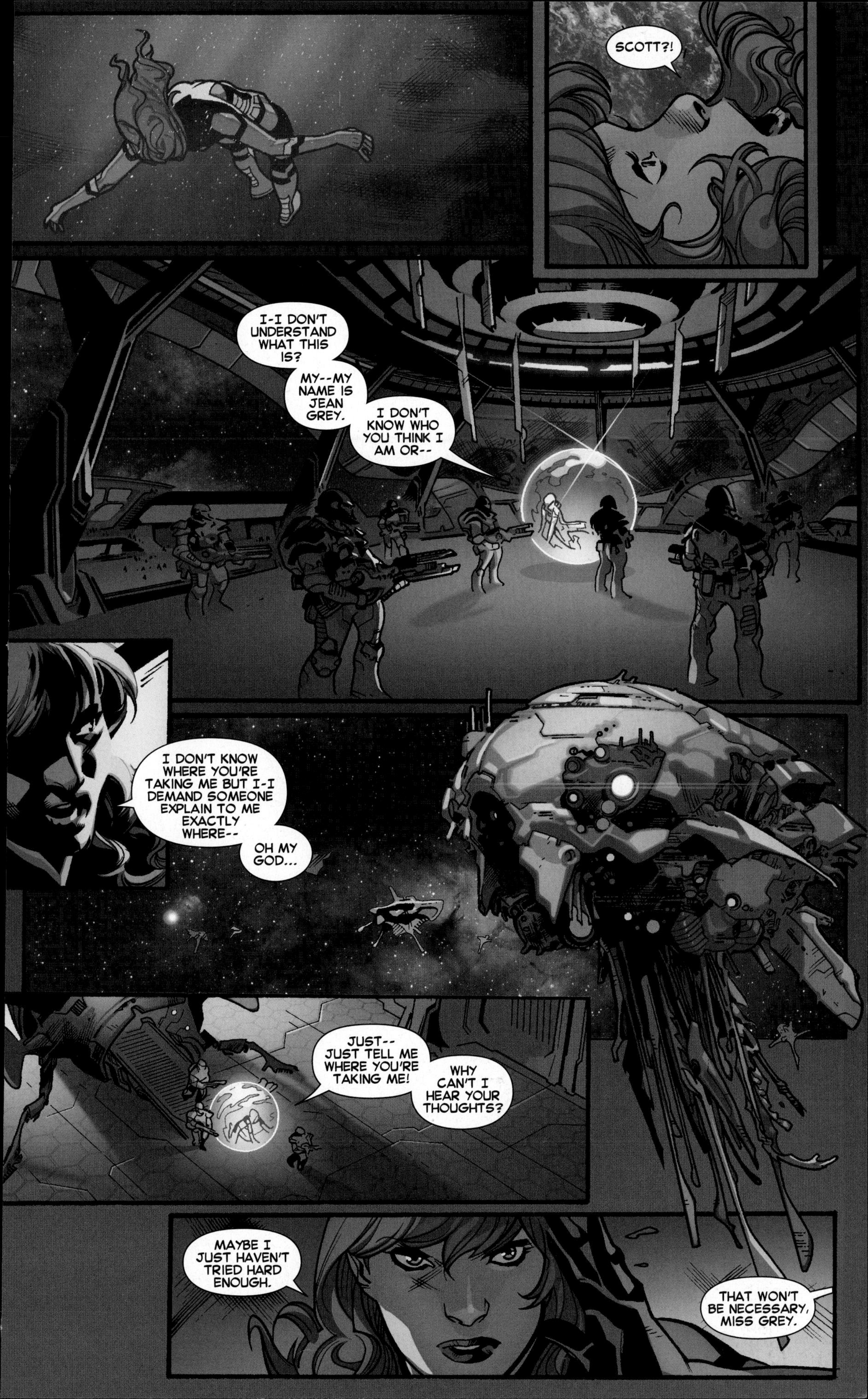
SCOTT?!
I-I DON'T UNDERSTAND WHAT THIS IS?
MY--MY NAME IS JEAN GREY.
I DON'T KNOW WHO YOU THINK I AM OR--
I DON'T KNOW WHERE YOU'RE TAKING ME BUT I-I DEMAND SOMEONE EXPLAIN TO ME EXACTLY WHERE--
OH MY GOD...
JUST-- JUST TELL ME WHERE YOU'RE TAKING ME!
WHY CAN'T I HEAR YOUR THOUGHTS?
MAYBE I JUST HAVEN'T TRIED HARD ENOUGH.
THAT WON'T BE NECESSARY, MISS GREY.

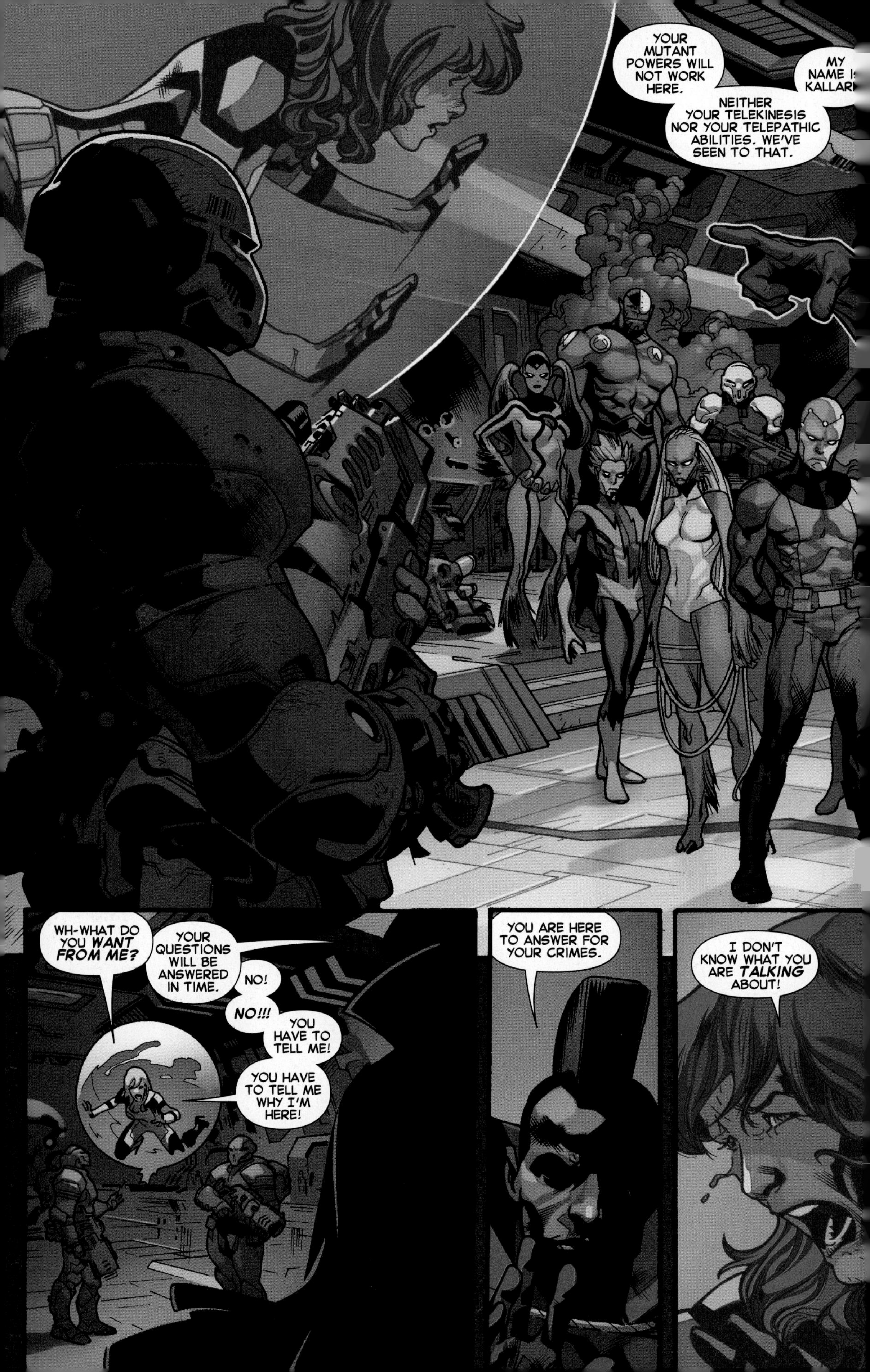
YOUR MUTANT POWERS WILL NOT WORK HERE.
NEITHER YOUR TELEKINESIS NOR YOUR TELEPATHIC ABILITIES. WE'VE SEEN TO THAT.
MY NAME IS KALLAR
WH-WHAT DO YOU WANT FROM ME?
YOUR QUESTIONS WILL BE ANSWERED IN TIME.
NO!
NO!!!
YOU HAVE TO TELL ME!
YOU HAVE TO TELL ME WHY I'M HERE!
YOU ARE HERE TO ANSWER FOR YOUR CRIMES.
I DON'T KNOW WHAT YOU ARE TALKING ABOUT!

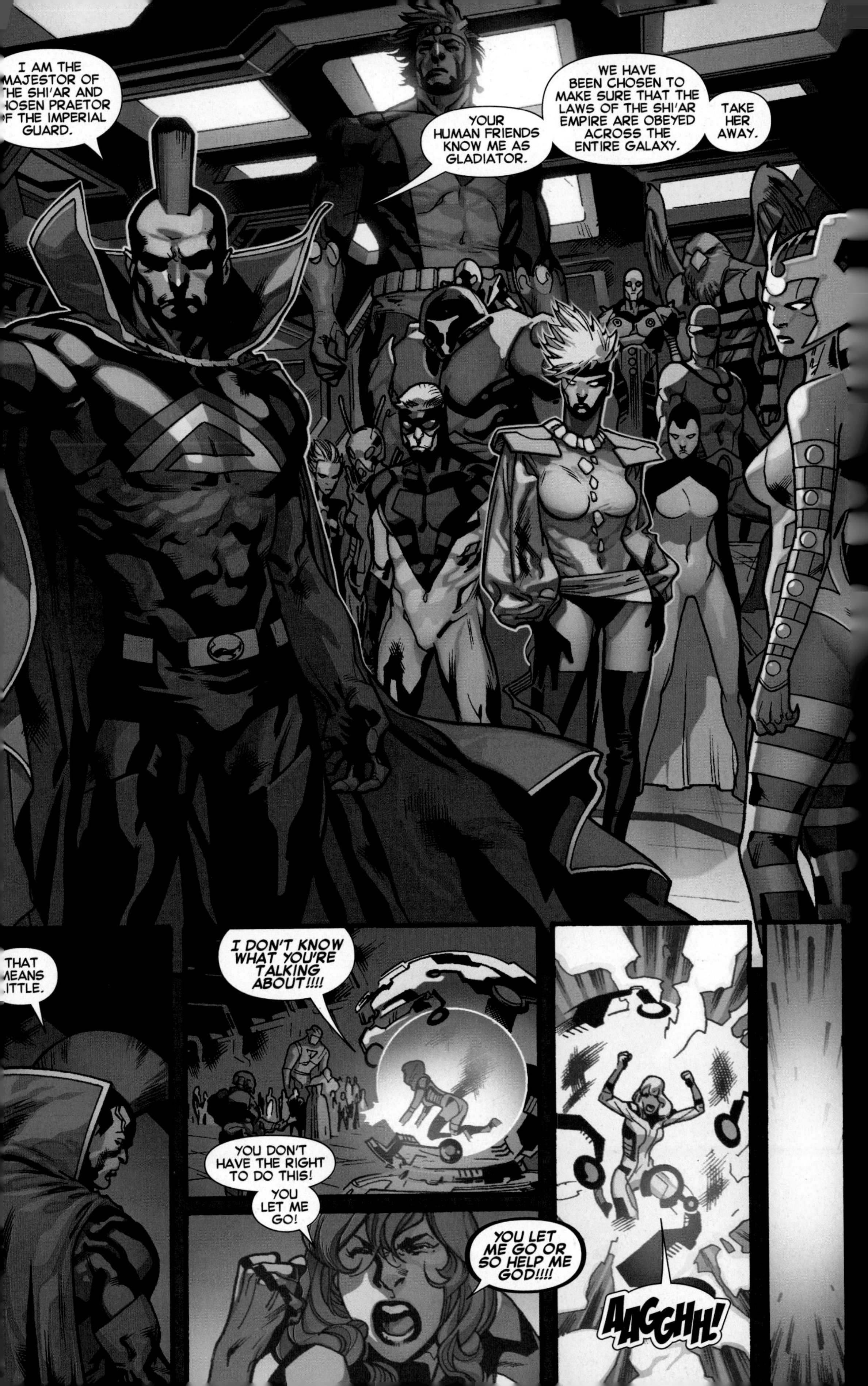

I AM THE MAJESTOR OF THE SHI'AR AND CHOSEN PRAETOR OF THE IMPERIAL GUARD.
YOUR HUMAN FRIENDS KNOW ME AS GLADIATOR.
WE HAVE BEEN CHOSEN TO MAKE SURE THAT THE LAWS OF THE SHI'AR EMPIRE ARE OBEYED ACROSS THE ENTIRE GALAXY.
TAKE HER AWAY.
THAT MEANS LITTLE.
I DON'T KNOW WHAT YOU'RE TALKING ABOUT!!!!
YOU DON'T HAVE THE RIGHT TO DO THIS!
YOU LET ME GO!
YOU LET ME GO OR SO HELP ME GOD!!!!
AAAGGHH!

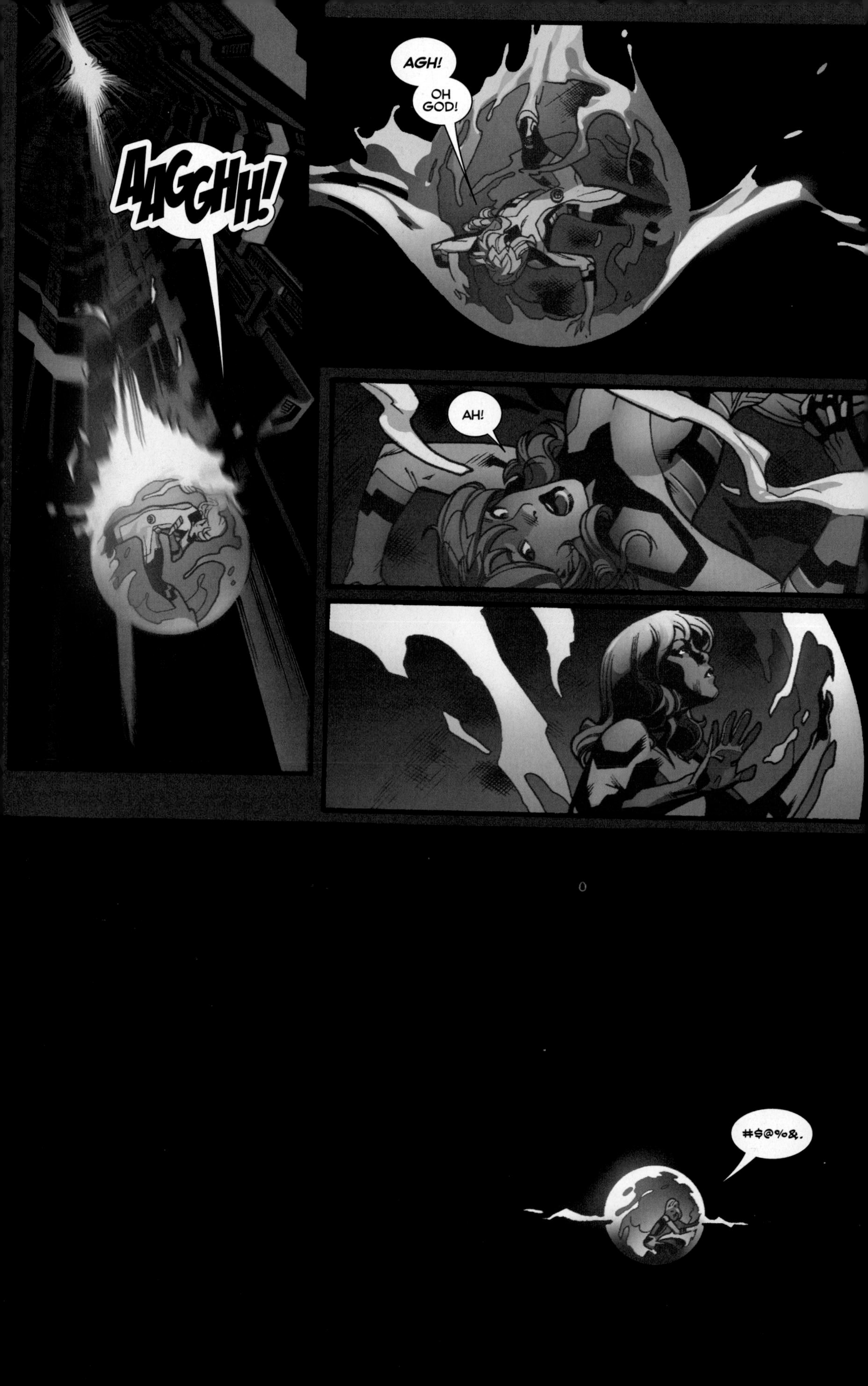
AAGGHH!
AGH!
OH GOD!
AH!
#$@%&.

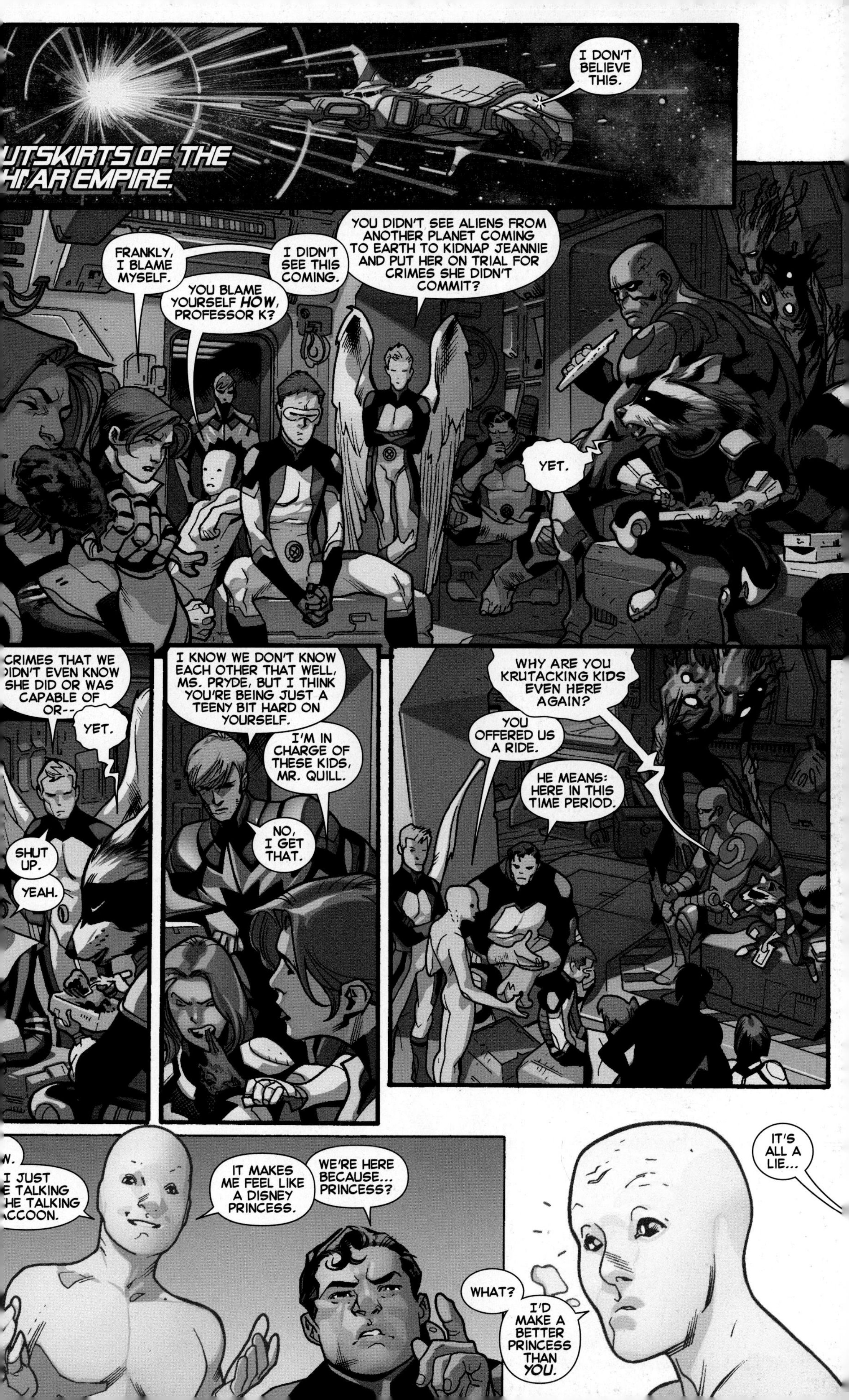
I DON'T BELIEVE THIS.
UTSKIRTS OF THE HI'AR EMPIRE.
FRANKLY, I BLAME MYSELF.
I DIDN'T SEE THIS COMING.
YOU BLAME YOURSELF HOW, PROFESSOR K?
YOU DIDN'T SEE ALIENS FROM ANOTHER PLANET COMING TO EARTH TO KIDNAP JEANNIE AND PUT HER ON TRIAL FOR CRIMES SHE DIDN'T COMMIT?
YET.
CRIMES THAT WE DIDN'T EVEN KNOW SHE DID OR WAS CAPABLE OF OR--
YET.
SHUT UP.
YEAH.
I KNOW WE DON'T KNOW EACH OTHER THAT WELL, MS. PRYDE, BUT I THINK YOU'RE BEING JUST A TEENY BIT HARD ON YOURSELF.
I'M IN CHARGE OF THESE KIDS, MR. QUILL.
NO, I GET THAT.
WHY ARE YOU KRUTACKING KIDS EVEN HERE AGAIN?
YOU OFFERED US A RIDE.
HE MEANS: HERE IN THIS TIME PERIOD.
W. I JUST E TALKING HE TALKING ACCOON.
IT MAKES ME FEEL LIKE A DISNEY PRINCESS.
WE'RE HERE BECAUSE... PRINCESS?
IT'S ALL A LIE...
WHAT?
I'D MAKE A BETTER PRINCESS THAN YOU.

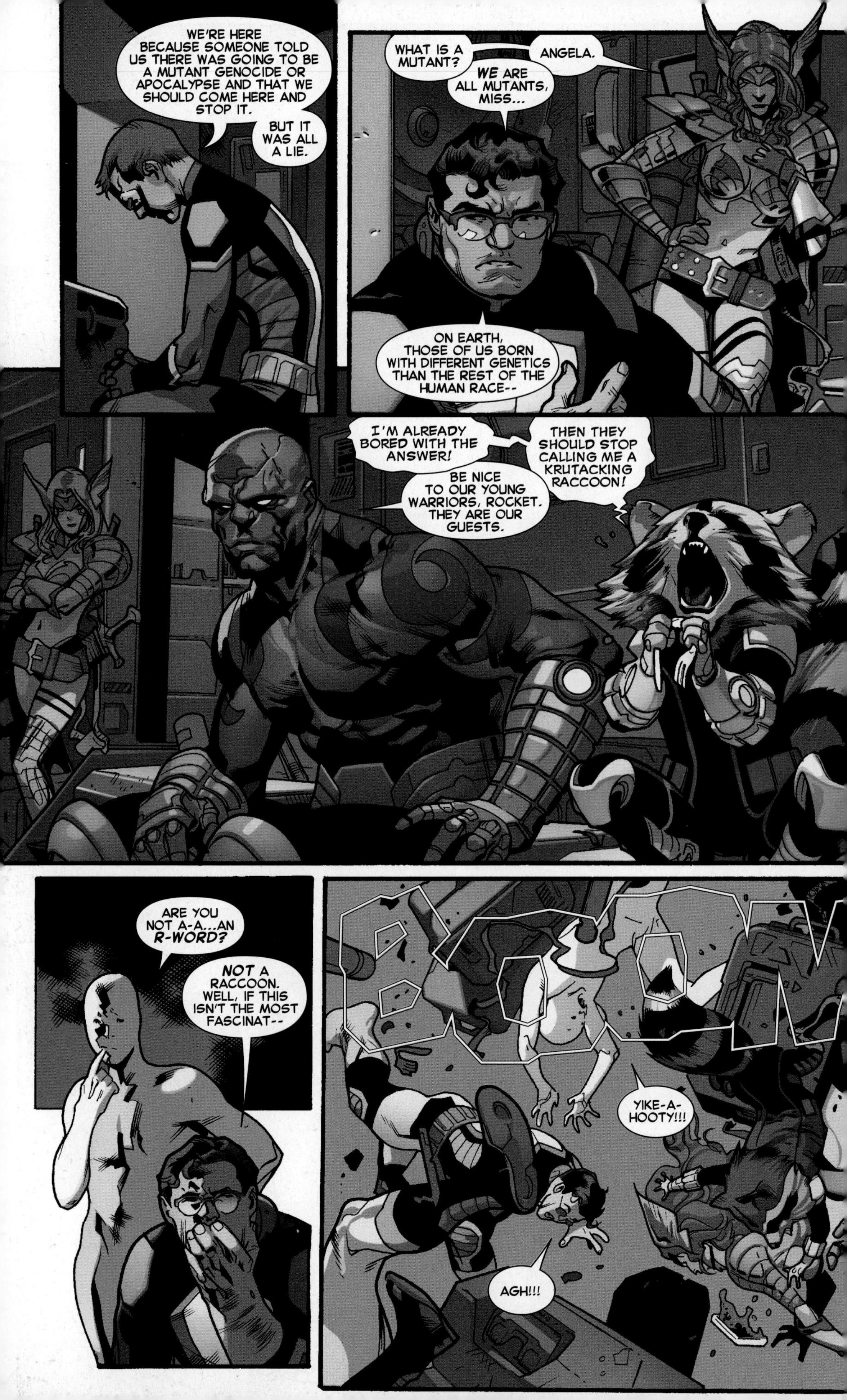
WE'RE HERE BECAUSE SOMEONE TOLD US THERE WAS GOING TO BE A MUTANT GENOCIDE OR APOCALYPSE AND THAT WE SHOULD COME HERE AND STOP IT.
BUT IT WAS ALL A LIE.
WHAT IS A MUTANT?
ANGELA.
WE ARE ALL MUTANTS, MISS...
ON EARTH, THOSE OF US BORN WITH DIFFERENT GENETICS THAN THE REST OF THE HUMAN RACE--
I'M ALREADY BORED WITH THE ANSWER!
THEN THEY SHOULD STOP CALLING ME A KRUTACKING RACCOON!
BE NICE TO OUR YOUNG WARRIORS, ROCKET. THEY ARE OUR GUESTS.
ARE YOU NOT A-A...AN R-WORD?
NOT A RACCOON. WELL, IF THIS ISN'T THE MOST FASCINAT--
BOOM
YIKE-A-HOOTY!!!
AGH!!!

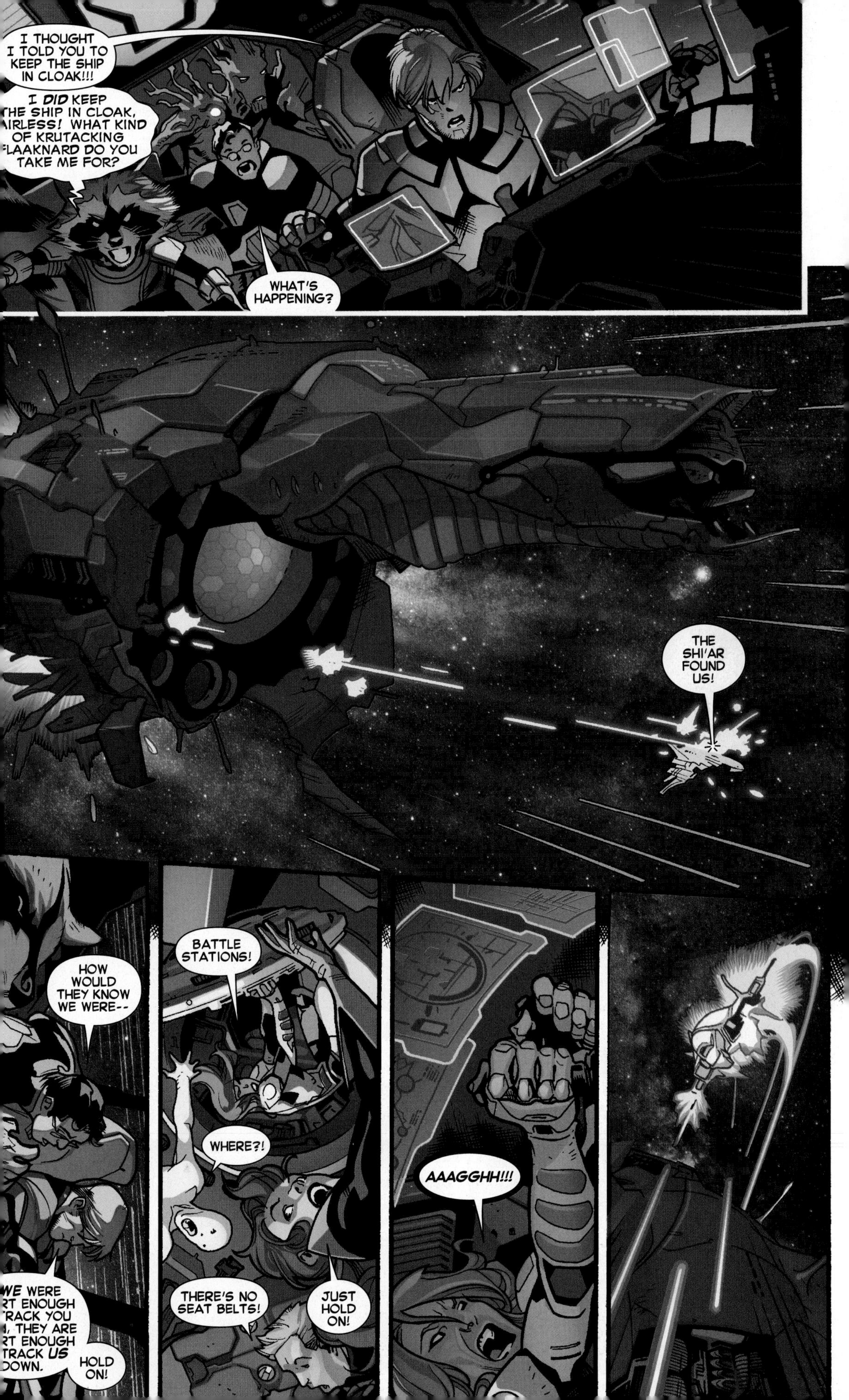

I THOUGHT I TOLD YOU TO KEEP THE SHIP IN CLOAK!!!
I *DID* KEEP THE SHIP IN CLOAK, AIRLESS! WHAT KIND OF KRUTACKING FLAAKNARD DO YOU TAKE ME FOR?
WHAT'S HAPPENING?
THE SHI'AR FOUND US!
HOW WOULD THEY KNOW WE WERE--
BATTLE STATIONS!
WHERE?!
AAAGGHH!!!
THERE'S NO SEAT BELTS!
JUST HOLD ON!
HOLD ON!

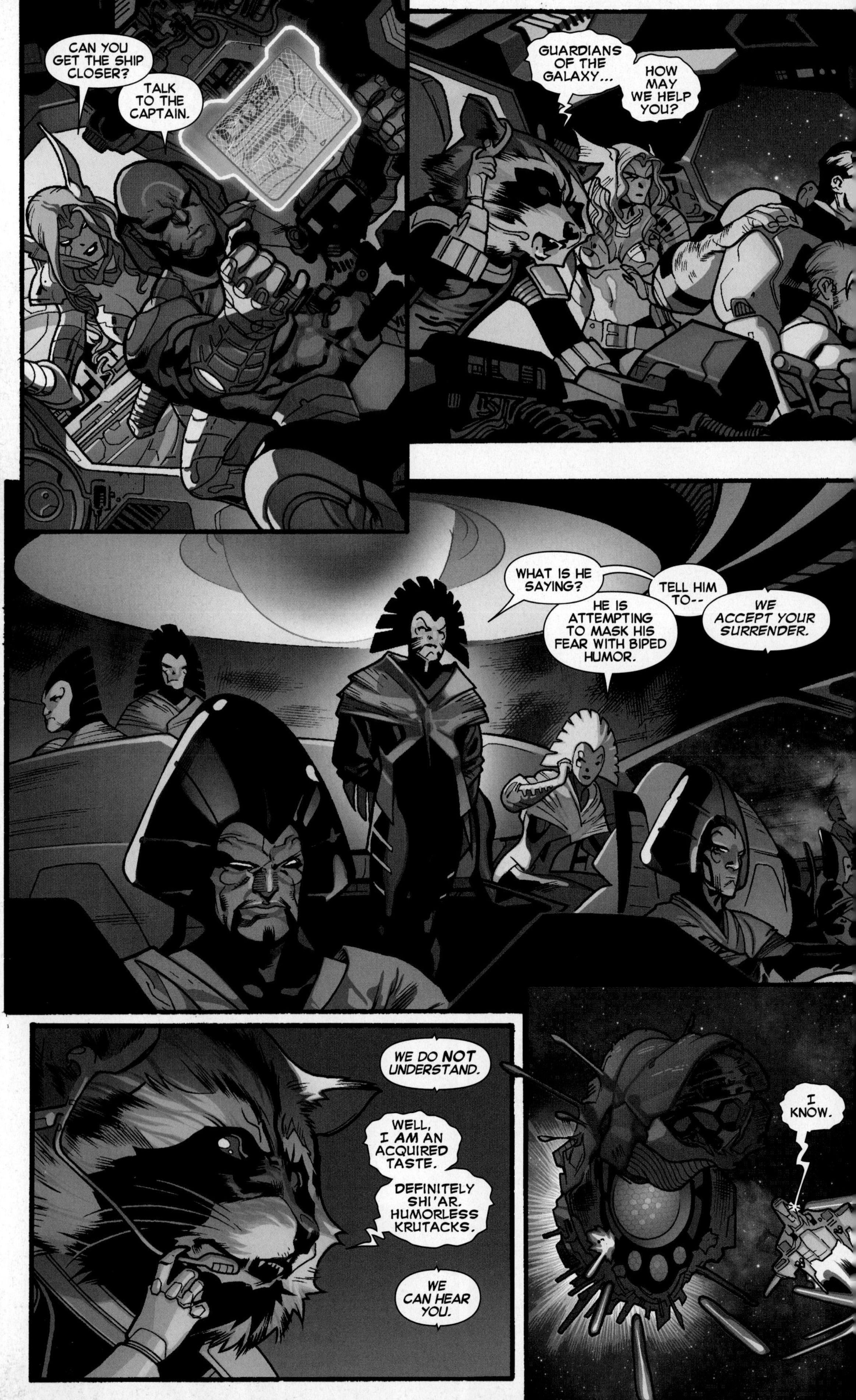
CAN YOU GET THE SHIP CLOSER?
TALK TO THE CAPTAIN.
GUARDIANS OF THE GALAXY...
HOW MAY WE HELP YOU?
WHAT IS HE SAYING?
TELL HIM TO--
HE IS ATTEMPTING TO MASK HIS FEAR WITH BIPED HUMOR.
WE ACCEPT YOUR SURRENDER.
WE DO NOT UNDERSTAND.
WELL, I AM AN ACQUIRED TASTE.
DEFINITELY SHI'AR. HUMORLESS KRUTACKS.
WE CAN HEAR YOU.
I KNOW.

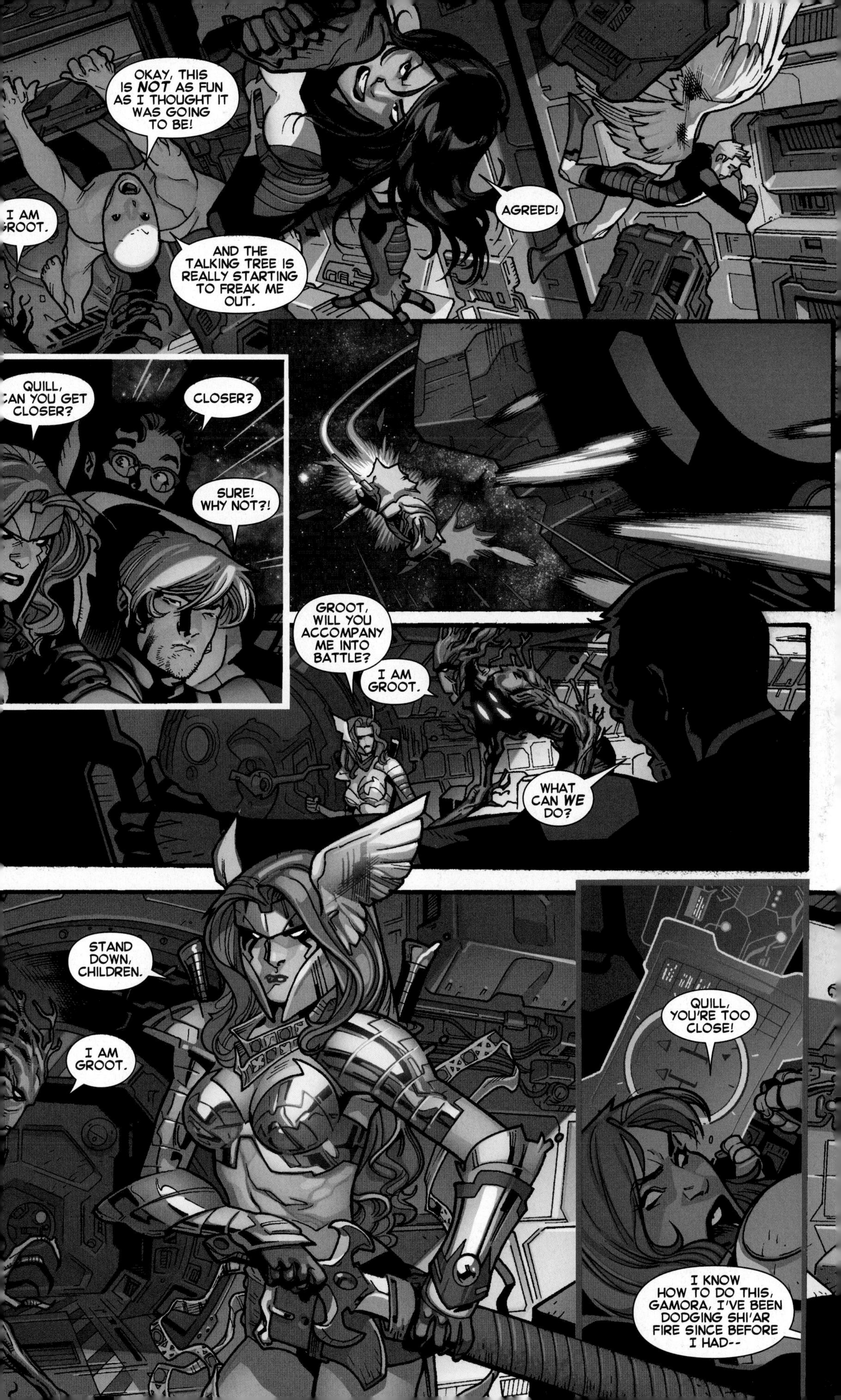
OKAY, THIS IS NOT AS FUN AS I THOUGHT IT WAS GOING TO BE!
I AM GROOT.
AND THE TALKING TREE IS REALLY STARTING TO FREAK ME OUT.
AGREED!
QUILL, CAN YOU GET CLOSER?
CLOSER?
SURE! WHY NOT?!
GROOT, WILL YOU ACCOMPANY ME INTO BATTLE?
I AM GROOT.
WHAT CAN WE DO?
STAND DOWN, CHILDREN.
I AM GROOT.
QUILL, YOU'RE TOO CLOSE!
I KNOW HOW TO DO THIS, GAMORA, I'VE BEEN DODGING SHI'AR FIRE SINCE BEFORE I HAD--

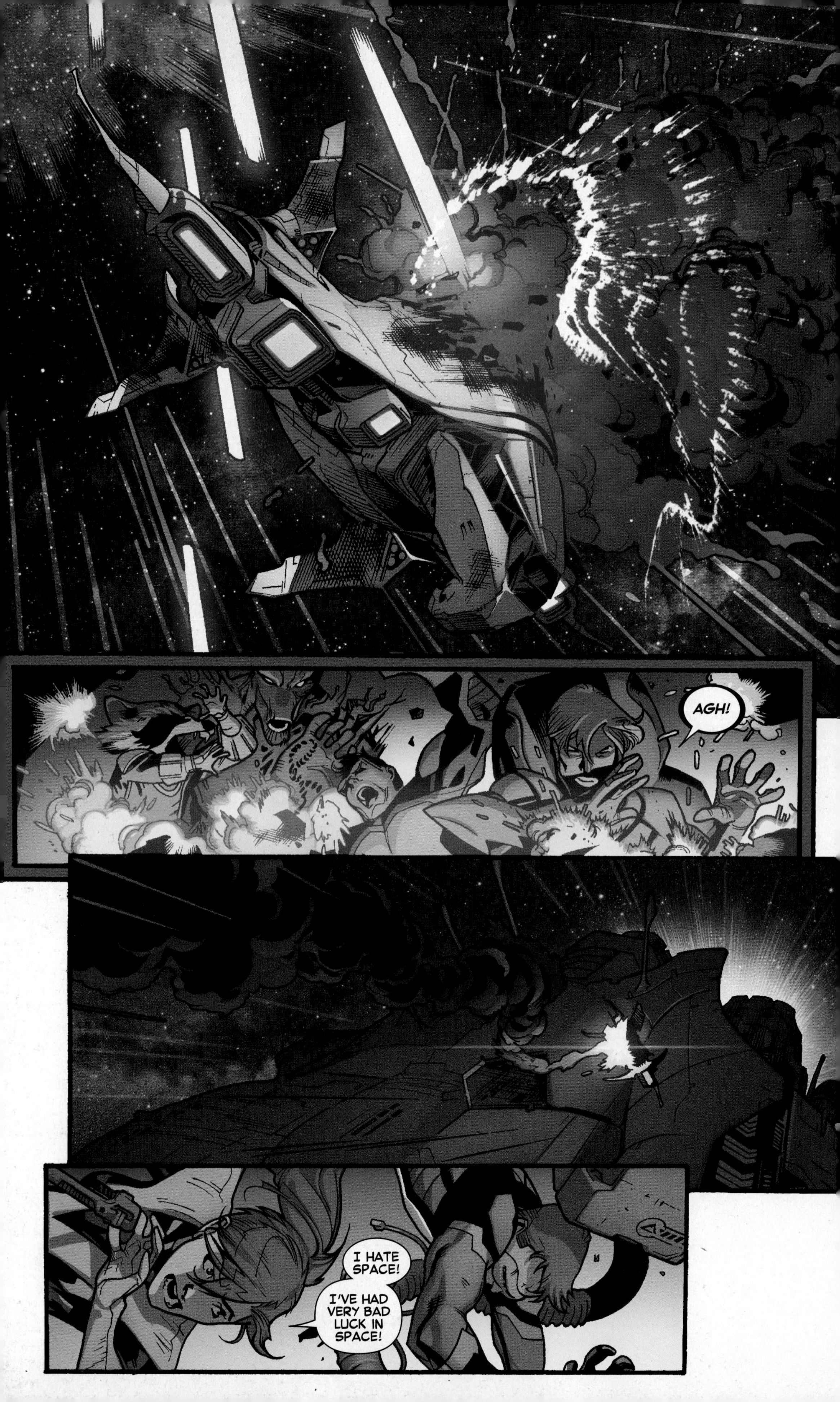
AGH!
I HATE SPACE!
I'VE HAD VERY BAD LUCK IN SPACE!

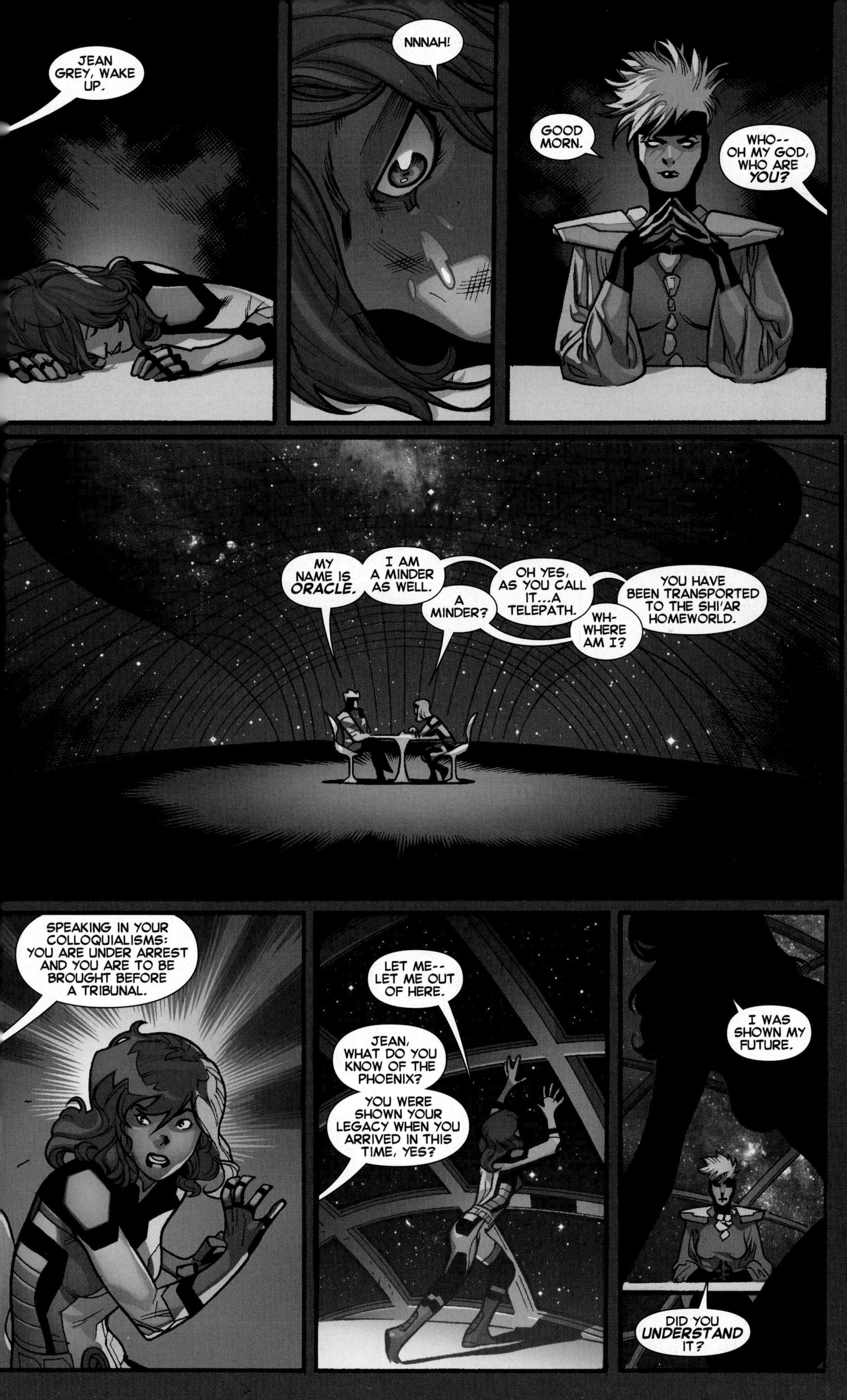
JEAN GREY, WAKE UP.
NNNAH!
GOOD MORN.
WHO-- OH MY GOD, WHO ARE YOU?
MY NAME IS ORACLE.
I AM A MINDER AS WELL.
A MINDER?
OH YES, AS YOU CALL IT...A TELEPATH.
WH- WHERE AM I?
YOU HAVE BEEN TRANSPORTED TO THE SHI'AR HOMEWORLD.
SPEAKING IN YOUR COLLOQUIALISMS: YOU ARE UNDER ARREST AND YOU ARE TO BE BROUGHT BEFORE A TRIBUNAL.
LET ME-- LET ME OUT OF HERE.
JEAN, WHAT DO YOU KNOW OF THE PHOENIX?
YOU WERE SHOWN YOUR LEGACY WHEN YOU ARRIVED IN THIS TIME, YES?
I WAS SHOWN MY FUTURE.
DID YOU UNDERSTAND IT?

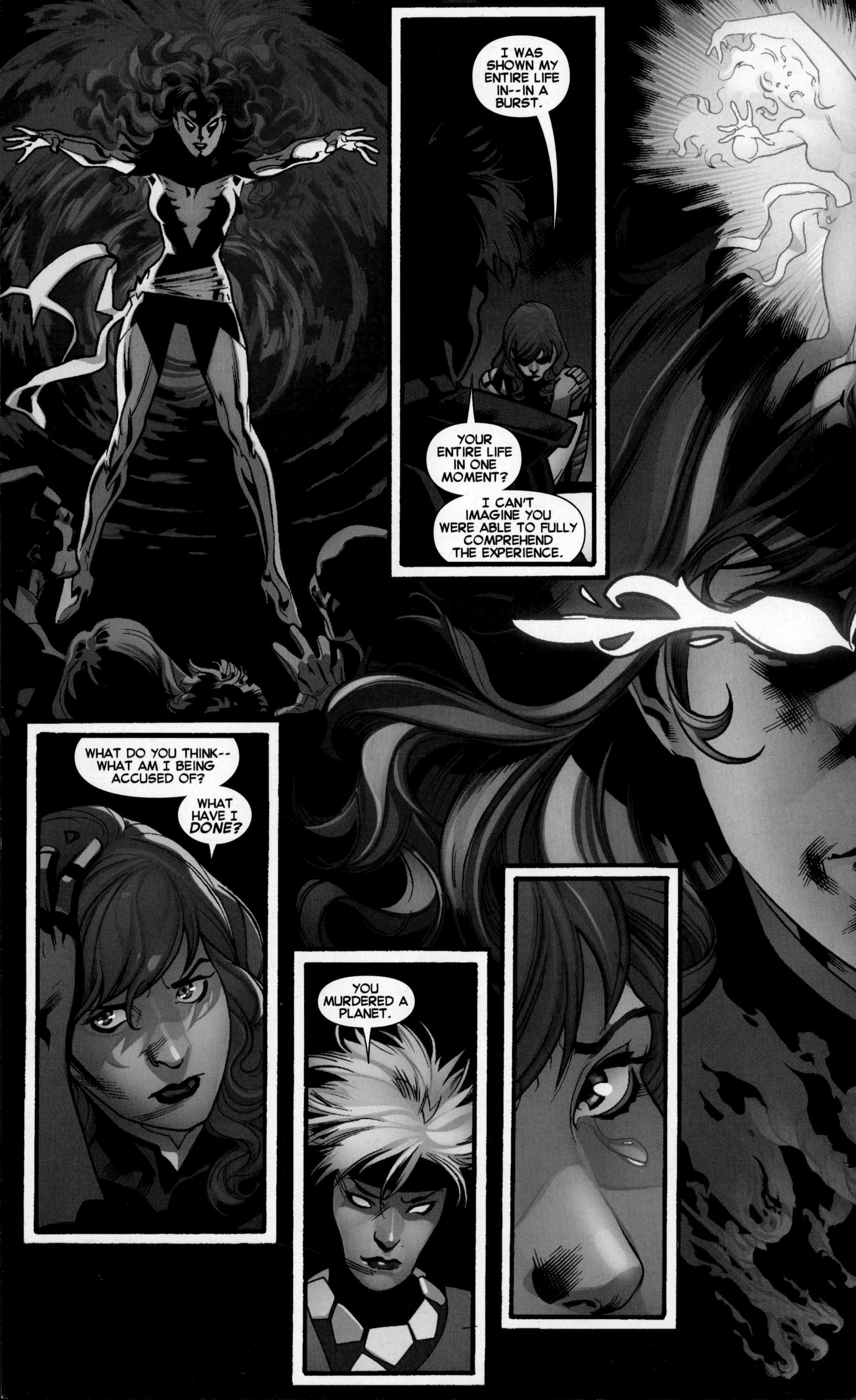
I WAS SHOWN MY ENTIRE LIFE IN--IN A BURST.
YOUR ENTIRE LIFE IN ONE MOMENT?
I CAN'T IMAGINE YOU WERE ABLE TO FULLY COMPREHEND THE EXPERIENCE.
WHAT DO YOU THINK-- WHAT AM I BEING ACCUSED OF?
WHAT HAVE I *DONE?*
YOU MURDERED A PLANET.

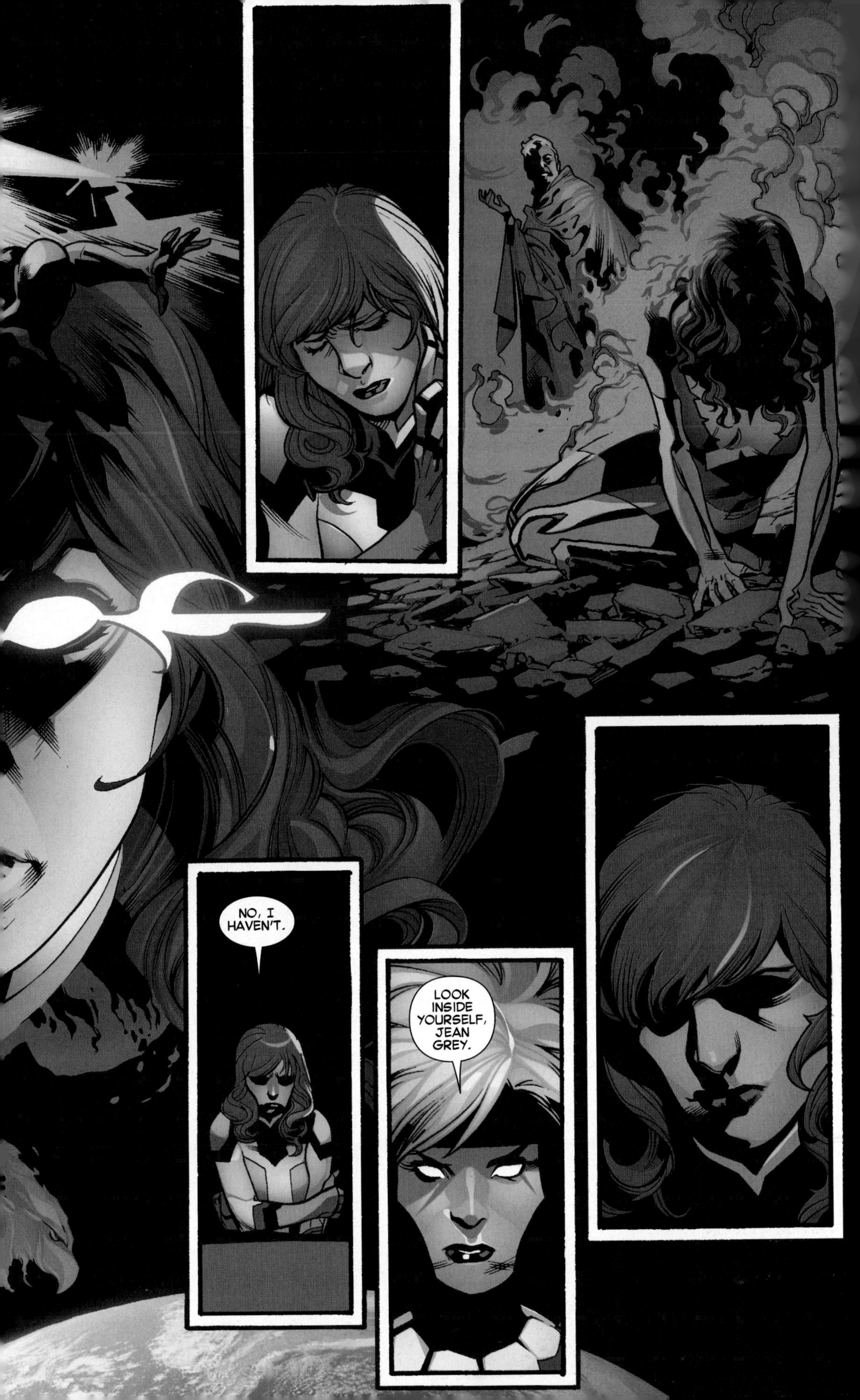
NO, I HAVEN'T.
LOOK INSIDE YOURSELF, JEAN GREY.

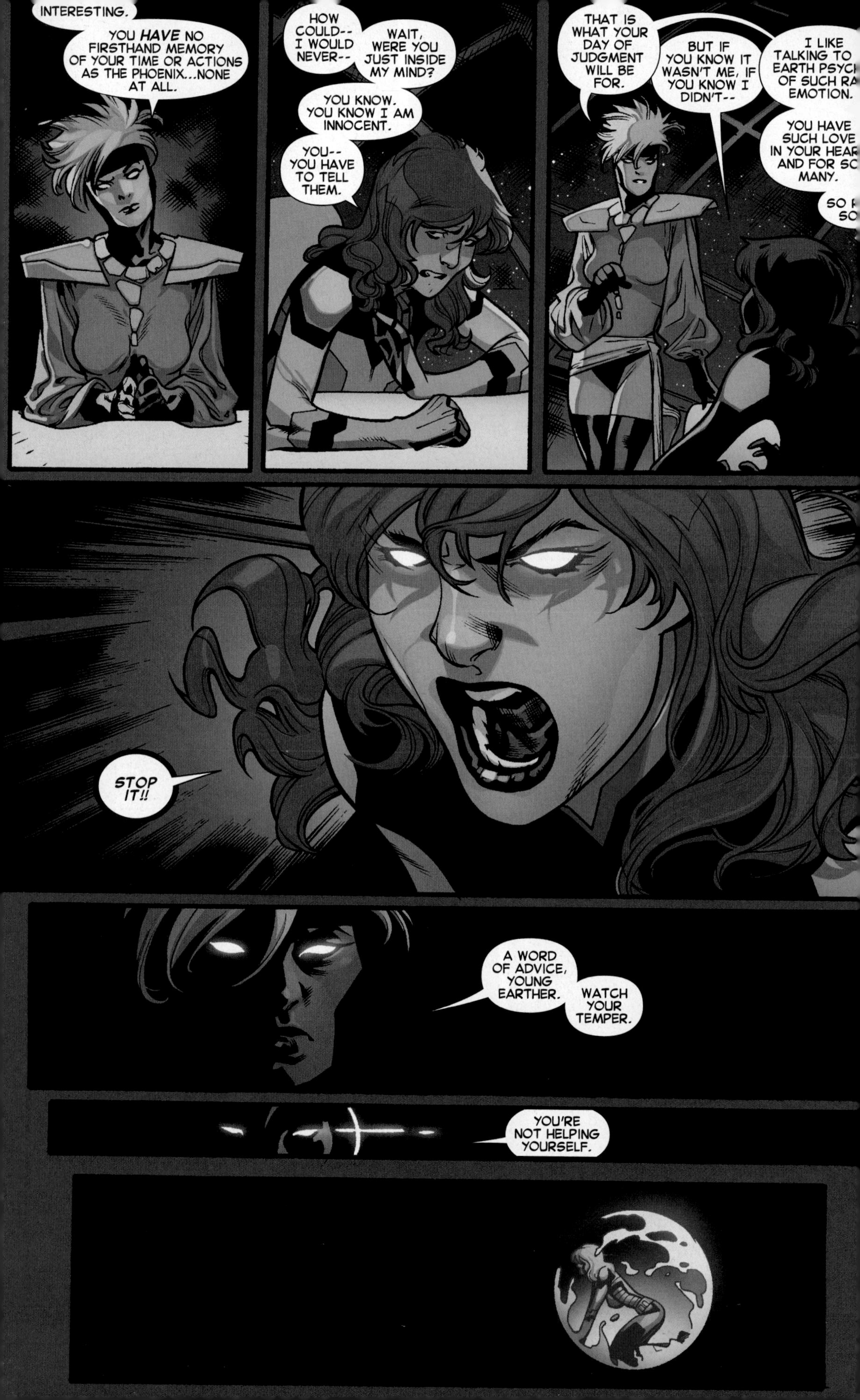
INTERESTING.
YOU *HAVE* NO FIRSTHAND MEMORY OF YOUR TIME OR ACTIONS AS THE PHOENIX...NONE AT ALL.
HOW COULD-- I WOULD NEVER--
WAIT, WERE YOU JUST INSIDE MY MIND?
YOU KNOW. YOU KNOW I AM INNOCENT.
YOU-- YOU HAVE TO TELL THEM.
THAT IS WHAT YOUR DAY OF JUDGMENT WILL BE FOR.
BUT IF YOU KNOW IT WASN'T ME, IF YOU KNOW I DIDN'T--
I LIKE TALKING TO EARTH PSYC OF SUCH RA EMOTION.
YOU HAVE SUCH LOVE IN YOUR HEAR AND FOR SC MANY.
SO SO
STOP IT!!
A WORD OF ADVICE, YOUNG EARTHER.
WATCH YOUR TEMPER.
YOU'RE NOT HELPING YOURSELF.

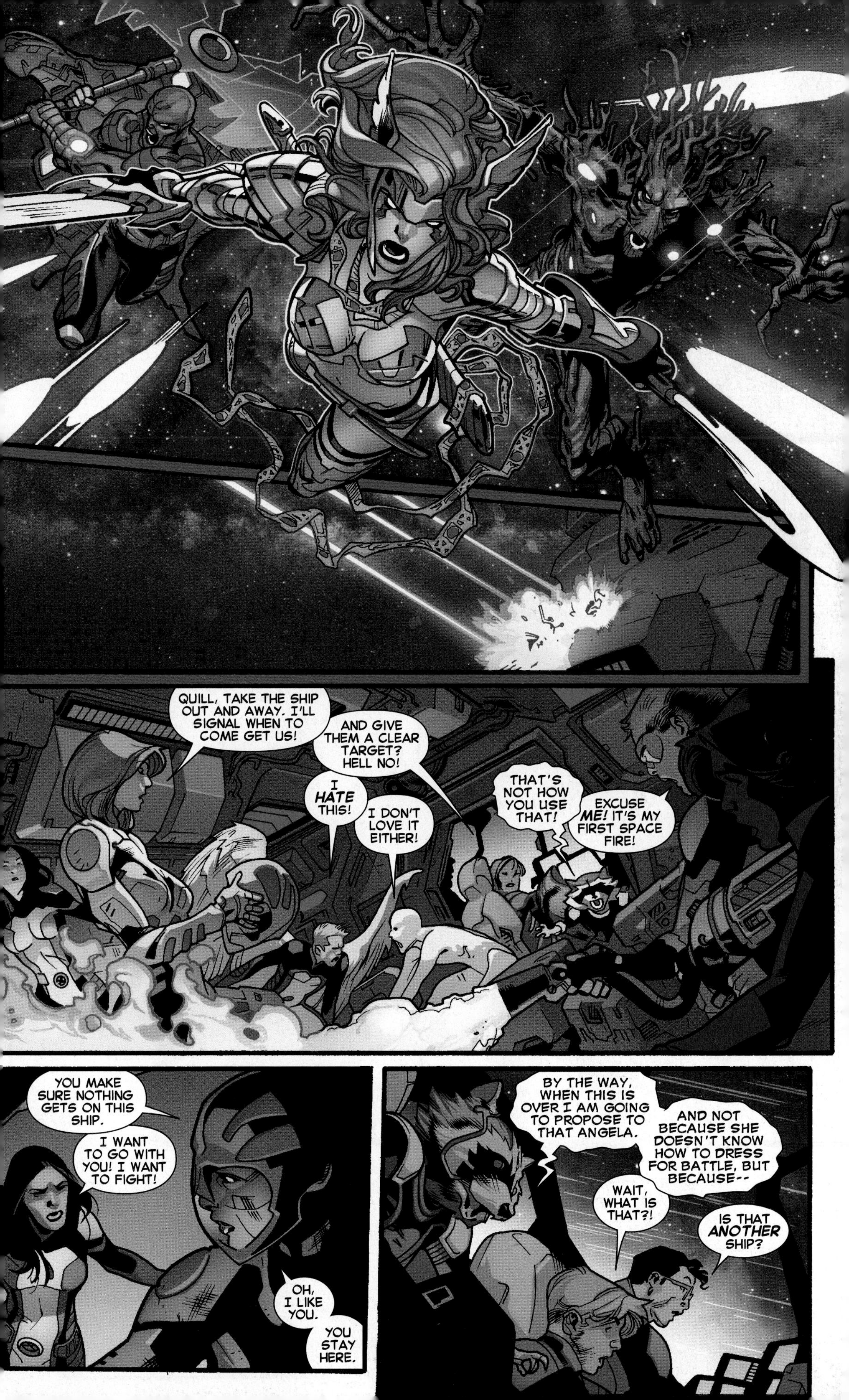
QUILL, TAKE THE SHIP OUT AND AWAY. I'LL SIGNAL WHEN TO COME GET US!
AND GIVE THEM A CLEAR TARGET? HELL NO!
I *HATE* THIS!
I DON'T LOVE IT EITHER!
THAT'S NOT HOW YOU USE THAT!
EXCUSE *ME!* IT'S MY FIRST SPACE FIRE!
YOU MAKE SURE NOTHING GETS ON THIS SHIP.
I WANT TO GO WITH YOU! I WANT TO FIGHT!
OH, I LIKE YOU.
YOU STAY HERE.
BY THE WAY, WHEN THIS IS OVER I AM GOING TO PROPOSE TO THAT ANGELA.
AND NOT BECAUSE SHE DOESN'T KNOW HOW TO DRESS FOR BATTLE, BUT BECAUSE--
WAIT, WHAT IS THAT?!
IS THAT *ANOTHER* SHIP?

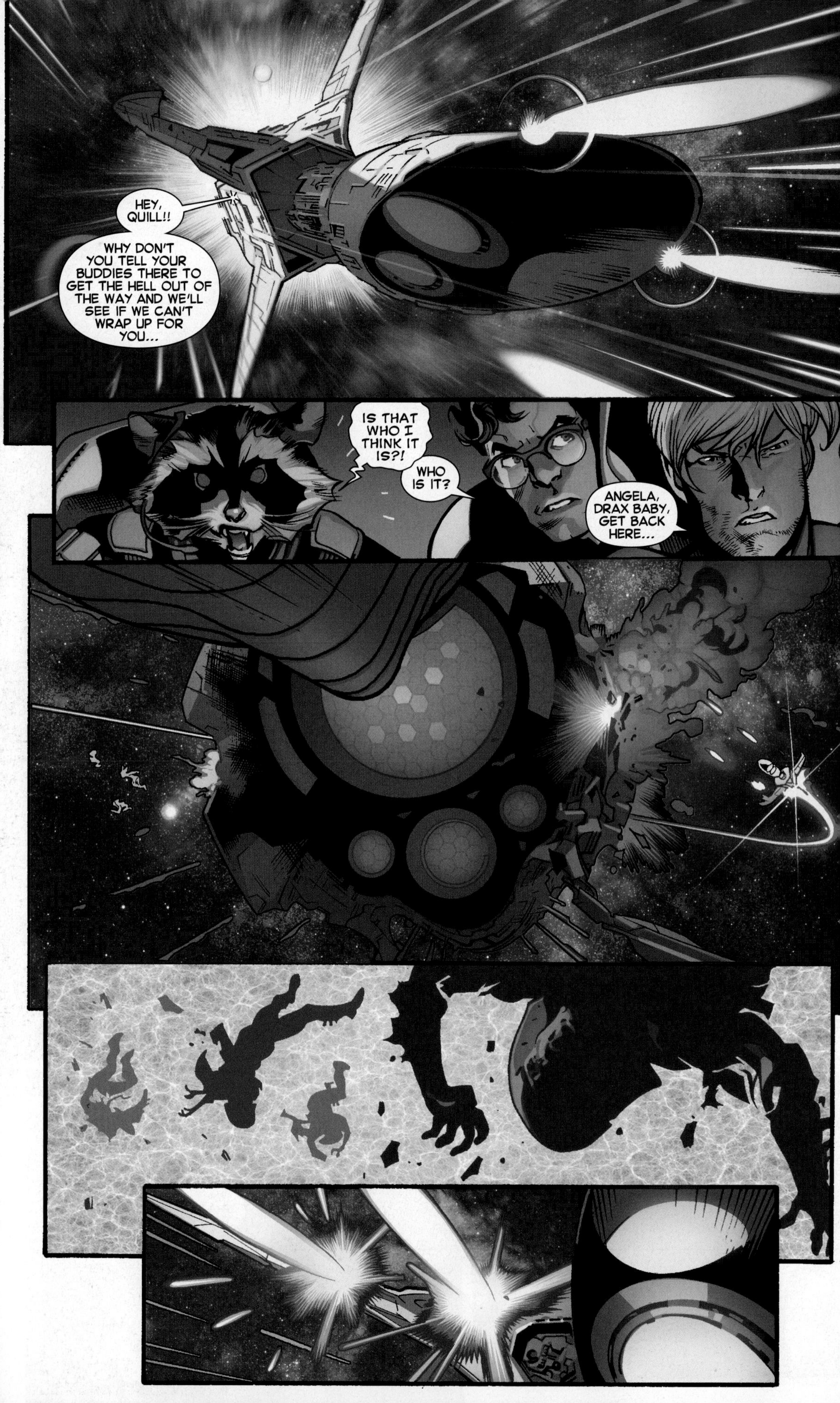
HEY, QUILL!!
WHY DON'T YOU TELL YOUR BUDDIES THERE TO GET THE HELL OUT OF THE WAY AND WE'LL SEE IF WE CAN'T WRAP UP FOR YOU...
IS THAT WHO I THINK IT IS?!
WHO IS IT?
ANGELA, DRAX BABY, GET BACK HERE...

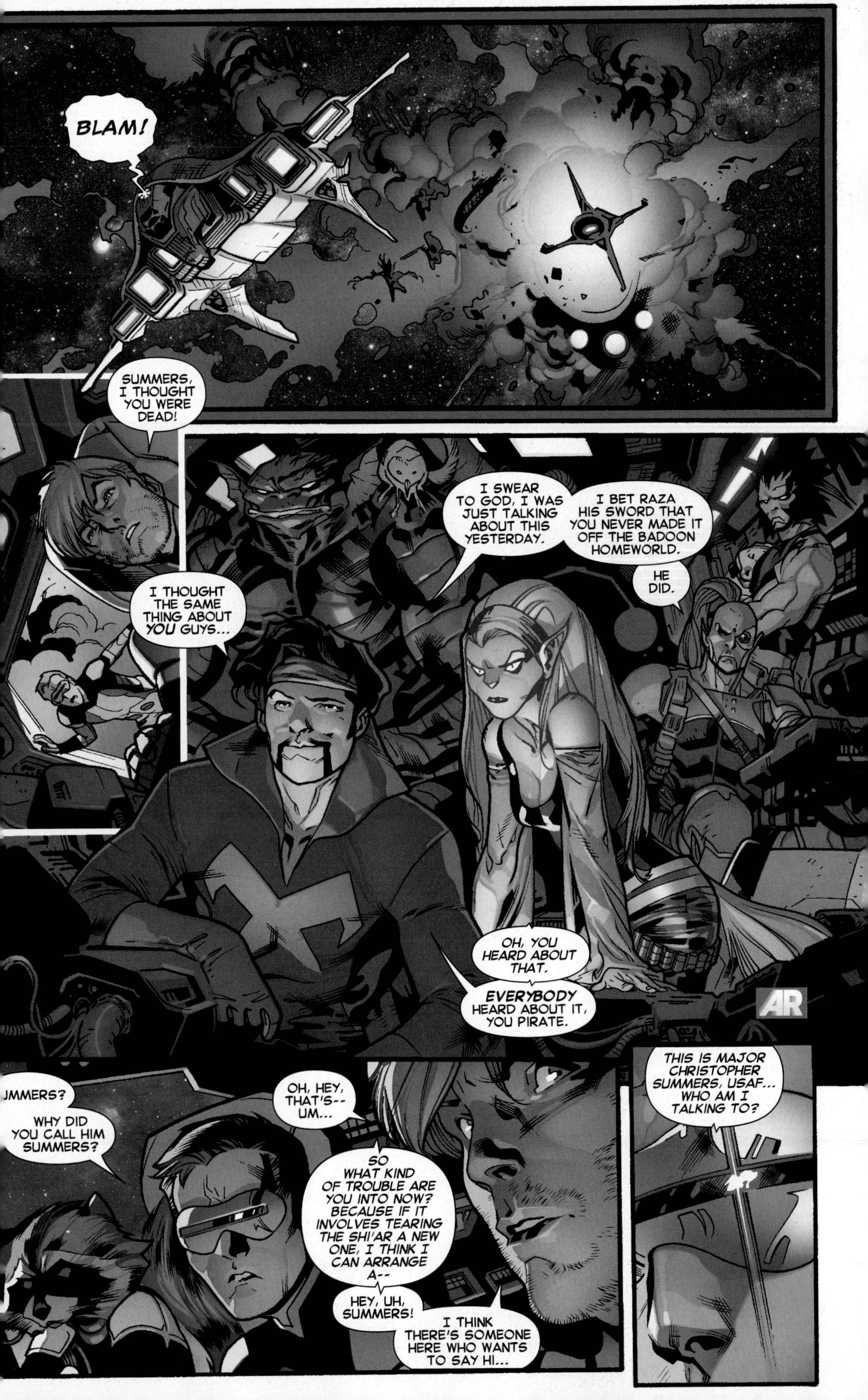
BLAM!
SUMMERS, I THOUGHT YOU WERE DEAD!
I THOUGHT THE SAME THING ABOUT YOU GUYS...
I SWEAR TO GOD, I WAS JUST TALKING ABOUT THIS YESTERDAY.
I BET RAZA HIS SWORD THAT YOU NEVER MADE IT OFF THE BADOON HOMEWORLD.
HE DID.
OH, YOU HEARD ABOUT THAT.
EVERYBODY HEARD ABOUT IT, YOU PIRATE.
AR
UMMERS?
WHY DID YOU CALL HIM SUMMERS?
OH, HEY, THAT'S-- UM...
SO WHAT KIND OF TROUBLE ARE YOU INTO NOW? BECAUSE IF IT INVOLVES TEARING THE SHI'AR A NEW ONE, I THINK I CAN ARRANGE A--
HEY, UH, SUMMERS!
I THINK THERE'S SOMEONE HERE WHO WANTS TO SAY HI...
THIS IS MAJOR CHRISTOPHER SUMMERS, USAF... WHO AM I TALKING TO?

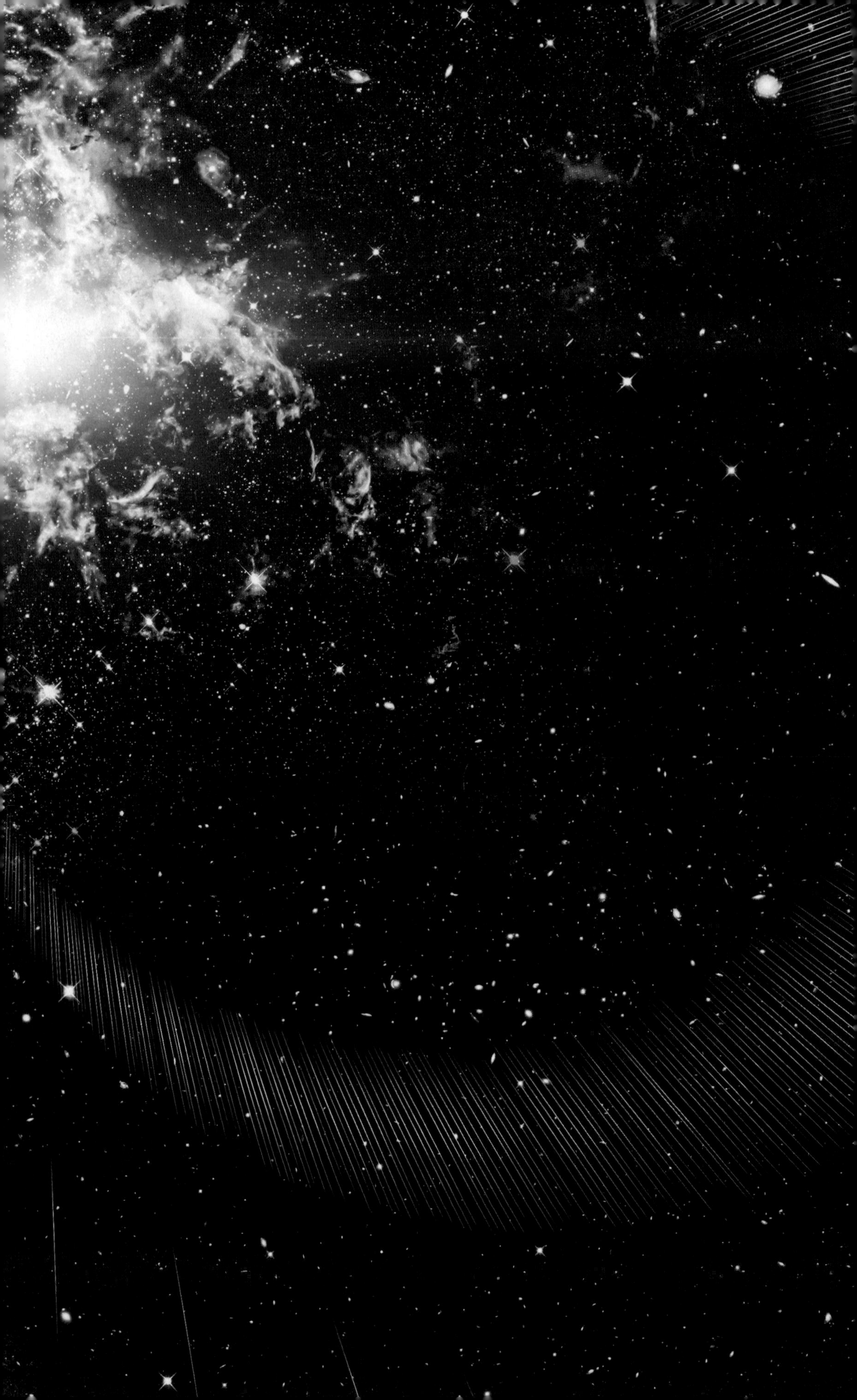

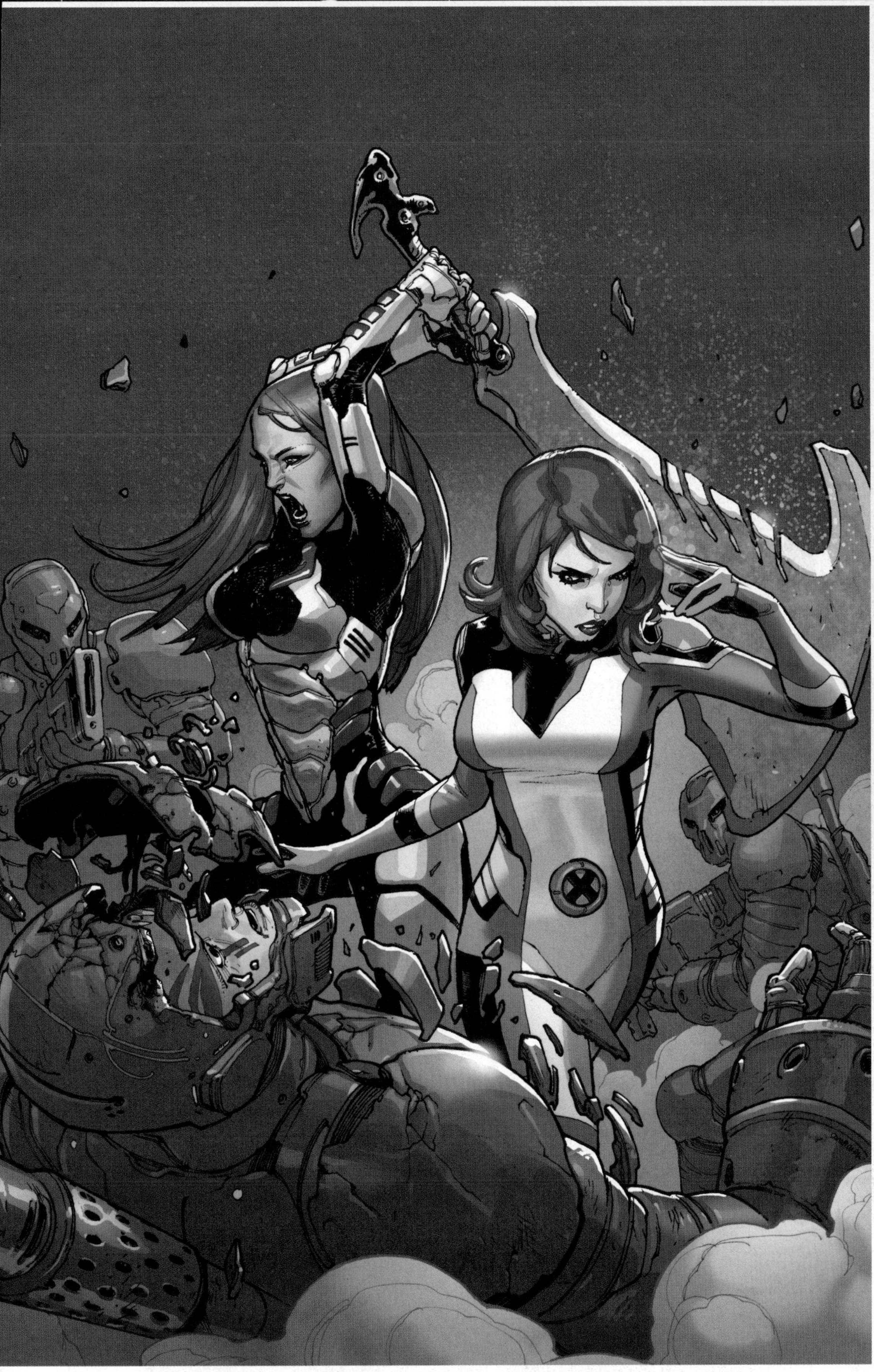

GUARDIANS OF THE GALAXY 12

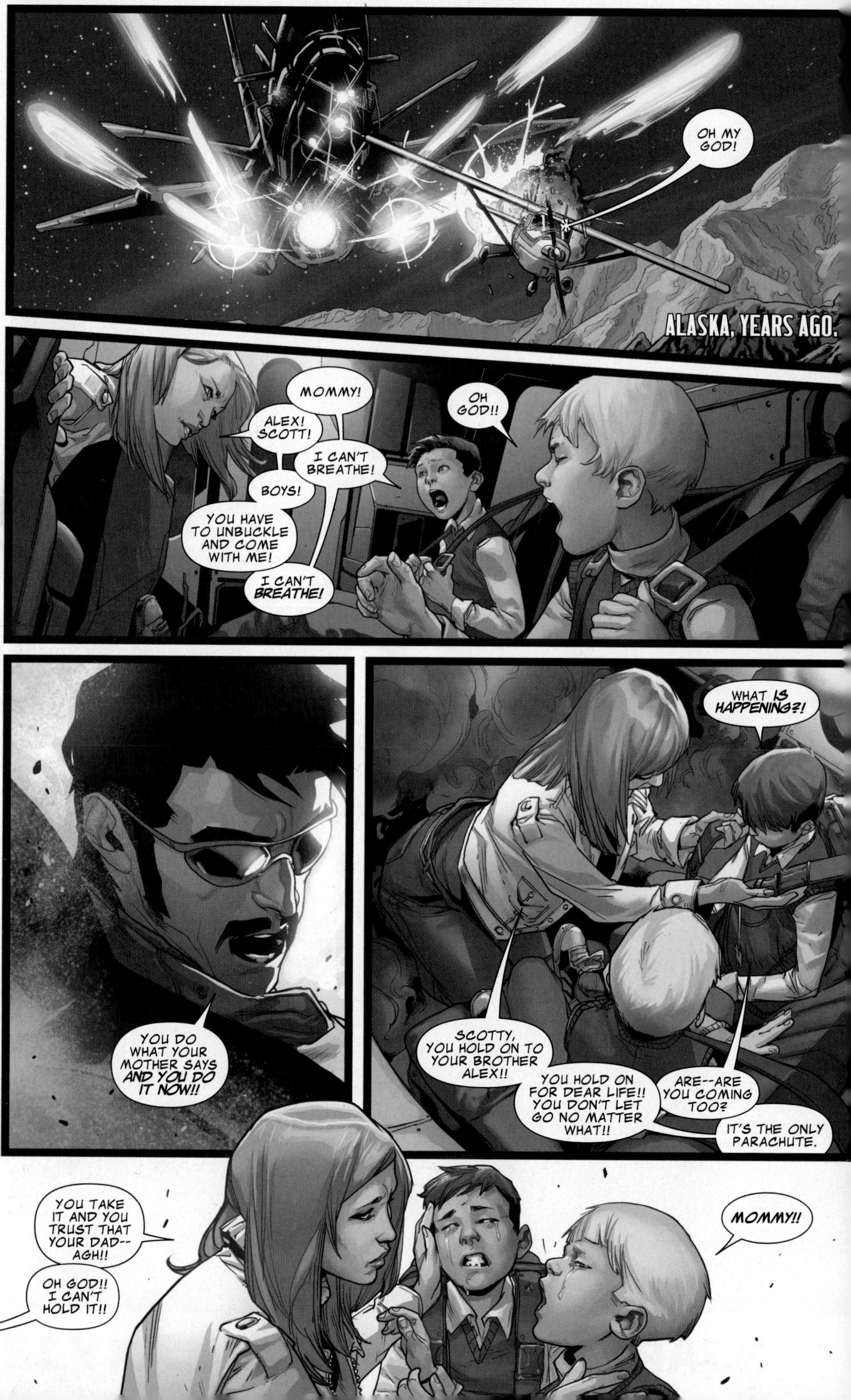
OH MY GOD!
ALASKA, YEARS AGO.
ALEX! SCOTT!
MOMMY!
OH GOD!!
I CAN'T BREATHE!
BOYS!
YOU HAVE TO UNBUCKLE AND COME WITH ME!
I CAN'T BREATHE!
YOU DO WHAT YOUR MOTHER SAYS AND YOU DO IT NOW!!
WHAT IS HAPPENING?!
SCOTTY, YOU HOLD ON TO YOUR BROTHER ALEX!!
YOU HOLD ON FOR DEAR LIFE!! YOU DON'T LET GO NO MATTER WHAT!!
ARE--ARE YOU COMING TOO?
IT'S THE ONLY PARACHUTE.
YOU TAKE IT AND YOU TRUST THAT YOUR DAD-- AGH!!
OH GOD!! I CAN'T HOLD IT!!
MOMMY!!

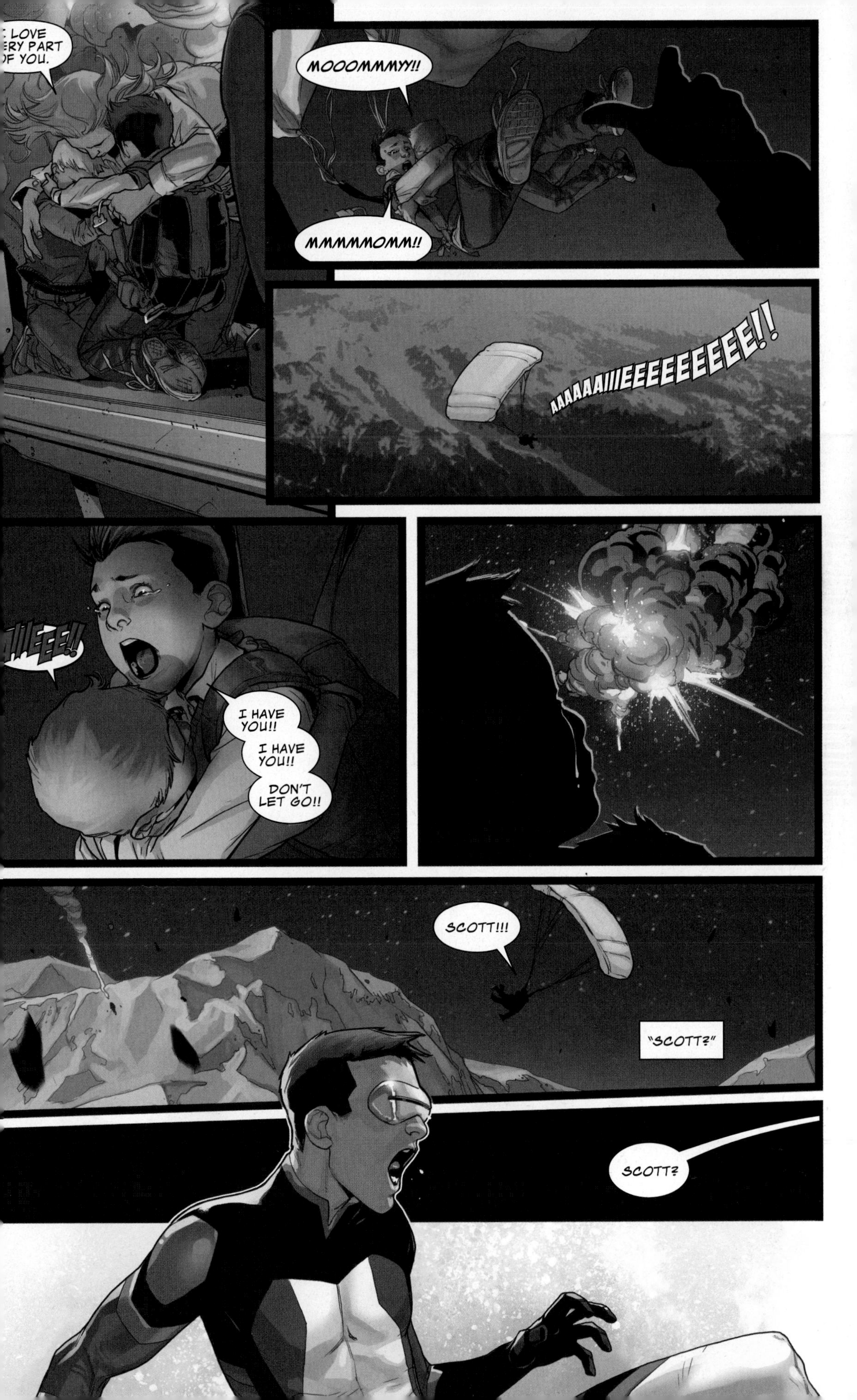
LOVE
ERY PART
OF YOU.
MOOOMMMYY!!
MMMMMOMM!!
AAAAAIIIIEEEEEEEEEE!!
IIEEE!!
I HAVE YOU!!
I HAVE YOU!!
DON'T LET GO!!
SCOTT!!!
"SCOTT?"
SCOTT?

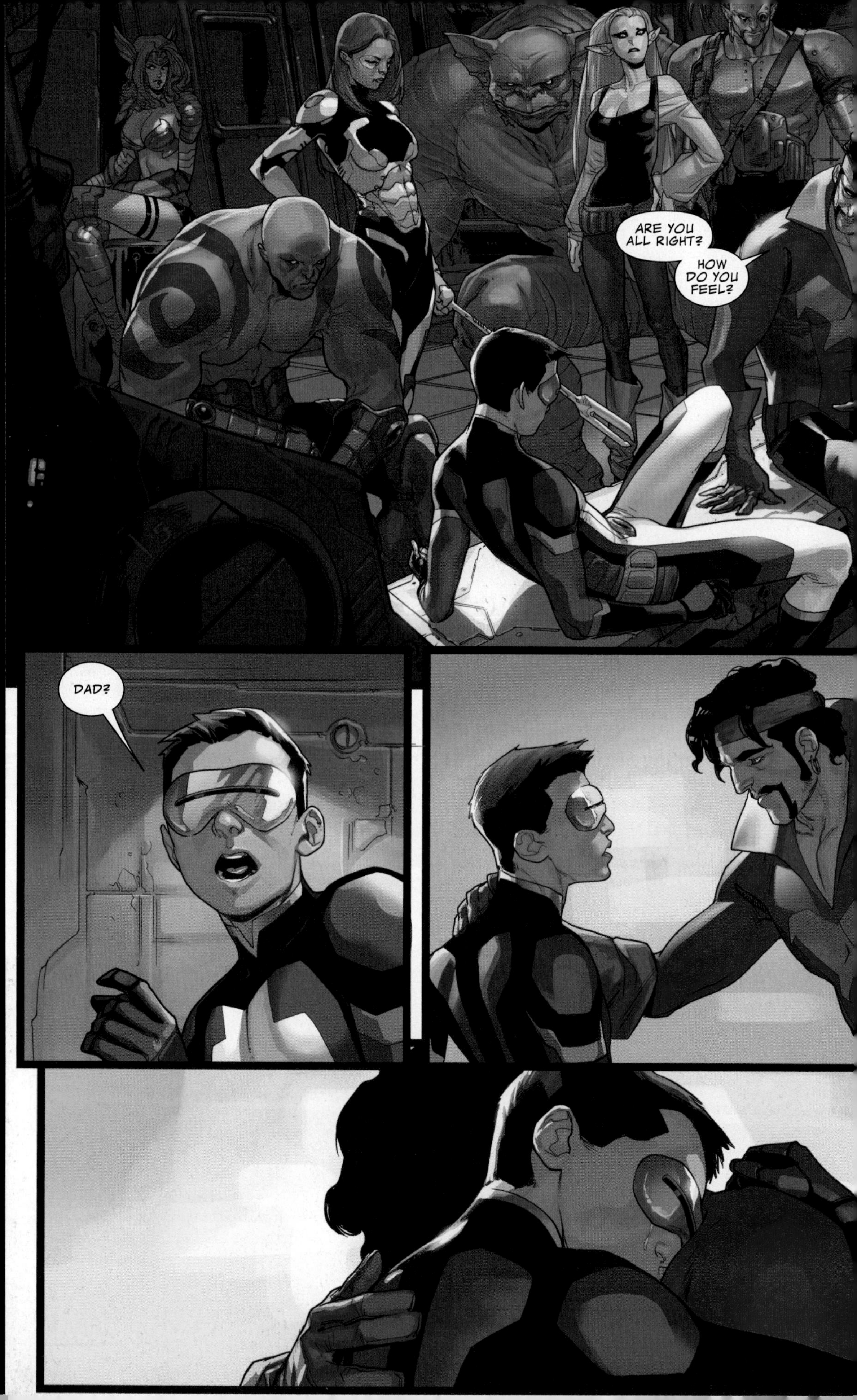
ARE YOU ALL RIGHT?
HOW DO YOU FEEL?
DAD?

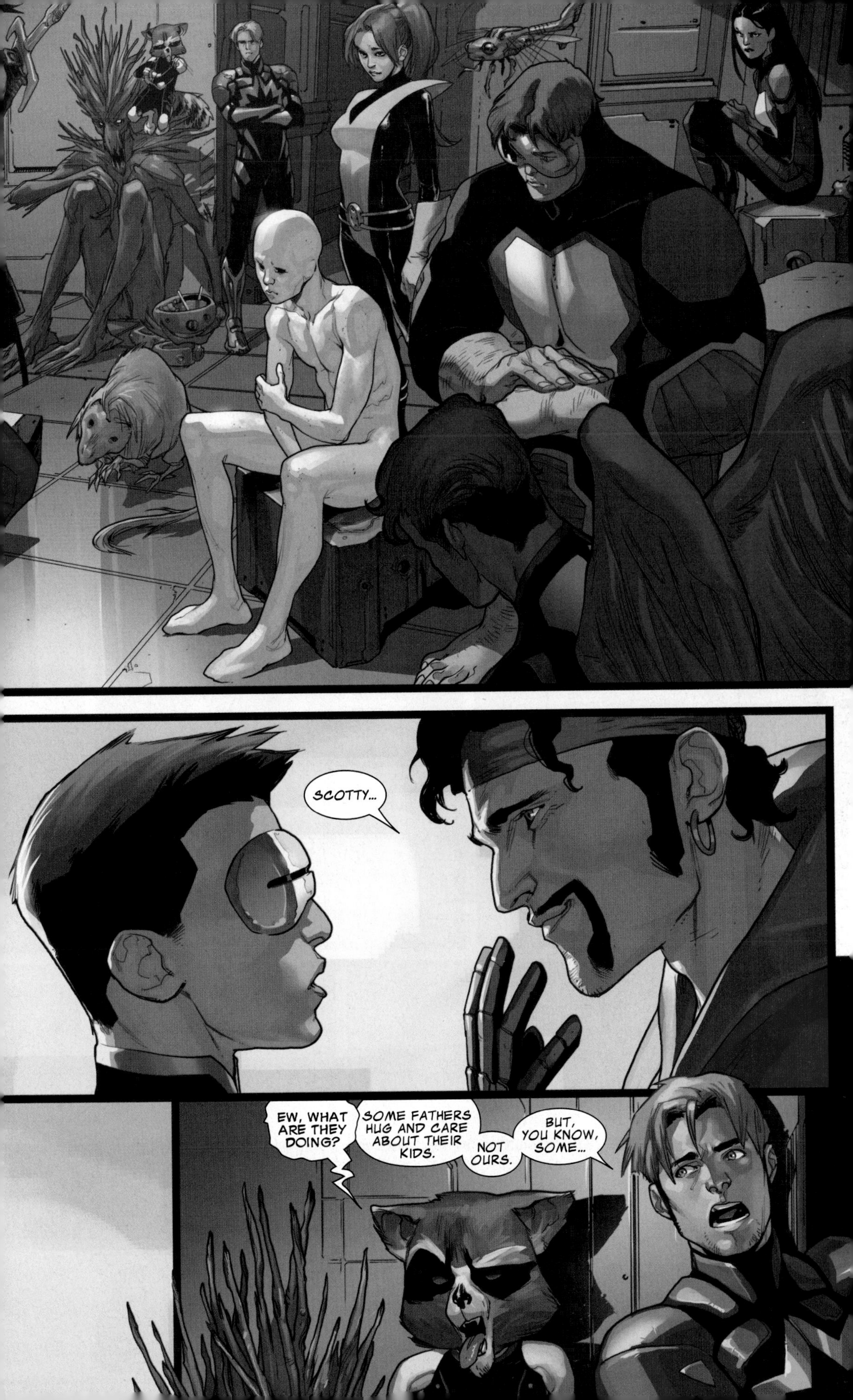
SCOTTY...
EW, WHAT ARE THEY DOING?
SOME FATHERS HUG AND CARE ABOUT THEIR KIDS.
NOT OURS.
BUT, YOU KNOW, SOME...

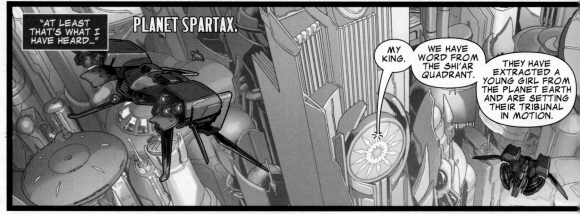

"AT LEAST THAT'S WHAT I HAVE HEARD..."

PLANET SPARTAX.

MY KING.

WE HAVE WORD FROM THE SHI'AR QUADRANT.

THEY HAVE EXTRACTED A YOUNG GIRL FROM THE PLANET EARTH AND ARE SETTING THEIR TRIBUNAL IN MOTION.

WHO AS YOU MAY KNOW WAS, AT ONE TIME OR ANOTHER, POSSESSED BY THE PHOENIX FORCE.

OUR INTEL CLEARLY SHOWS THAT JEAN GREY IS DEAD AND HAS BEEN FOR SOME TIME.

SO THIS NEW INTEL MUST BE FALSE.

DAMNED SHI'AR AND THEIR RELIGIOUS PRECISION.

I'M SORRY, SIR...DO YOU ALREADY **KNOW** OF THIS?

I DIDN'T THINK IT WAS GOING TO HAPPEN SO QUICKLY.

HAS THE EARTH RESPONDED?

WE DON'T BELIEVE THEY EVEN KNOW.

THE EXTRACTION HAPPENED COVERTLY.

WHY?

WHY D EVERYC ME IN POSIT

YOUR SON...

AND HIS GUARDIANS...

HOW DOES HE DO IT?

HOW DOES MY SON ALWAYS FIND A WAY TO PUT HIMSELF IN THE MIDDLE OF EVERYTHING??

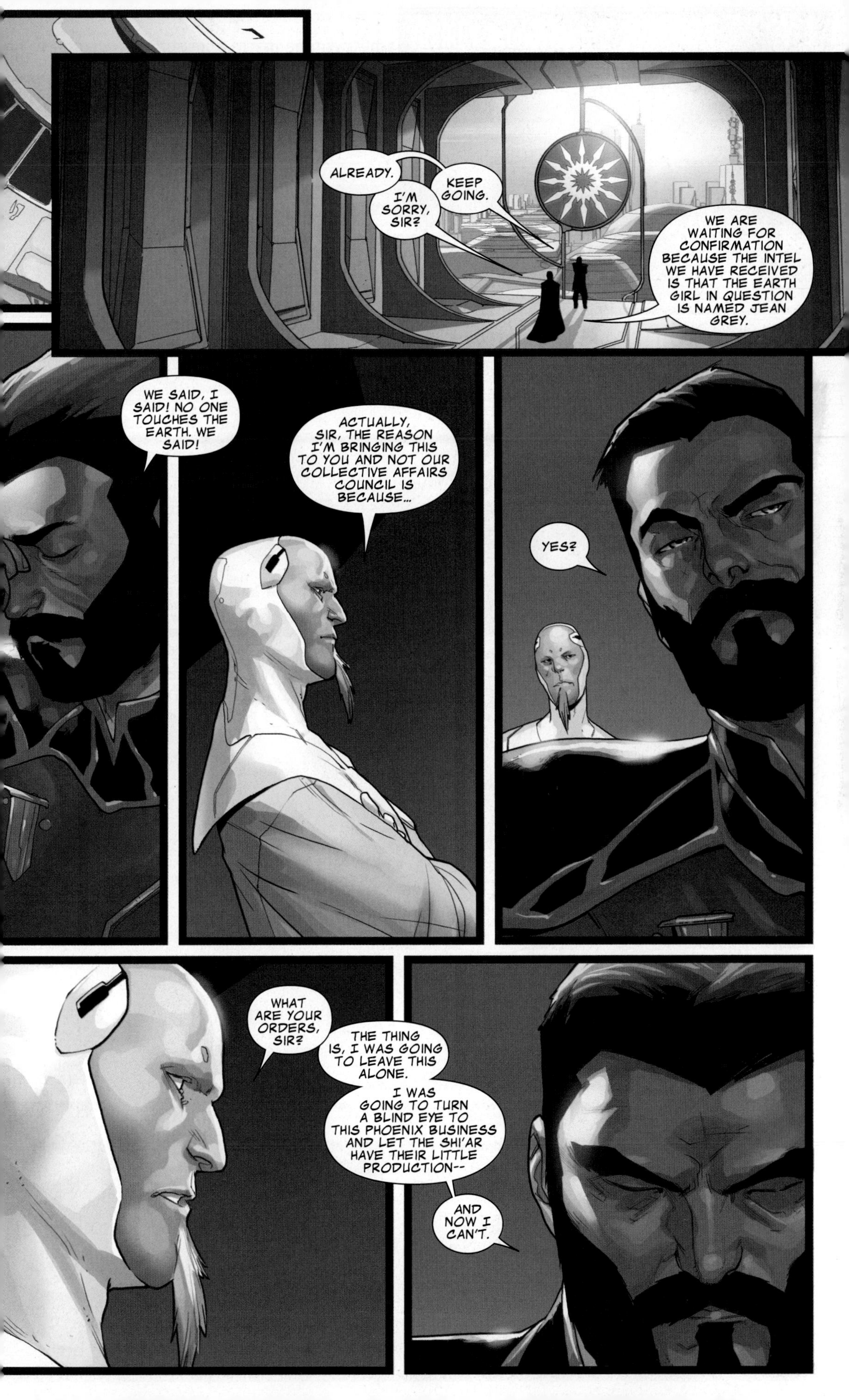
ALREADY.
KEEP GOING.
I'M SORRY, SIR?
WE ARE WAITING FOR CONFIRMATION BECAUSE THE INTEL WE HAVE RECEIVED IS THAT THE EARTH GIRL IN QUESTION IS NAMED JEAN GREY.
WE SAID, I SAID! NO ONE TOUCHES THE EARTH. WE SAID!
ACTUALLY, SIR, THE REASON I'M BRINGING THIS TO YOU AND NOT OUR COLLECTIVE AFFAIRS COUNCIL IS BECAUSE...
YES?
WHAT ARE YOUR ORDERS, SIR?
THE THING IS, I WAS GOING TO LEAVE THIS ALONE.
I WAS GOING TO TURN A BLIND EYE TO THIS PHOENIX BUSINESS AND LET THE SHI'AR HAVE THEIR LITTLE PRODUCTION--
AND NOW I CAN'T.

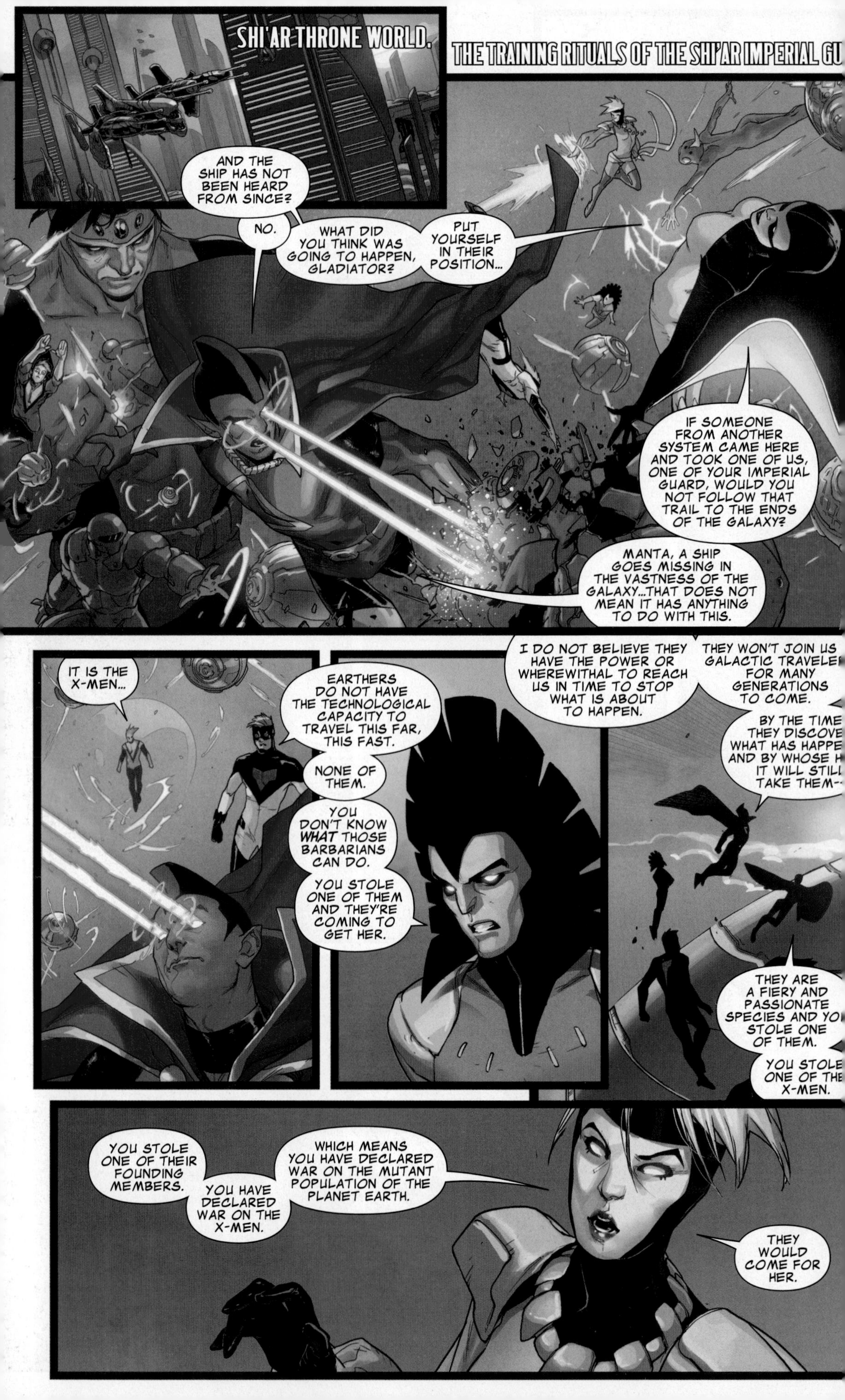
SHI'AR THRONE WORLD.
THE TRAINING RITUALS OF THE SHI'AR IMPERIAL GU
AND THE SHIP HAS NOT BEEN HEARD FROM SINCE?
NO.
WHAT DID YOU THINK WAS GOING TO HAPPEN, GLADIATOR?
PUT YOURSELF IN THEIR POSITION...
IF SOMEONE FROM ANOTHER SYSTEM CAME HERE AND TOOK ONE OF US, ONE OF YOUR IMPERIAL GUARD, WOULD YOU NOT FOLLOW THAT TRAIL TO THE ENDS OF THE GALAXY?
MANTA, A SHIP GOES MISSING IN THE VASTNESS OF THE GALAXY...THAT DOES NOT MEAN IT HAS ANYTHING TO DO WITH THIS.
IT IS THE X-MEN...
EARTHERS DO NOT HAVE THE TECHNOLOGICAL CAPACITY TO TRAVEL THIS FAR, THIS FAST.
NONE OF THEM.
YOU DON'T KNOW WHAT THOSE BARBARIANS CAN DO.
YOU STOLE ONE OF THEM AND THEY'RE COMING TO GET HER.
I DO NOT BELIEVE THEY HAVE THE POWER OR WHEREWITHAL TO REACH US IN TIME TO STOP WHAT IS ABOUT TO HAPPEN.
THEY WON'T JOIN US GALACTIC TRAVELE FOR MANY GENERATIONS TO COME.
BY THE TIME THEY DISCOVE WHAT HAS HAPPE AND BY WHOSE H IT WILL STILL TAKE THEM--
THEY ARE A FIERY AND PASSIONATE SPECIES AND YO STOLE ONE OF THEM.
YOU STOLE ONE OF THE X-MEN.
YOU STOLE ONE OF THEIR FOUNDING MEMBERS.
YOU HAVE DECLARED WAR ON THE X-MEN.
WHICH MEANS YOU HAVE DECLARED WAR ON THE MUTANT POPULATION OF THE PLANET EARTH.
THEY WOULD COME FOR HER.

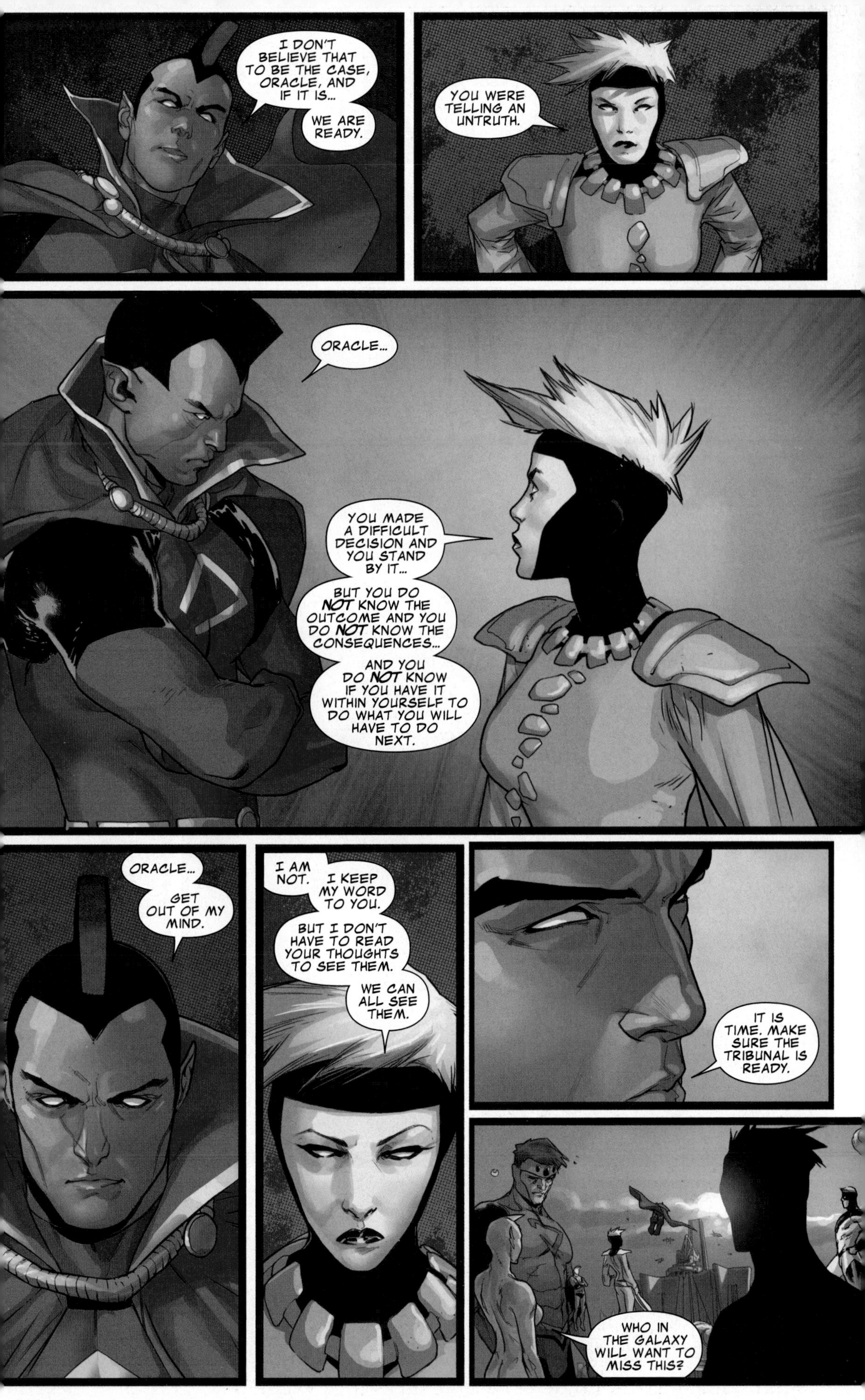
I DON'T BELIEVE THAT TO BE THE CASE, ORACLE, AND IF IT IS...
WE ARE READY.
YOU WERE TELLING AN UNTRUTH.
ORACLE...
YOU MADE A DIFFICULT DECISION AND YOU STAND BY IT...
BUT YOU DO NOT KNOW THE OUTCOME AND YOU DO NOT KNOW THE CONSEQUENCES...
AND YOU DO NOT KNOW IF YOU HAVE IT WITHIN YOURSELF TO DO WHAT YOU WILL HAVE TO DO NEXT.
ORACLE...
GET OUT OF MY MIND.
I AM NOT.
I KEEP MY WORD TO YOU.
BUT I DON'T HAVE TO READ YOUR THOUGHTS TO SEE THEM.
WE CAN ALL SEE THEM.
IT IS TIME. MAKE SURE THE TRIBUNAL IS READY.
WHO IN THE GALAXY WILL WANT TO MISS THIS?

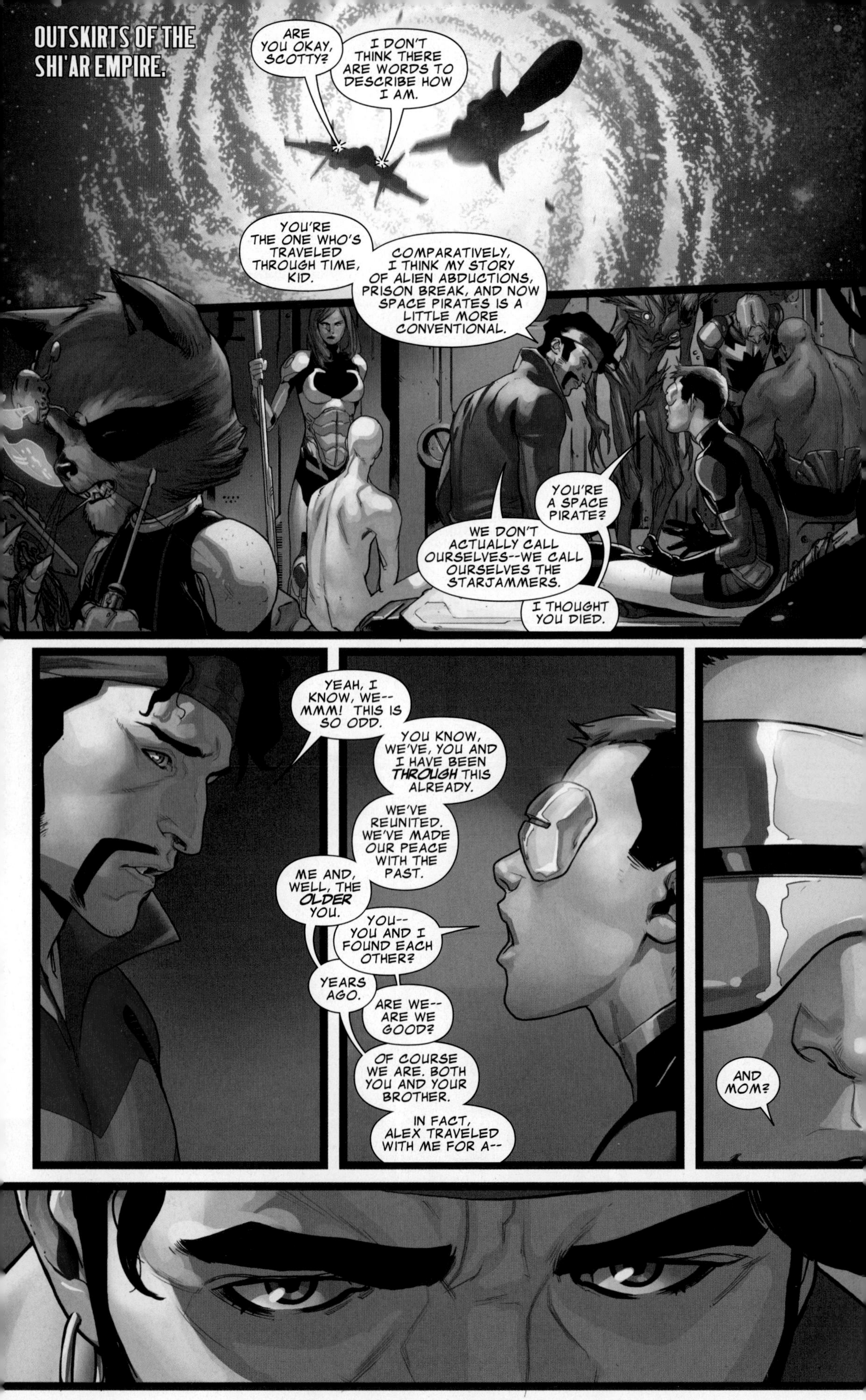
OUTSKIRTS OF THE SHI'AR EMPIRE.
ARE YOU OKAY, SCOTTY?
I DON'T THINK THERE ARE WORDS TO DESCRIBE HOW I AM.
YOU'RE THE ONE WHO'S TRAVELED THROUGH TIME, KID.
COMPARATIVELY, I THINK MY STORY OF ALIEN ABDUCTIONS, PRISON BREAK, AND NOW SPACE PIRATES IS A LITTLE MORE CONVENTIONAL.
YOU'RE A SPACE PIRATE?
WE DON'T ACTUALLY CALL OURSELVES--WE CALL OURSELVES THE STARJAMMERS.
I THOUGHT YOU DIED.
YEAH, I KNOW, WE-- MMM! THIS IS SO ODD.
YOU KNOW, WE'VE, YOU AND I HAVE BEEN THROUGH THIS ALREADY.
WE'VE REUNITED. WE'VE MADE OUR PEACE WITH THE PAST.
ME AND, WELL, THE OLDER YOU.
YOU-- YOU AND I FOUND EACH OTHER?
YEARS AGO.
ARE WE-- ARE WE GOOD?
OF COURSE WE ARE. BOTH YOU AND YOUR BROTHER.
IN FACT, ALEX TRAVELED WITH ME FOR A--
AND MOM?

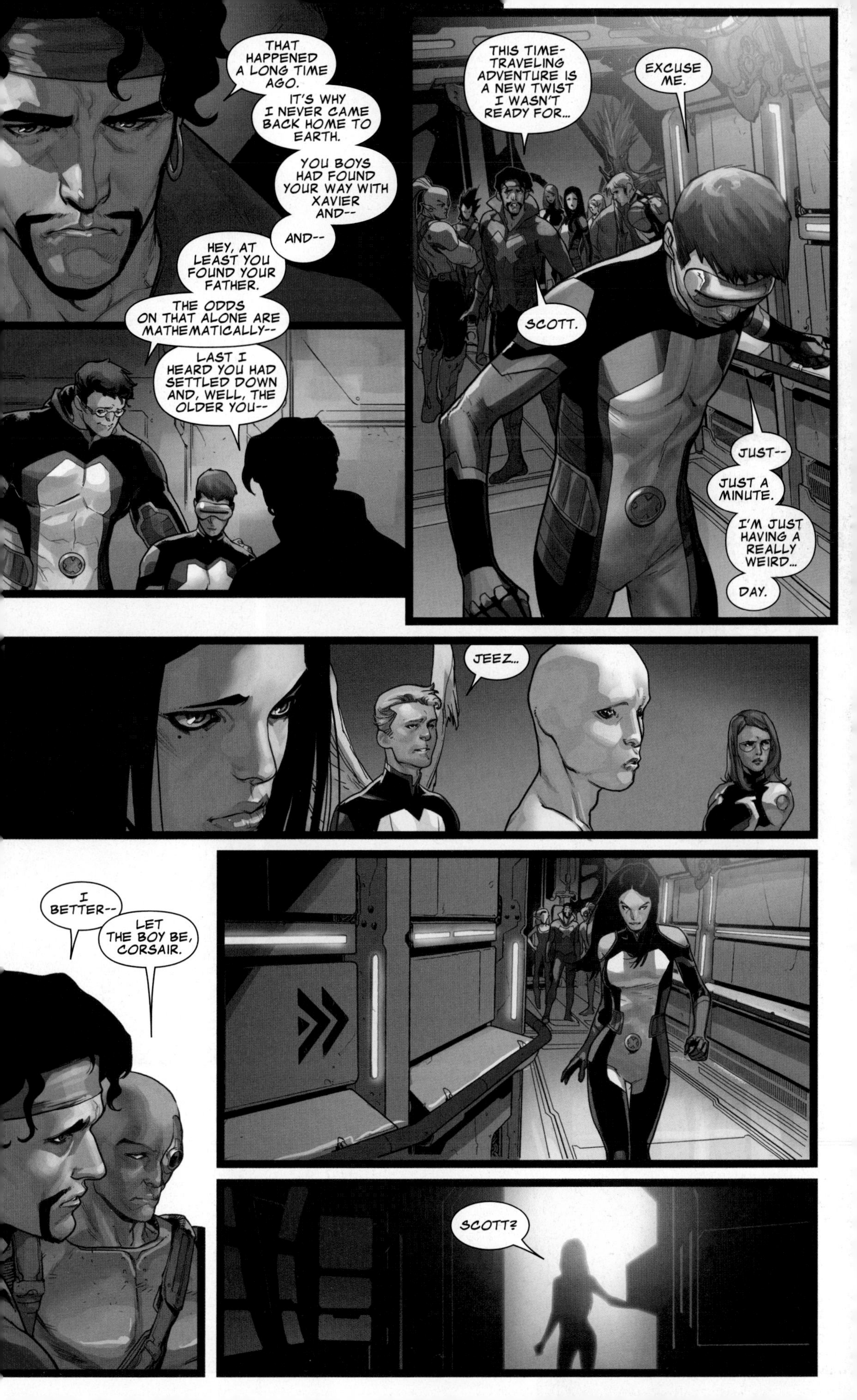

THAT HAPPENED A LONG TIME AGO.
IT'S WHY I NEVER CAME BACK HOME TO EARTH.
YOU BOYS HAD FOUND YOUR WAY WITH XAVIER AND--
AND--
HEY, AT LEAST YOU FOUND YOUR FATHER.
THE ODDS ON THAT ALONE ARE MATHEMATICALLY--
LAST I HEARD YOU HAD SETTLED DOWN AND, WELL, THE OLDER YOU--
THIS TIME-TRAVELING ADVENTURE IS A NEW TWIST I WASN'T READY FOR...
EXCUSE ME.
SCOTT.
JUST--
JUST A MINUTE.
I'M JUST HAVING A REALLY WEIRD...
DAY.
JEEZ...
I BETTER--
LET THE BOY BE, CORSAIR.
SCOTT?

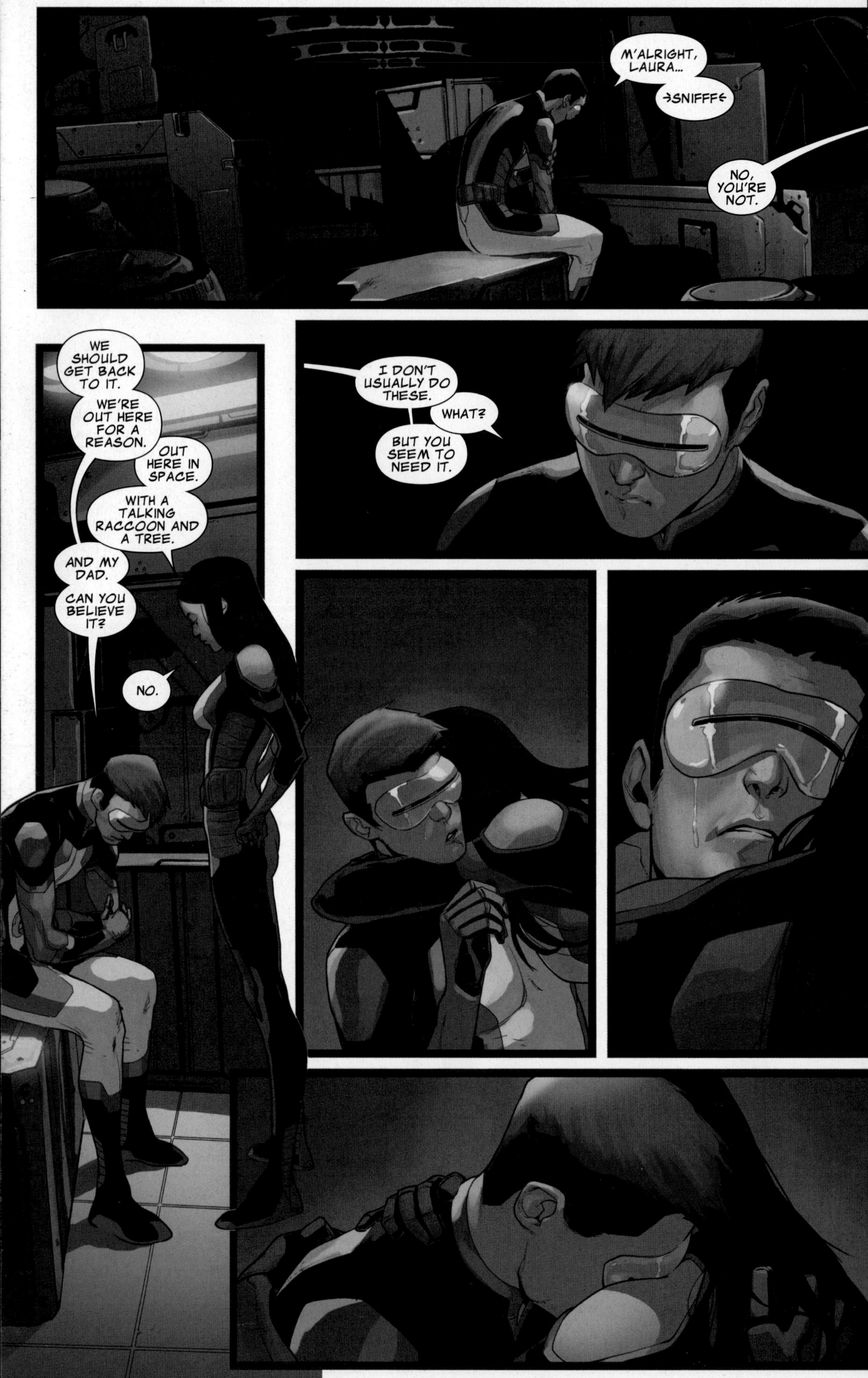
M'ALRIGHT, LAURA...
→SNIFFF←
NO, YOU'RE NOT.
WE SHOULD GET BACK TO IT.
WE'RE OUT HERE FOR A REASON.
OUT HERE IN SPACE.
WITH A TALKING RACCOON AND A TREE.
AND MY DAD.
CAN YOU BELIEVE IT?
NO.
I DON'T USUALLY DO THESE.
WHAT?
BUT YOU SEEM TO NEED IT.

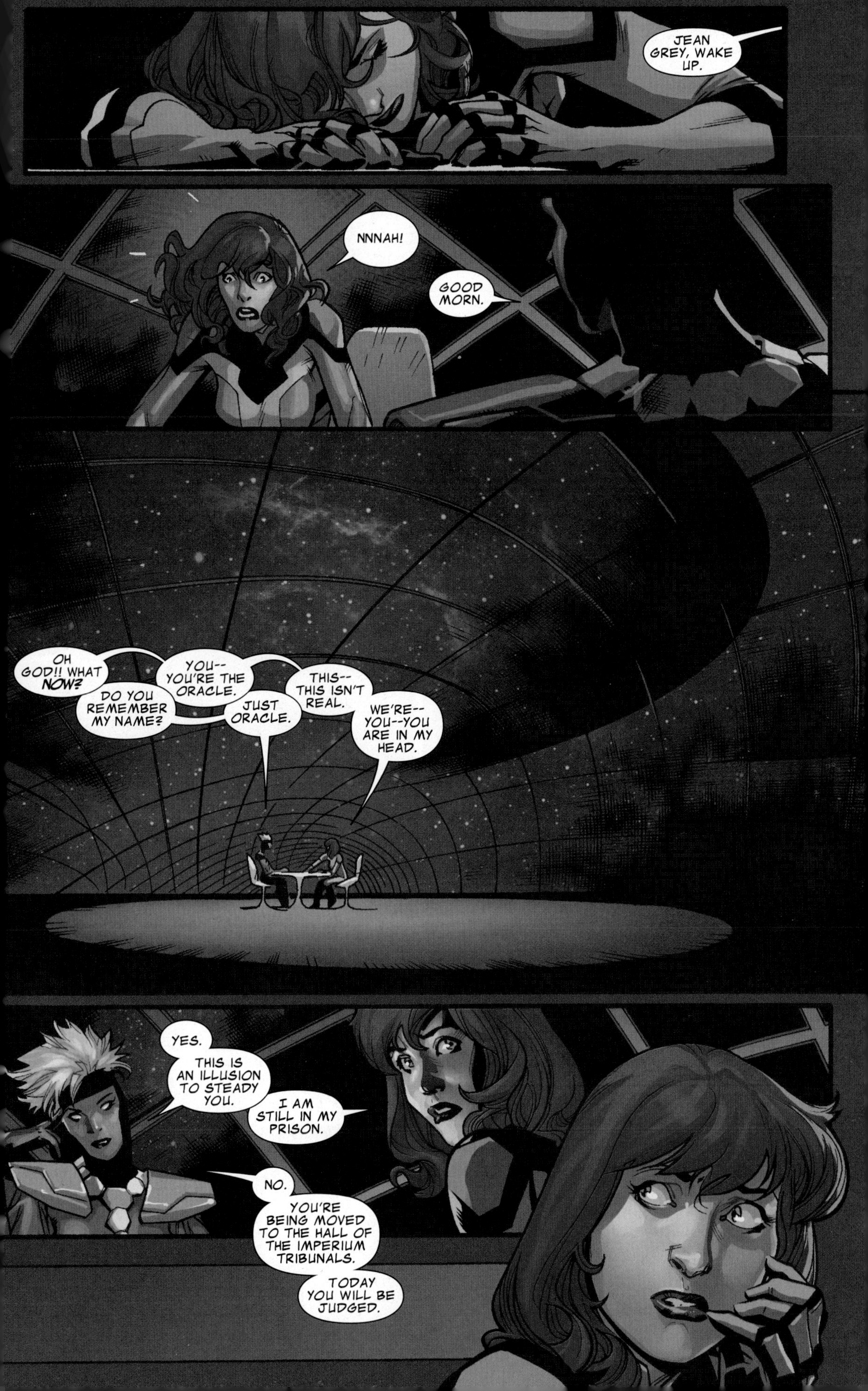
JEAN GREY, WAKE UP.
NNNAH!
GOOD MORN.
OH GOD!! WHAT NOW?
DO YOU REMEMBER MY NAME?
YOU-- YOU'RE THE ORACLE.
JUST ORACLE.
THIS-- THIS ISN'T REAL.
WE'RE-- YOU--YOU ARE IN MY HEAD.
YES.
THIS IS AN ILLUSION TO STEADY YOU.
I AM STILL IN MY PRISON.
NO.
YOU'RE BEING MOVED TO THE HALL OF THE IMPERIUM TRIBUNALS.
TODAY YOU WILL BE JUDGED.

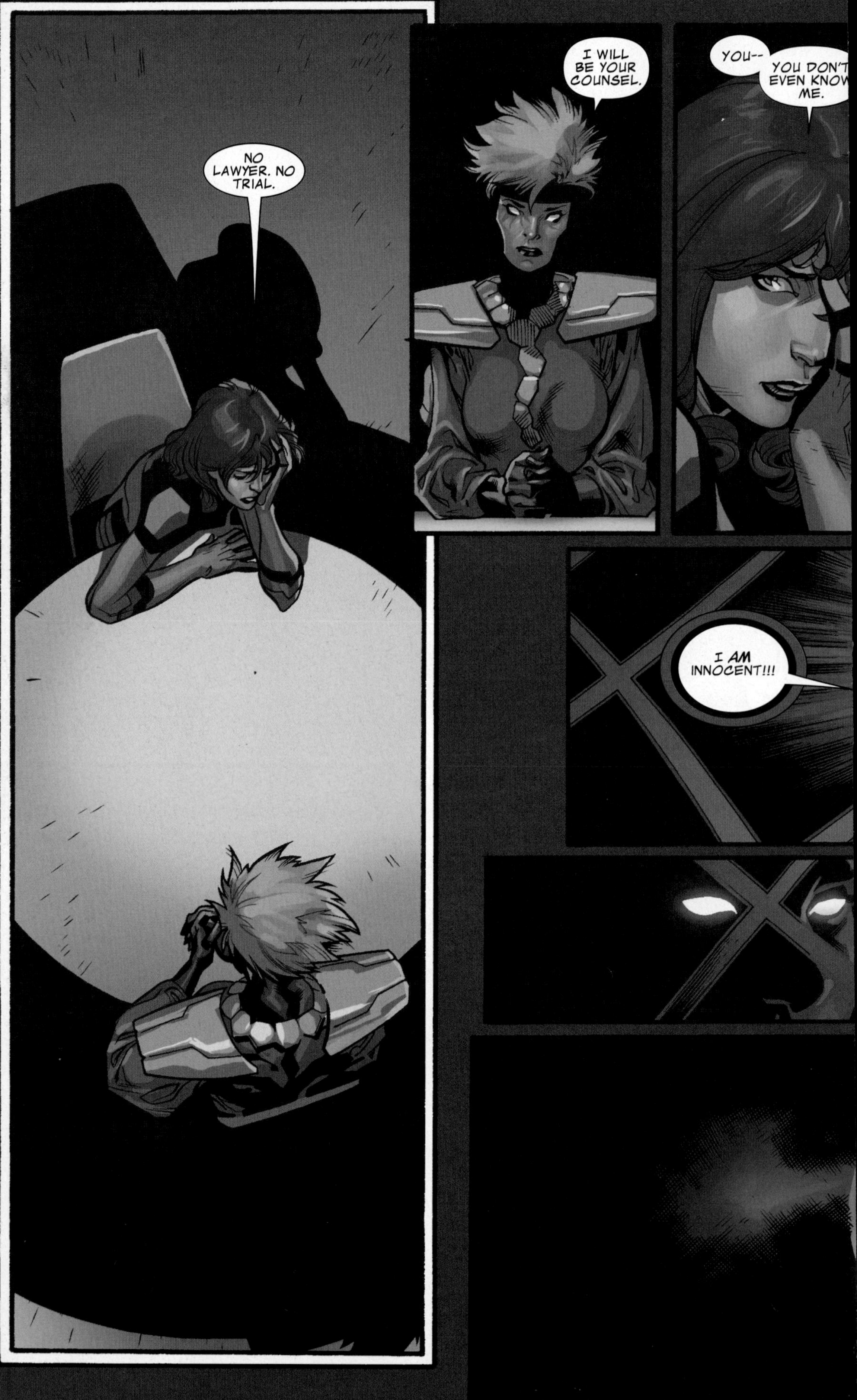
NO LAWYER. NO TRIAL.
I WILL BE YOUR COUNSEL.
YOU--
YOU DON'T EVEN KNOW ME.
I AM INNOCENT!!!

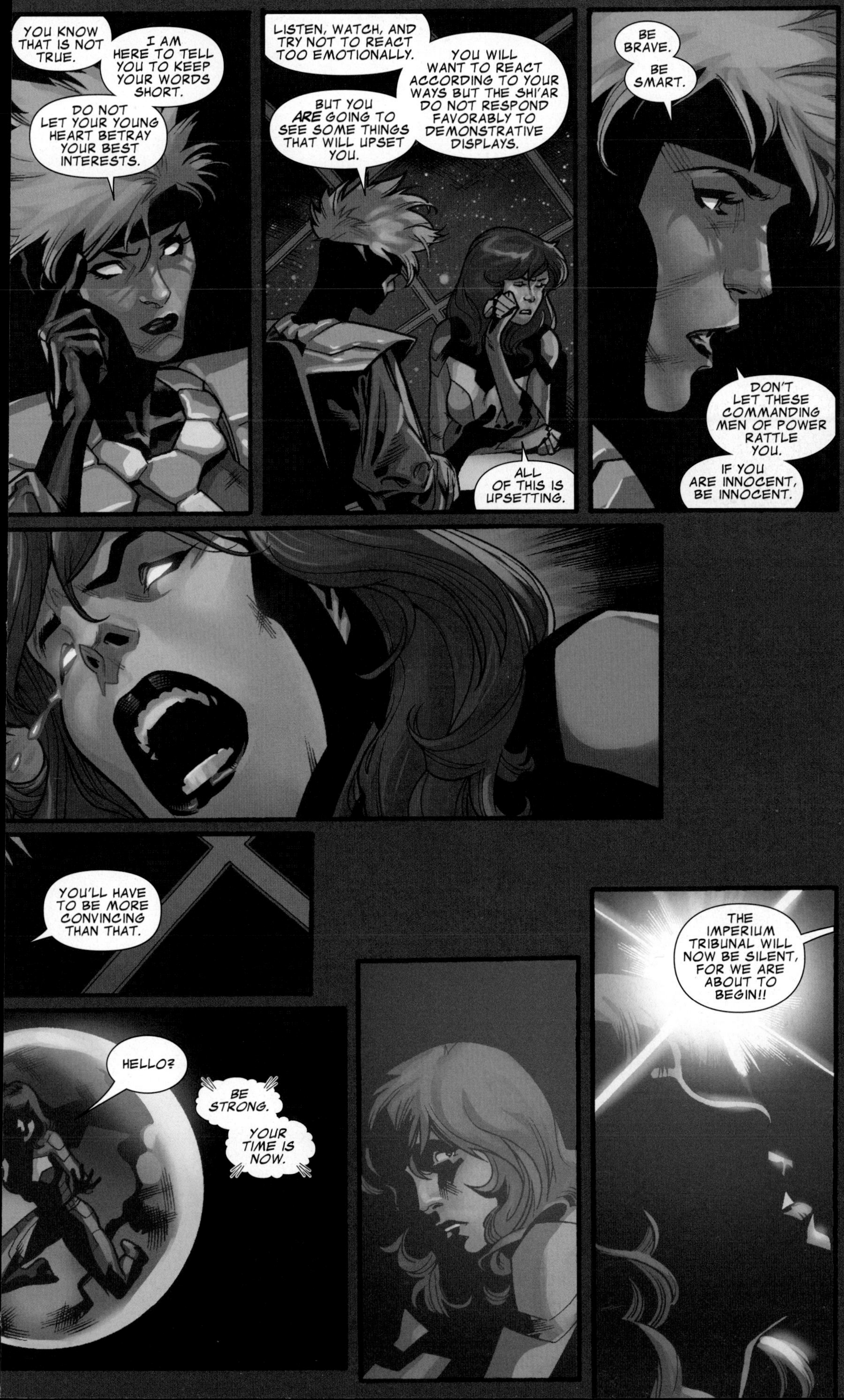
YOU KNOW THAT IS NOT TRUE.
I AM HERE TO TELL YOU TO KEEP YOUR WORDS SHORT.
DO NOT LET YOUR YOUNG HEART BETRAY YOUR BEST INTERESTS.
LISTEN, WATCH, AND TRY NOT TO REACT TOO EMOTIONALLY.
BUT YOU ARE GOING TO SEE SOME THINGS THAT WILL UPSET YOU.
YOU WILL WANT TO REACT ACCORDING TO YOUR WAYS BUT THE SHI'AR DO NOT RESPOND FAVORABLY TO DEMONSTRATIVE DISPLAYS.
ALL OF THIS IS UPSETTING.
BE BRAVE.
BE SMART.
DON'T LET THESE COMMANDING MEN OF POWER RATTLE YOU.
IF YOU ARE INNOCENT, BE INNOCENT.
YOU'LL HAVE TO BE MORE CONVINCING THAN THAT.
HELLO?
BE STRONG.
YOUR TIME IS NOW.
THE IMPERIUM TRIBUNAL WILL NOW BE SILENT, FOR WE ARE ABOUT TO BEGIN!!

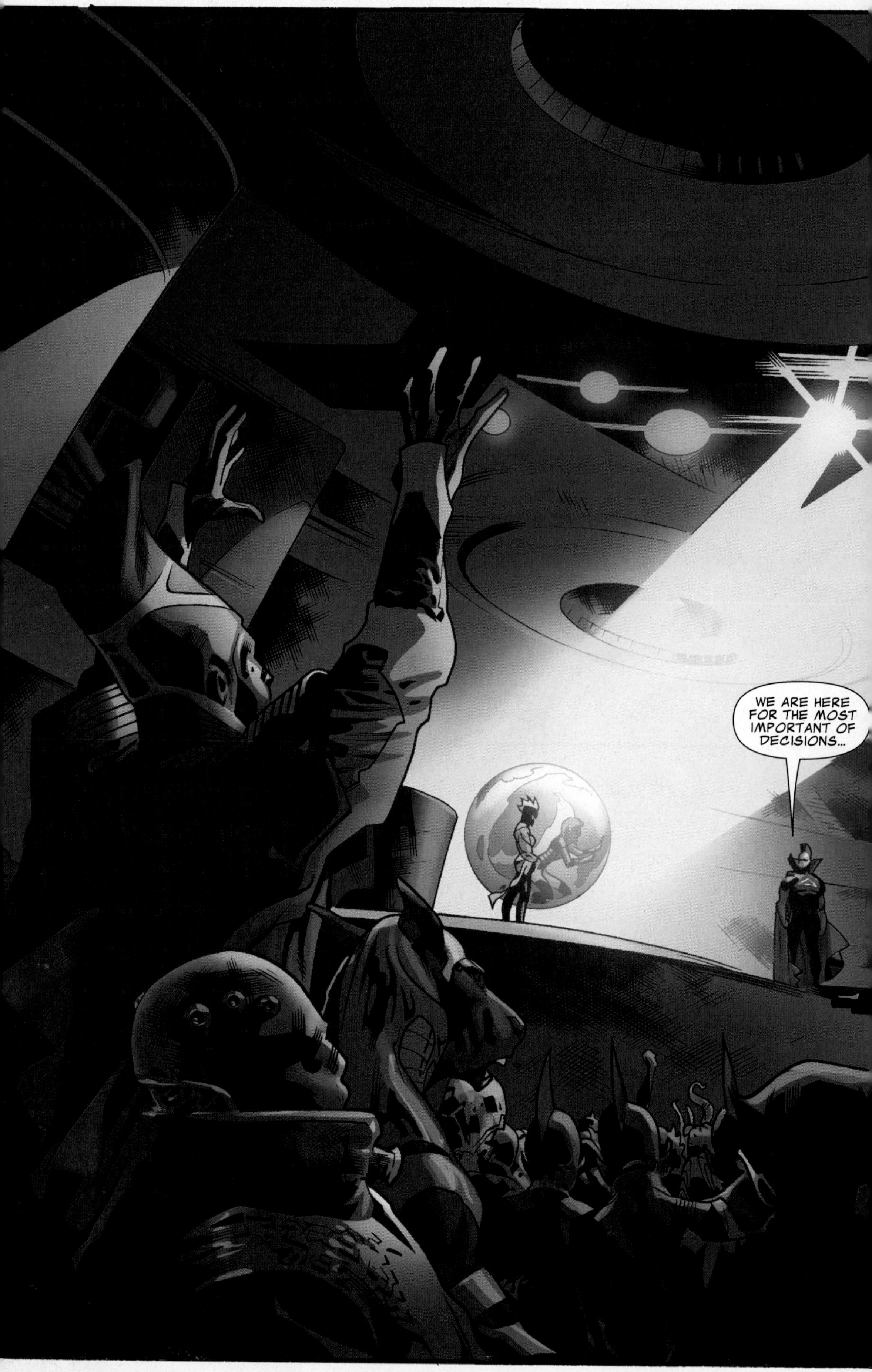
WE ARE HERE FOR THE MOST IMPORTANT OF DECISIONS...

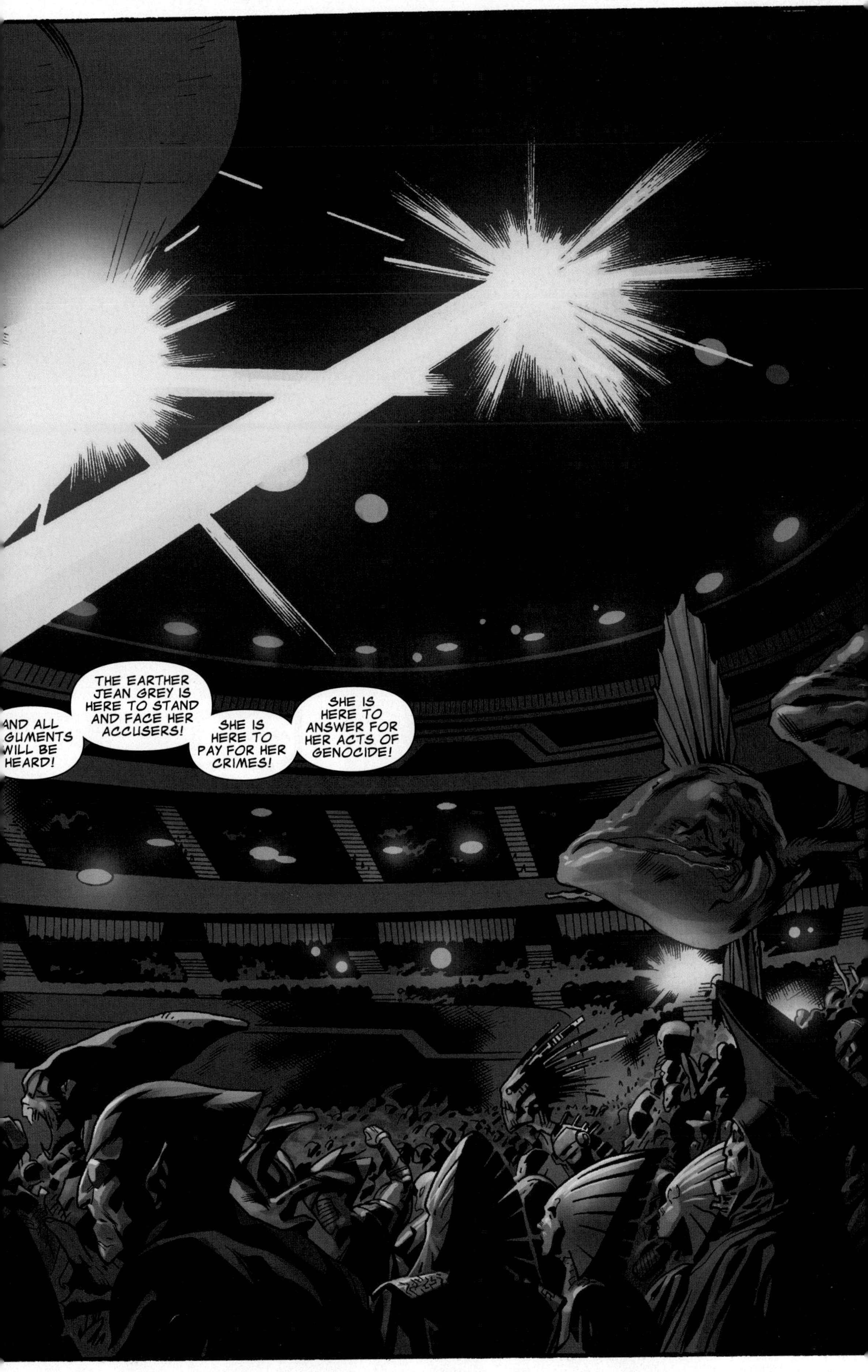
AND ALL GUMENTS WILL BE HEARD!
THE EARTHER JEAN GREY IS HERE TO STAND AND FACE HER ACCUSERS!
SHE IS HERE TO PAY FOR HER CRIMES!
SHE IS HERE TO ANSWER FOR HER ACTS OF GENOCIDE!

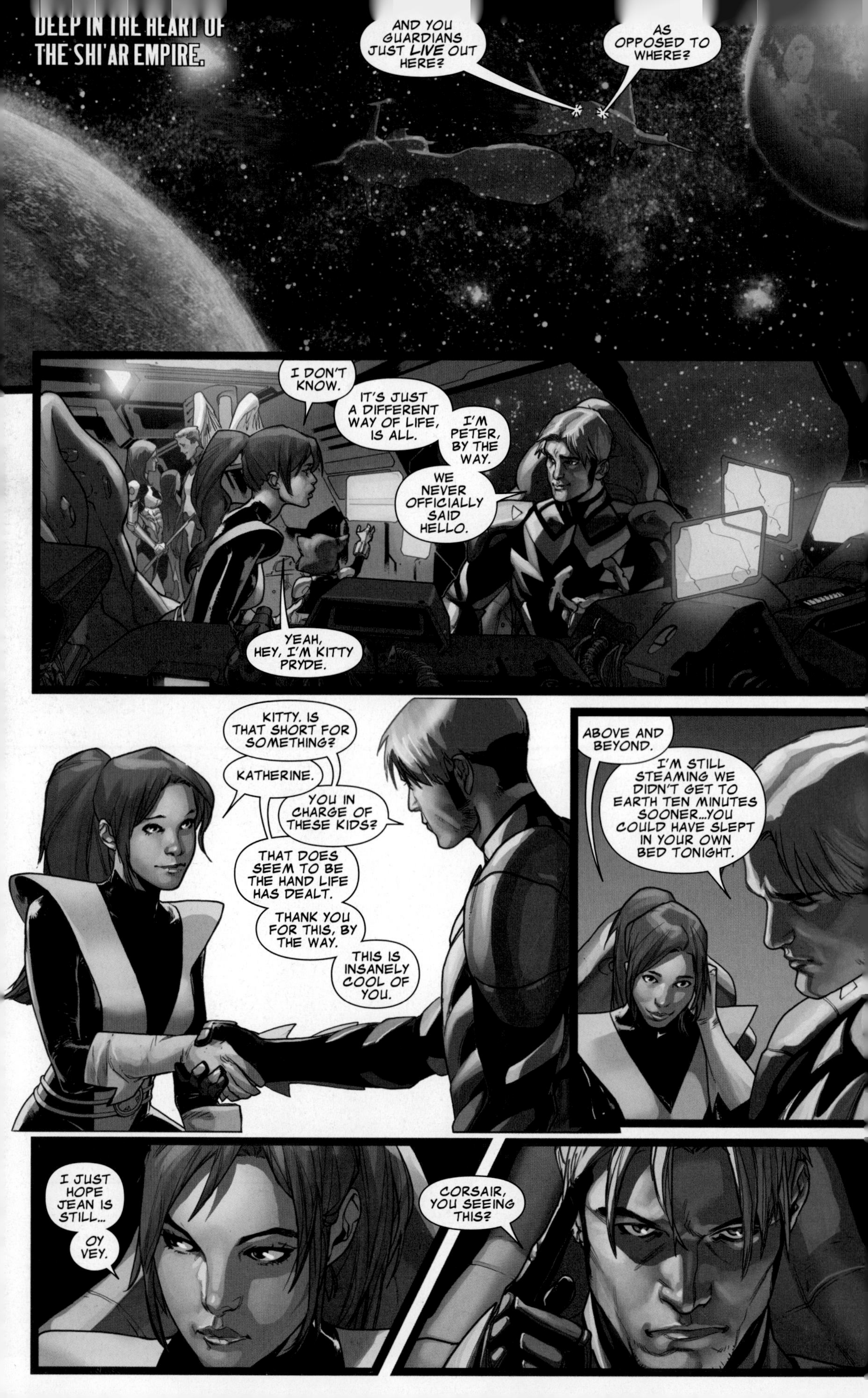
DEEP IN THE HEART OF THE SHI'AR EMPIRE.
AND YOU GUARDIANS JUST LIVE OUT HERE?
AS OPPOSED TO WHERE?
I DON'T KNOW.
IT'S JUST A DIFFERENT WAY OF LIFE, IS ALL.
I'M PETER, BY THE WAY.
WE NEVER OFFICIALLY SAID HELLO.
YEAH, HEY, I'M KITTY PRYDE.
KITTY. IS THAT SHORT FOR SOMETHING?
KATHERINE.
YOU IN CHARGE OF THESE KIDS?
THAT DOES SEEM TO BE THE HAND LIFE HAS DEALT.
THANK YOU FOR THIS, BY THE WAY.
THIS IS INSANELY COOL OF YOU.
ABOVE AND BEYOND.
I'M STILL STEAMING WE DIDN'T GET TO EARTH TEN MINUTES SOONER...YOU COULD HAVE SLEPT IN YOUR OWN BED TONIGHT.
I JUST HOPE JEAN IS STILL...
OY VEY.
CORSAIR, YOU SEEING THIS?

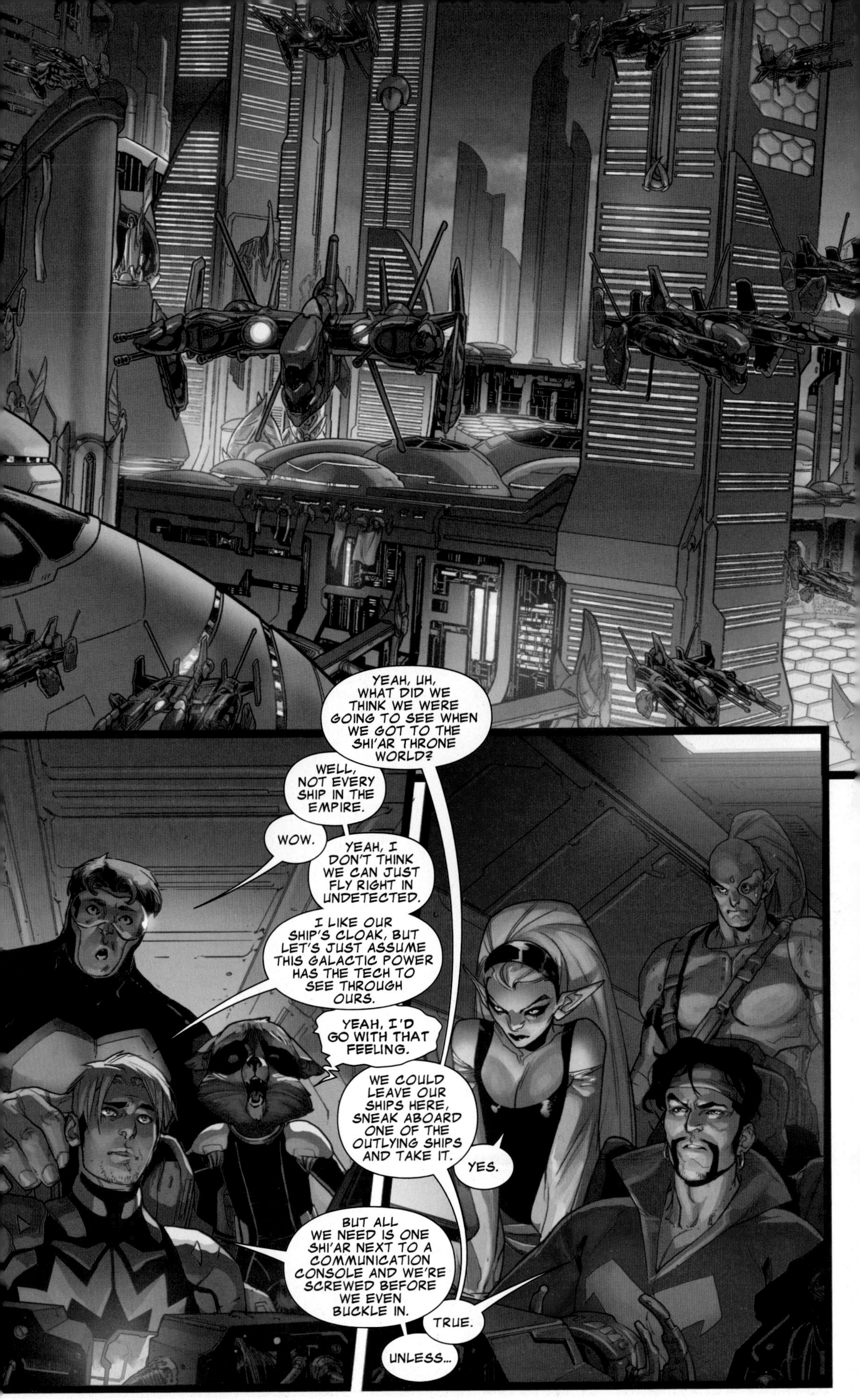
YEAH, UH, WHAT DID WE THINK WE WERE GOING TO SEE WHEN WE GOT TO THE SHI'AR THRONE WORLD?
WELL, NOT EVERY SHIP IN THE EMPIRE.
WOW.
YEAH, I DON'T THINK WE CAN JUST FLY RIGHT IN UNDETECTED.
I LIKE OUR SHIP'S CLOAK, BUT LET'S JUST ASSUME THIS GALACTIC POWER HAS THE TECH TO SEE THROUGH OURS.
YEAH, I'D GO WITH THAT FEELING.
WE COULD LEAVE OUR SHIPS HERE, SNEAK ABOARD ONE OF THE OUTLYING SHIPS AND TAKE IT.
YES.
BUT ALL WE NEED IS ONE SHI'AR NEXT TO A COMMUNICATION CONSOLE AND WE'RE SCREWED BEFORE WE EVEN BUCKLE IN.
TRUE.
UNLESS...

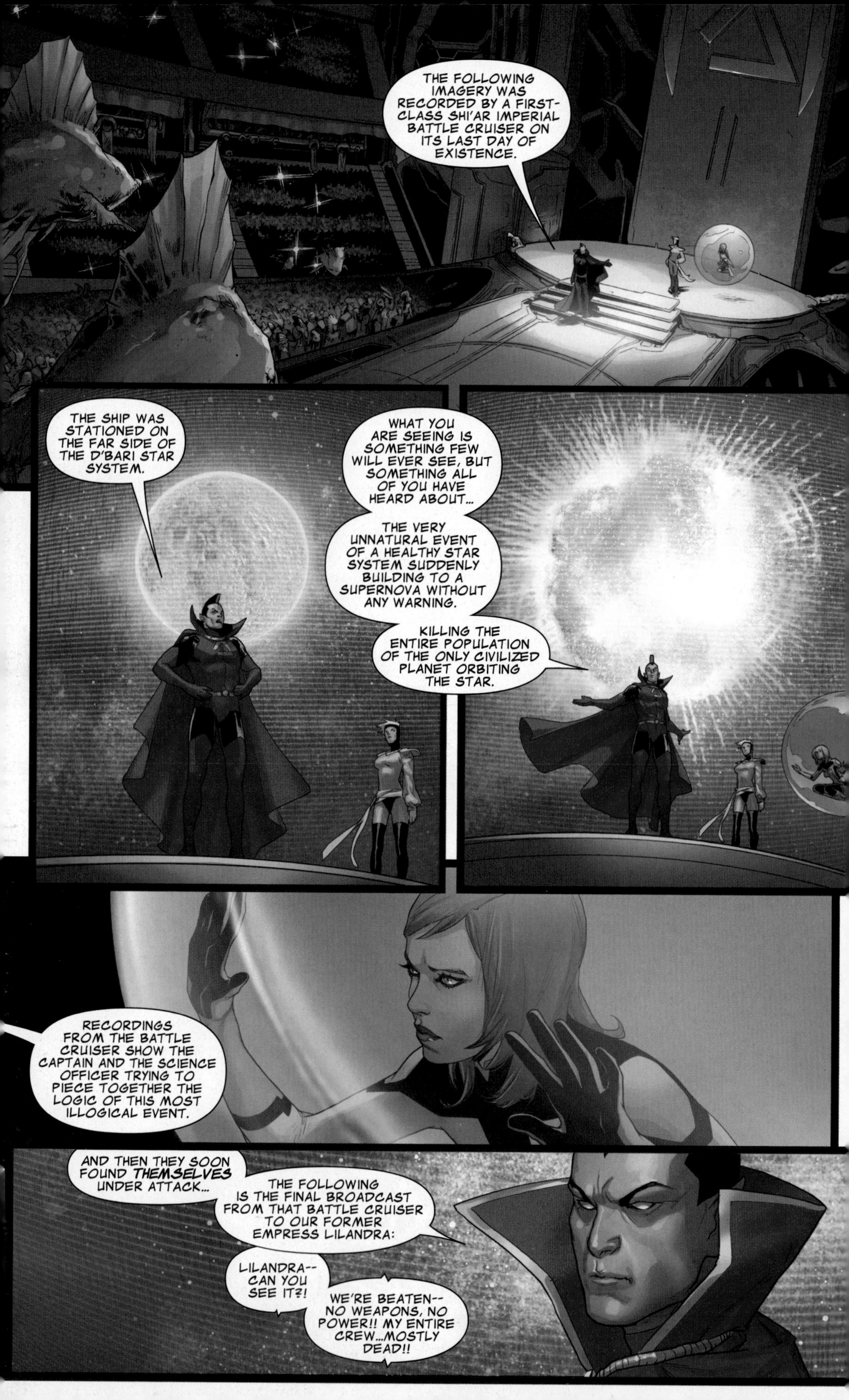
THE FOLLOWING IMAGERY WAS RECORDED BY A FIRST-CLASS SHI'AR IMPERIAL BATTLE CRUISER ON ITS LAST DAY OF EXISTENCE.
THE SHIP WAS STATIONED ON THE FAR SIDE OF THE D'BARI STAR SYSTEM.
WHAT YOU ARE SEEING IS SOMETHING FEW WILL EVER SEE, BUT SOMETHING ALL OF YOU HAVE HEARD ABOUT...
THE VERY UNNATURAL EVENT OF A HEALTHY STAR SYSTEM SUDDENLY BUILDING TO A SUPERNOVA WITHOUT ANY WARNING.
KILLING THE ENTIRE POPULATION OF THE ONLY CIVILIZED PLANET ORBITING THE STAR.
RECORDINGS FROM THE BATTLE CRUISER SHOW THE CAPTAIN AND THE SCIENCE OFFICER TRYING TO PIECE TOGETHER THE LOGIC OF THIS MOST ILLOGICAL EVENT.
AND THEN THEY SOON FOUND ***THEMSELVES*** UNDER ATTACK...
THE FOLLOWING IS THE FINAL BROADCAST FROM THAT BATTLE CRUISER TO OUR FORMER EMPRESS LILANDRA:
LILANDRA-- CAN YOU SEE IT?!
WE'RE BEATEN-- NO WEAPONS, NO POWER!! MY ENTIRE CREW...MOSTLY DEAD!!

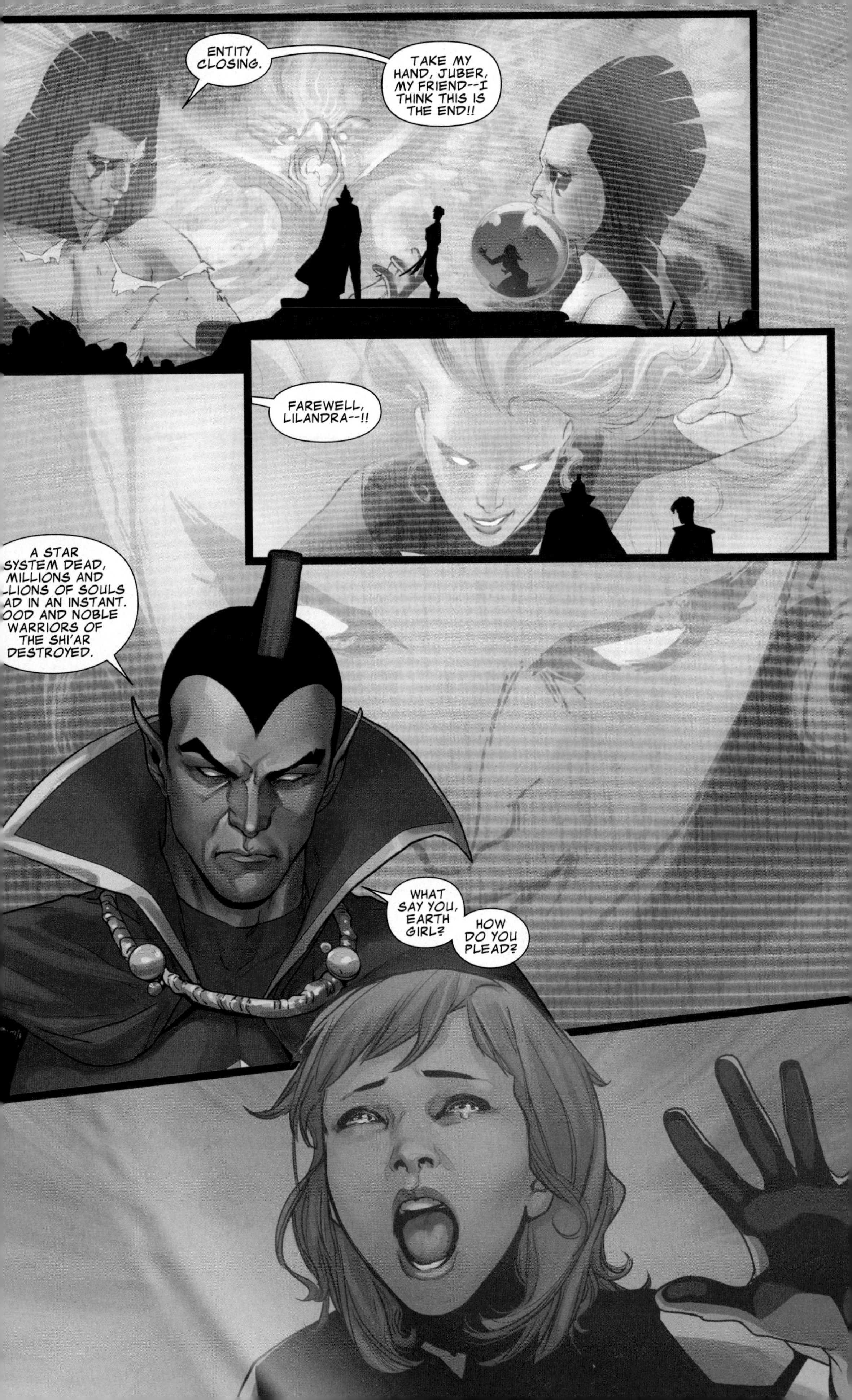
ENTITY CLOSING.
TAKE MY HAND, JUBER, MY FRIEND--I THINK THIS IS THE END!!
FAREWELL, LILANDRA--!!
A STAR SYSTEM DEAD, MILLIONS AND LLIONS OF SOULS AD IN AN INSTANT. OOD AND NOBLE WARRIORS OF THE SHI'AR DESTROYED.
WHAT SAY YOU, EARTH GIRL?
HOW DO YOU PLEAD?

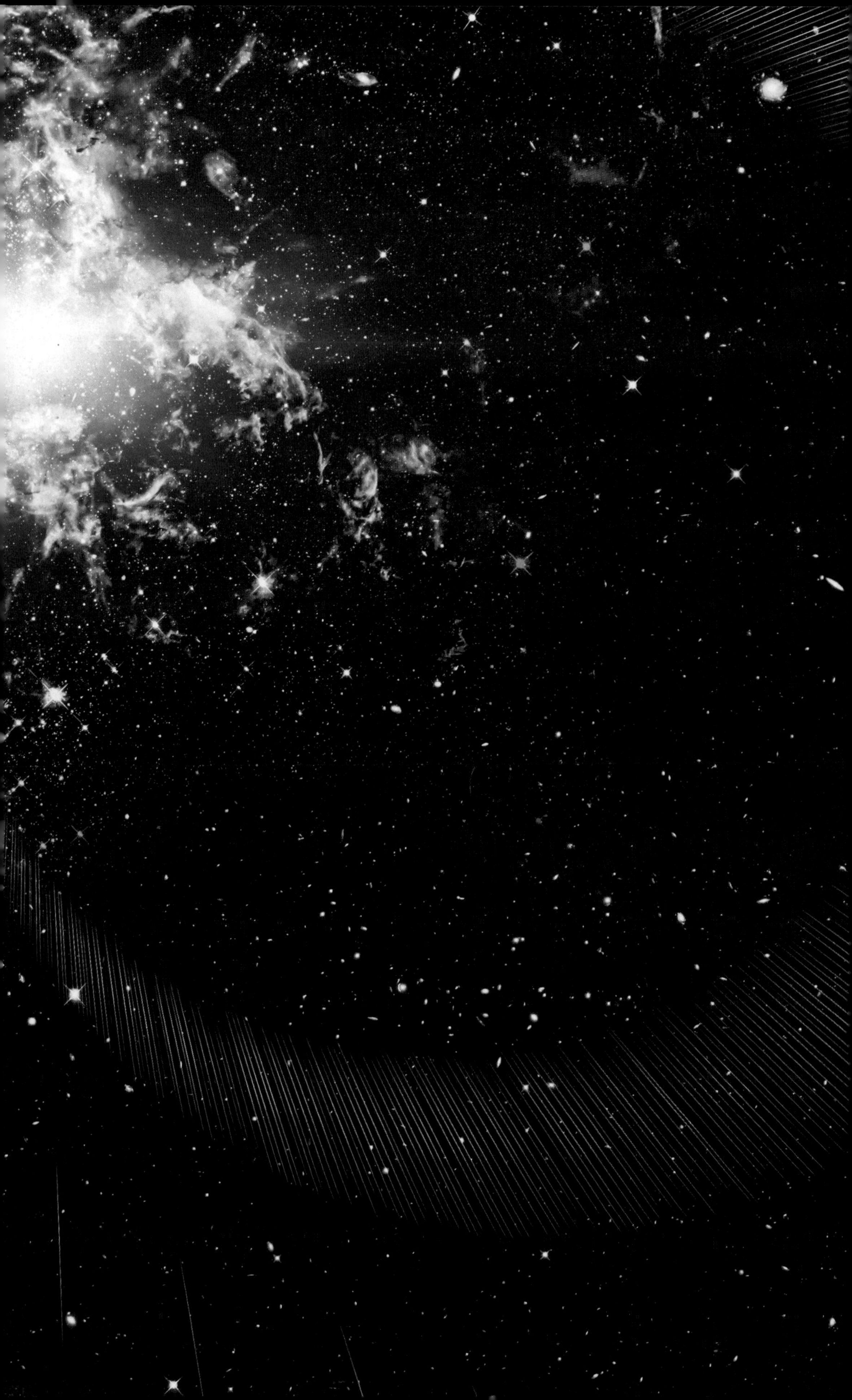

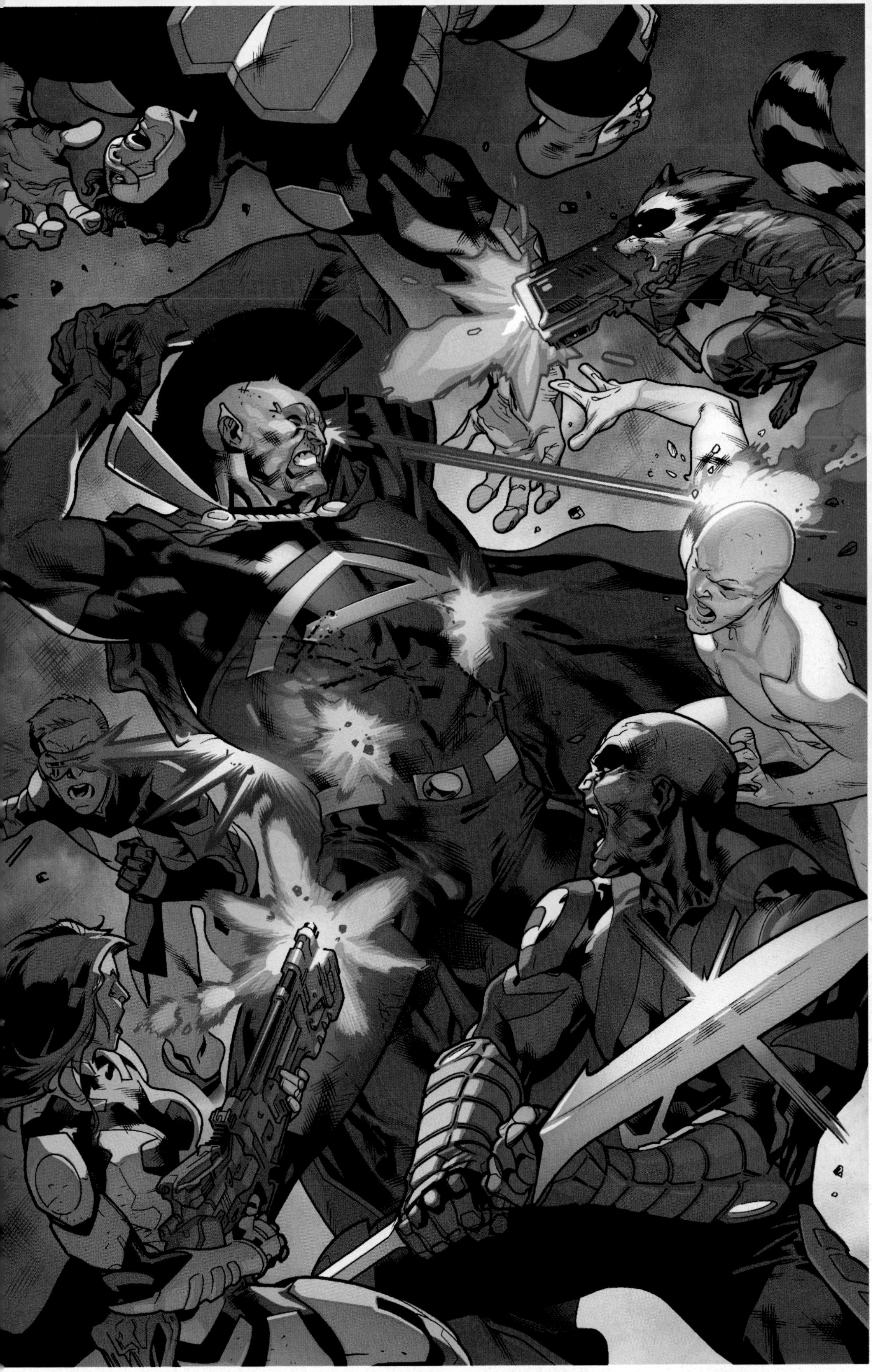

ALL-NEW X-MEN 24

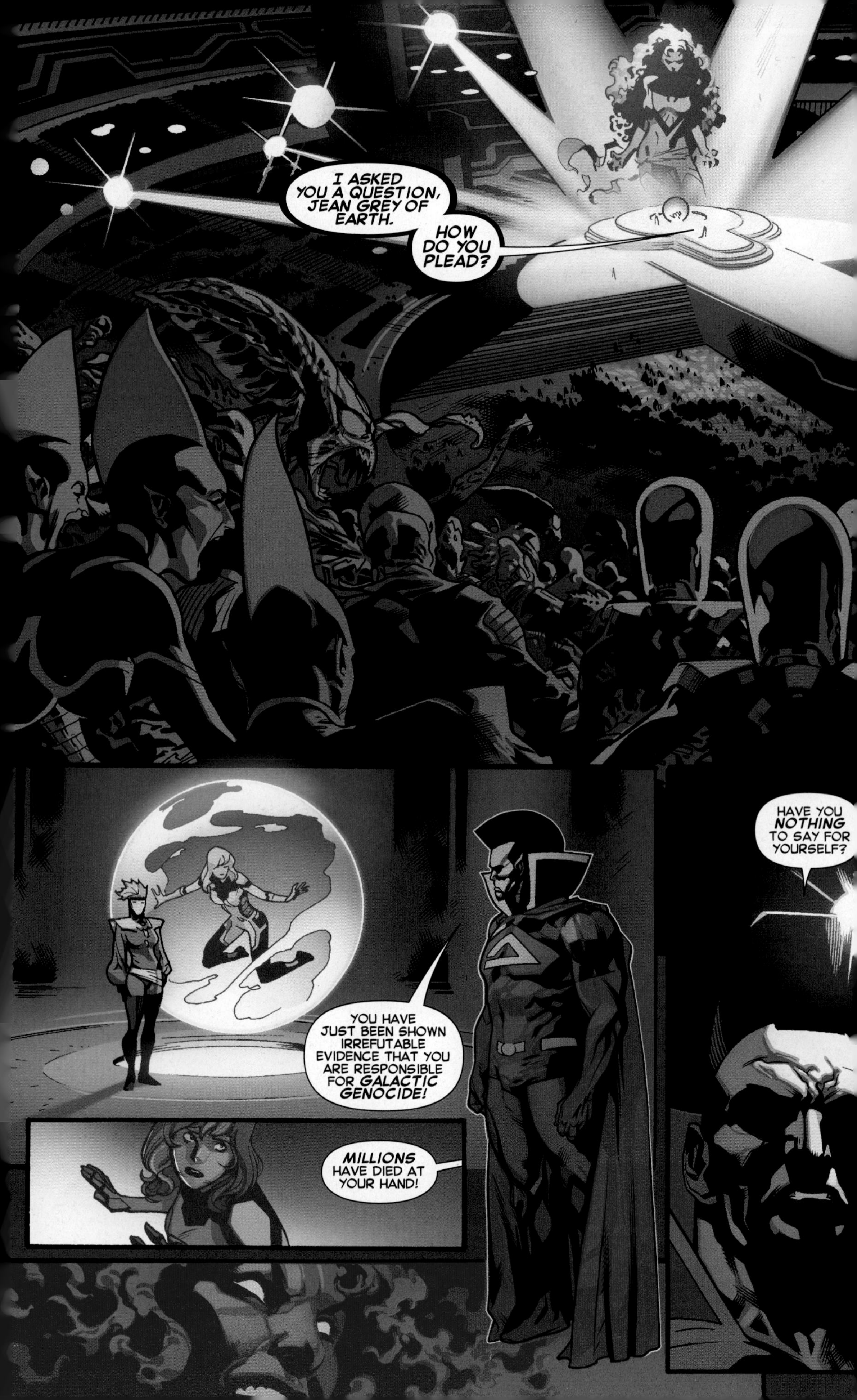
I ASKED YOU A QUESTION, JEAN GREY OF EARTH.
HOW DO YOU PLEAD?
YOU HAVE JUST BEEN SHOWN IRREFUTABLE EVIDENCE THAT YOU ARE RESPONSIBLE FOR GALACTIC GENOCIDE!
MILLIONS HAVE DIED AT YOUR HAND!
HAVE YOU NOTHING TO SAY FOR YOURSELF?

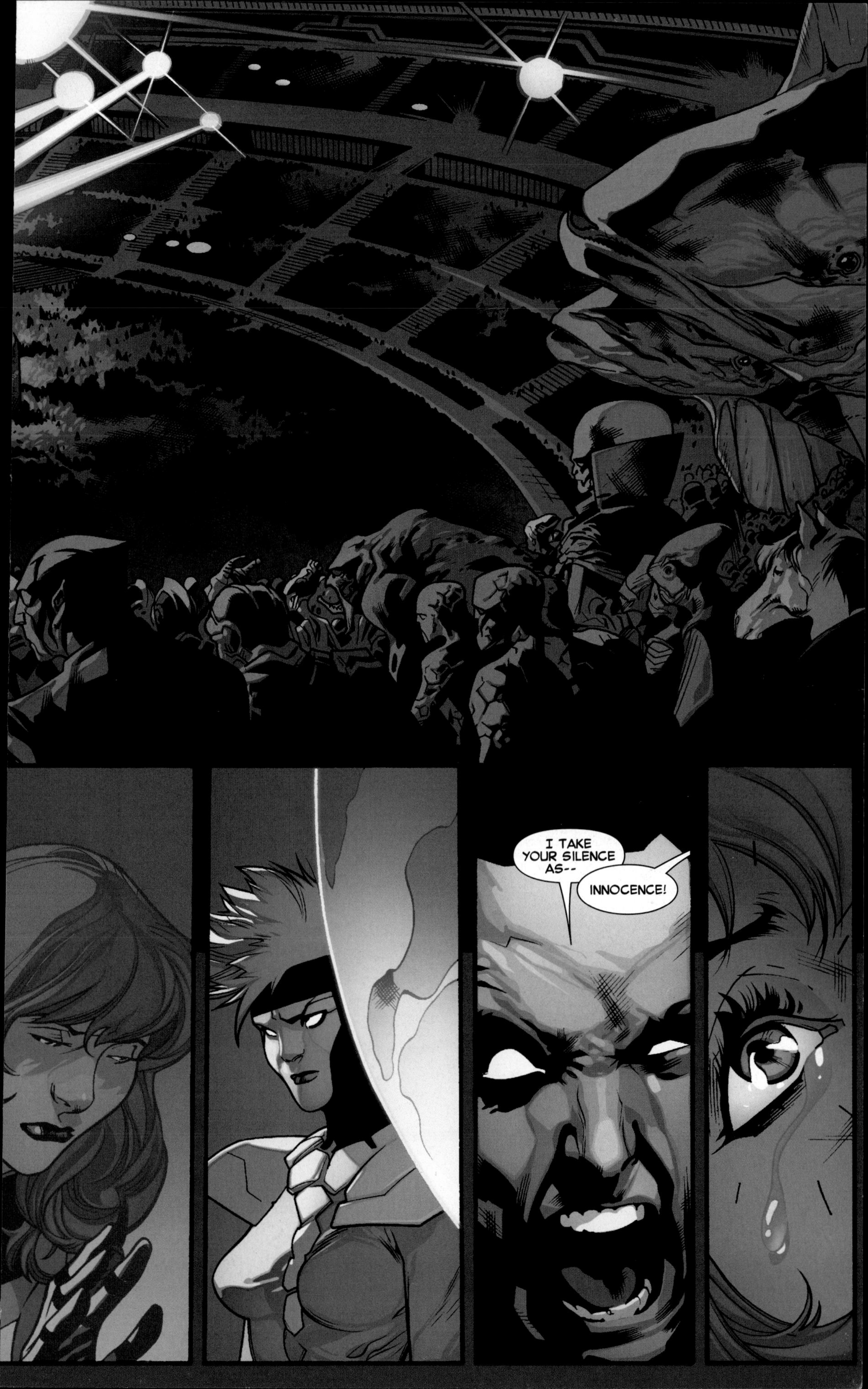
I TAKE YOUR SILENCE AS--
INNOCENCE!

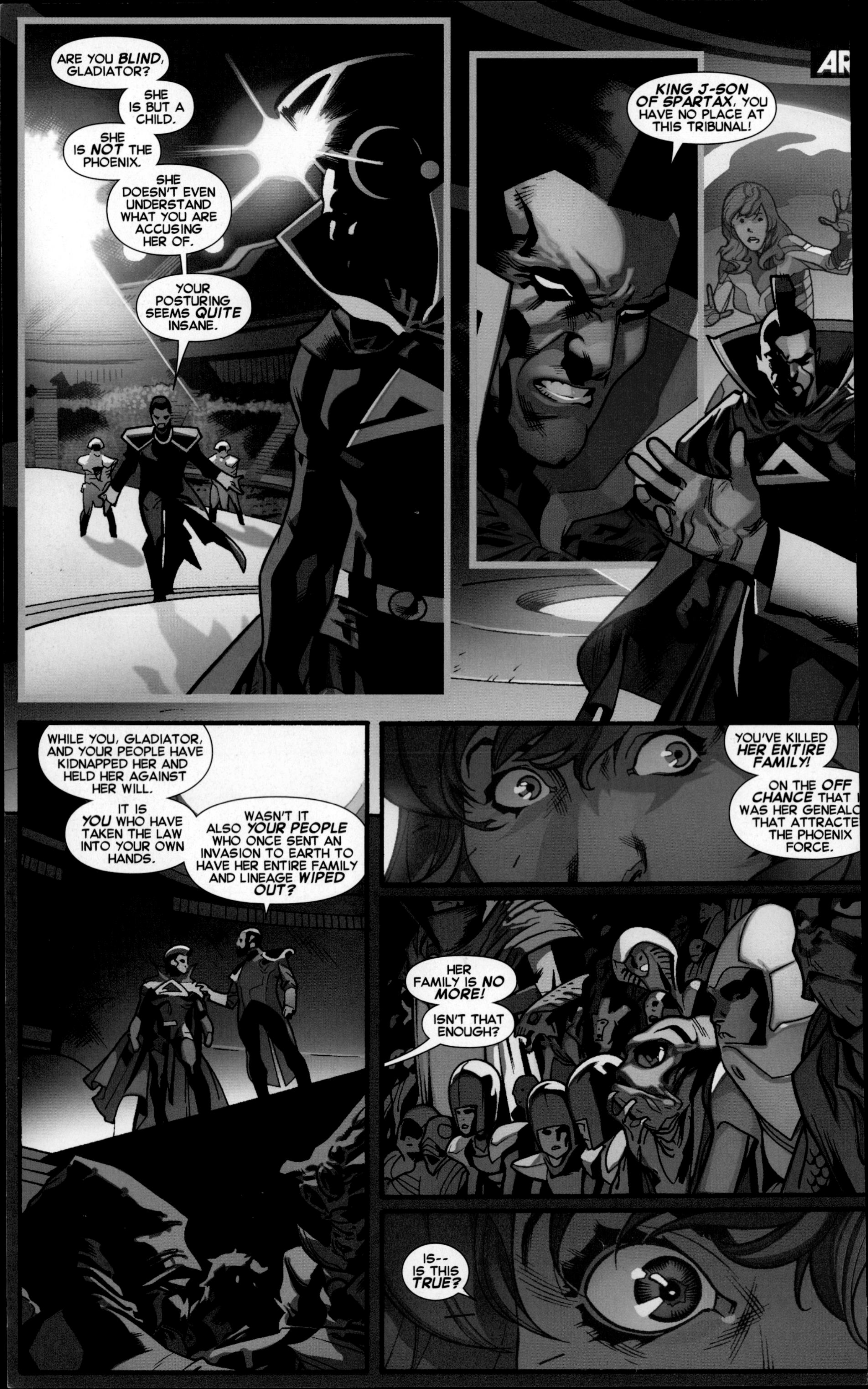

ARE YOU BLIND, GLADIATOR?
SHE IS BUT A CHILD.
SHE IS NOT THE PHOENIX.
SHE DOESN'T EVEN UNDERSTAND WHAT YOU ARE ACCUSING HER OF.
YOUR POSTURING SEEMS QUITE INSANE.
KING J-SON OF SPARTAX, YOU HAVE NO PLACE AT THIS TRIBUNAL!
WHILE YOU, GLADIATOR, AND YOUR PEOPLE HAVE KIDNAPPED HER AND HELD HER AGAINST HER WILL.
IT IS YOU WHO HAVE TAKEN THE LAW INTO YOUR OWN HANDS.
WASN'T IT ALSO YOUR PEOPLE WHO ONCE SENT AN INVASION TO EARTH TO HAVE HER ENTIRE FAMILY AND LINEAGE WIPED OUT?
YOU'VE KILLED HER ENTIRE FAMILY!
ON THE OFF CHANCE THAT I WAS HER GENEALO THAT ATTRACTE THE PHOENIX FORCE.
HER FAMILY IS NO MORE!
ISN'T THAT ENOUGH?
IS-- IS THIS TRUE?

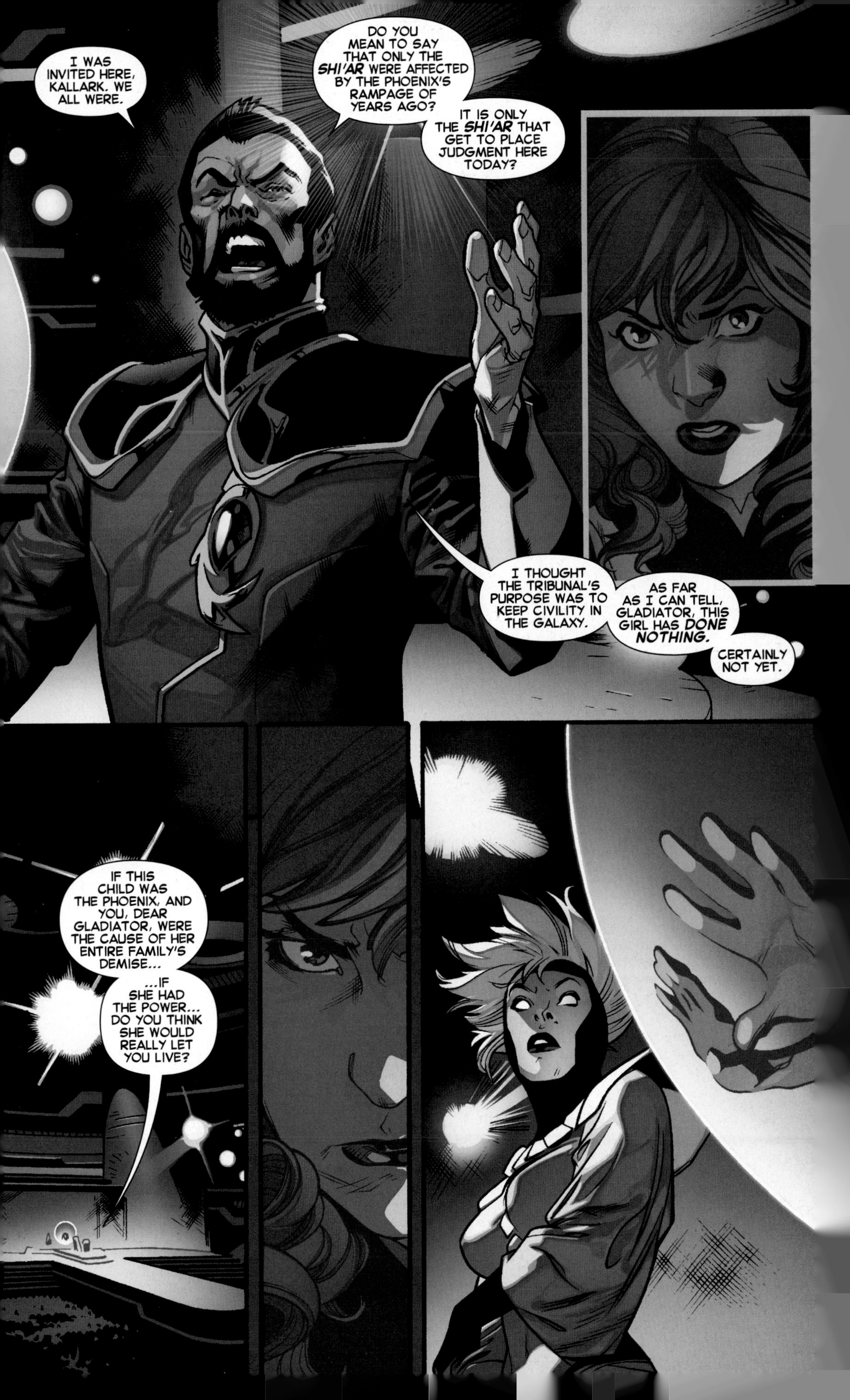
I WAS INVITED HERE, KALLARK. WE ALL WERE.
DO YOU MEAN TO SAY THAT ONLY THE SHI'AR WERE AFFECTED BY THE PHOENIX'S RAMPAGE OF YEARS AGO?
IT IS ONLY THE SHI'AR THAT GET TO PLACE JUDGMENT HERE TODAY?
I THOUGHT THE TRIBUNAL'S PURPOSE WAS TO KEEP CIVILITY IN THE GALAXY.
AS FAR AS I CAN TELL, GLADIATOR, THIS GIRL HAS DONE NOTHING.
CERTAINLY NOT YET.
IF THIS CHILD WAS THE PHOENIX, AND YOU, DEAR GLADIATOR, WERE THE CAUSE OF HER ENTIRE FAMILY'S DEMISE...
...IF SHE HAD THE POWER... DO YOU THINK SHE WOULD REALLY LET YOU LIVE?

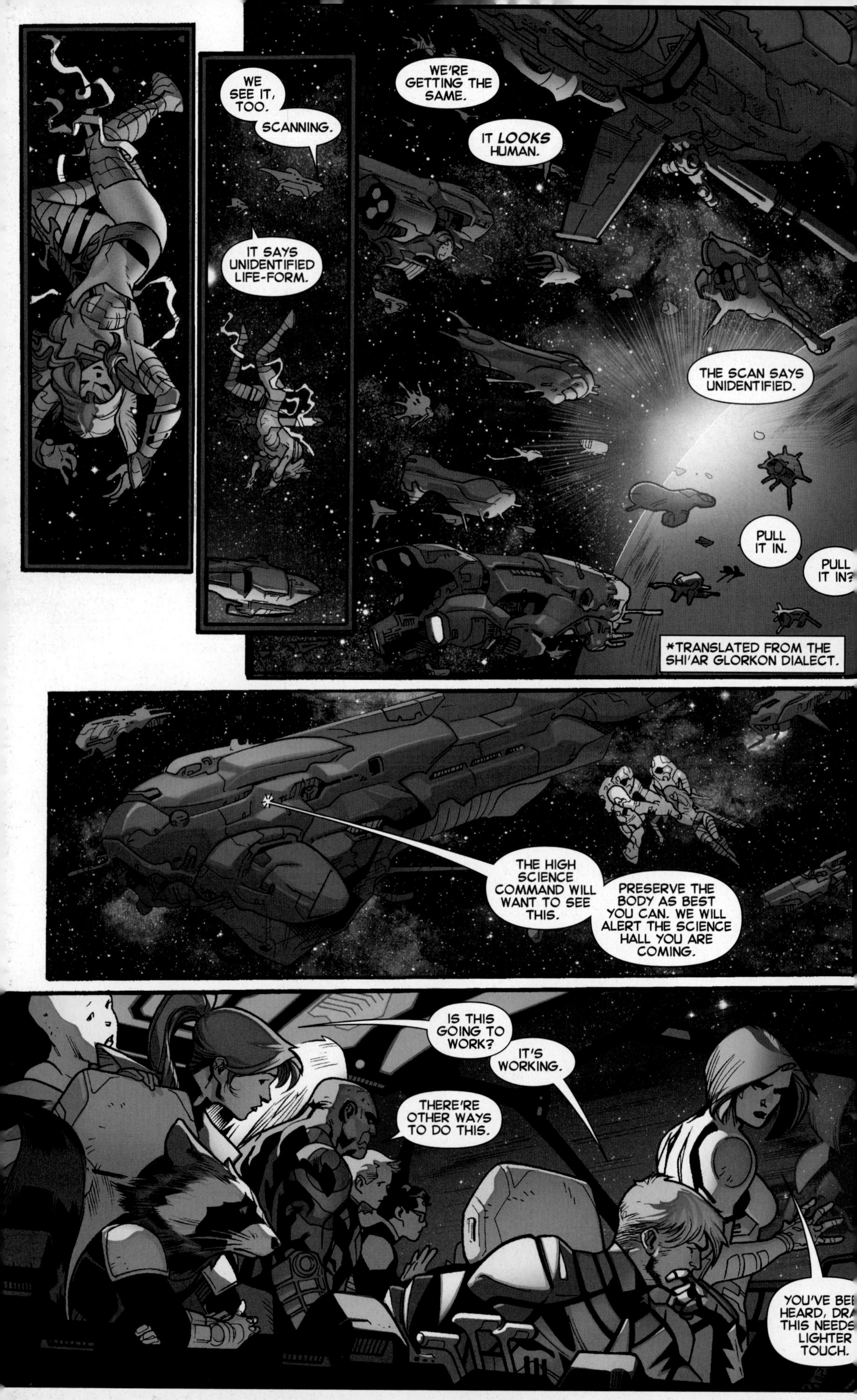

WE SEE IT, TOO.
SCANNING.
IT SAYS UNIDENTIFIED LIFE-FORM.
WE'RE GETTING THE SAME.
IT LOOKS HUMAN.
THE SCAN SAYS UNIDENTIFIED.
PULL IT IN.
PULL IT IN?
*TRANSLATED FROM THE SHI'AR GLORKON DIALECT.
THE HIGH SCIENCE COMMAND WILL WANT TO SEE THIS.
PRESERVE THE BODY AS BEST YOU CAN. WE WILL ALERT THE SCIENCE HALL YOU ARE COMING.
IS THIS GOING TO WORK?
IT'S WORKING.
THERE'RE OTHER WAYS TO DO THIS.
YOU'VE BEE HEARD, DRA THIS NEEDS LIGHTER TOUCH.

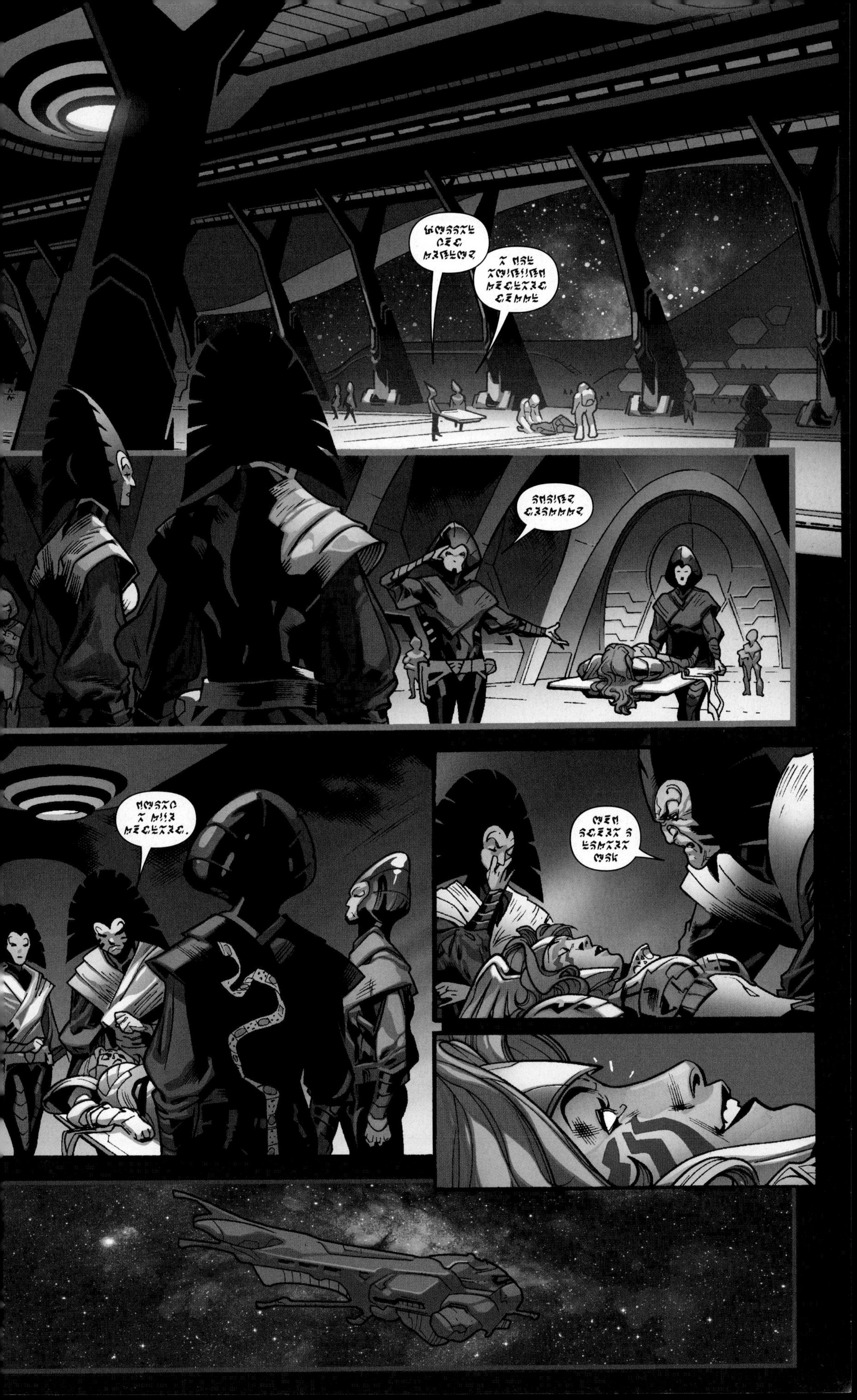

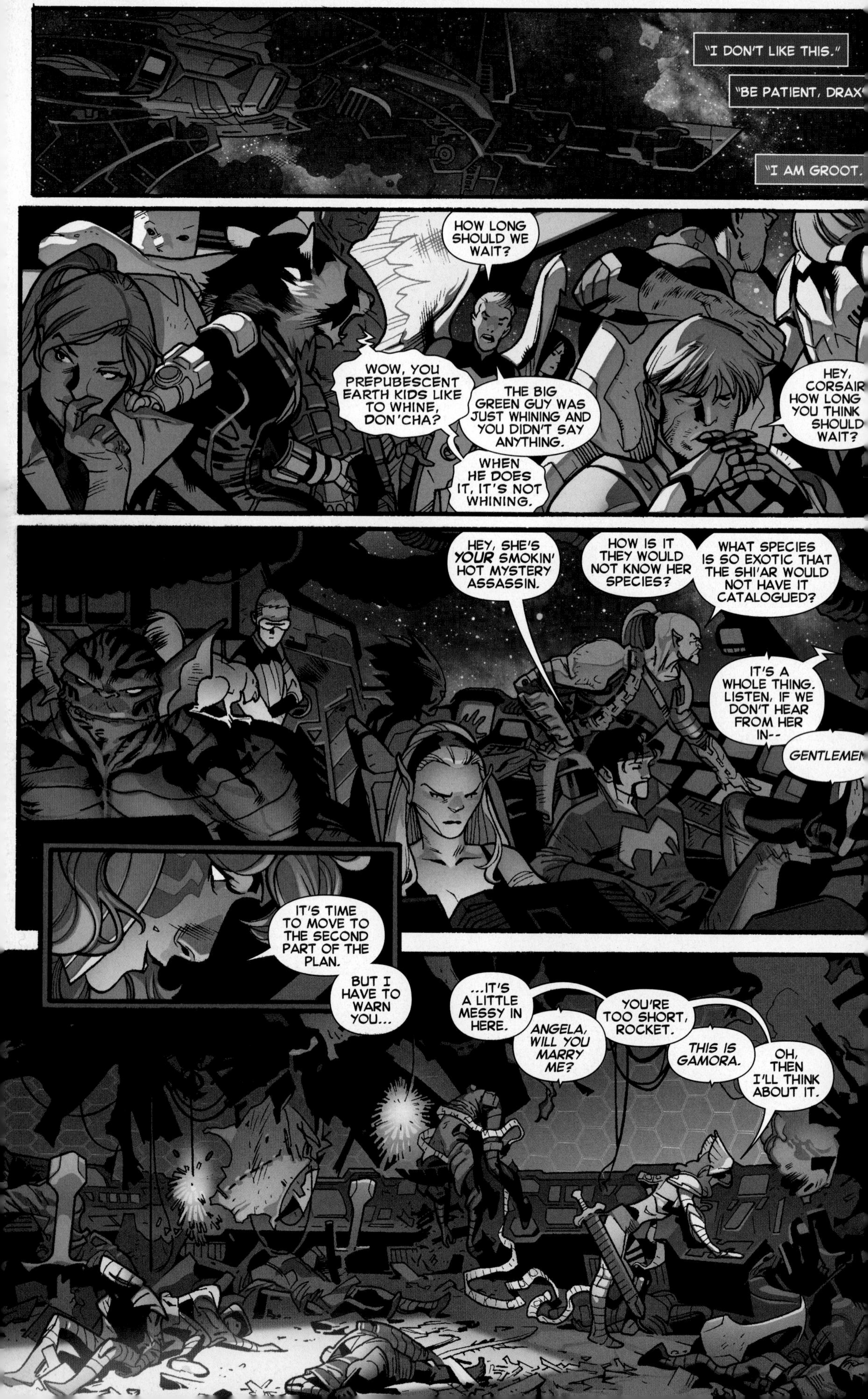
"I DON'T LIKE THIS."
"BE PATIENT, DRAX
"I AM GROOT.
HOW LONG SHOULD WE WAIT?
WOW, YOU PREPUBESCENT EARTH KIDS LIKE TO WHINE, DON'CHA?
THE BIG GREEN GUY WAS JUST WHINING AND YOU DIDN'T SAY ANYTHING.
WHEN HE DOES IT, IT'S NOT WHINING.
HEY, CORSAIR HOW LONG YOU THINK SHOULD WAIT?
HEY, SHE'S YOUR SMOKIN' HOT MYSTERY ASSASSIN.
HOW IS IT THEY WOULD NOT KNOW HER SPECIES?
WHAT SPECIES IS SO EXOTIC THAT THE SHI'AR WOULD NOT HAVE IT CATALOGUED?
IT'S A WHOLE THING. LISTEN, IF WE DON'T HEAR FROM HER IN--
GENTLEMEN
IT'S TIME TO MOVE TO THE SECOND PART OF THE PLAN.
BUT I HAVE TO WARN YOU...
...IT'S A LITTLE MESSY IN HERE.
ANGELA, WILL YOU MARRY ME?
YOU'RE TOO SHORT, ROCKET.
THIS IS GAMORA.
OH, THEN I'LL THINK ABOUT IT.

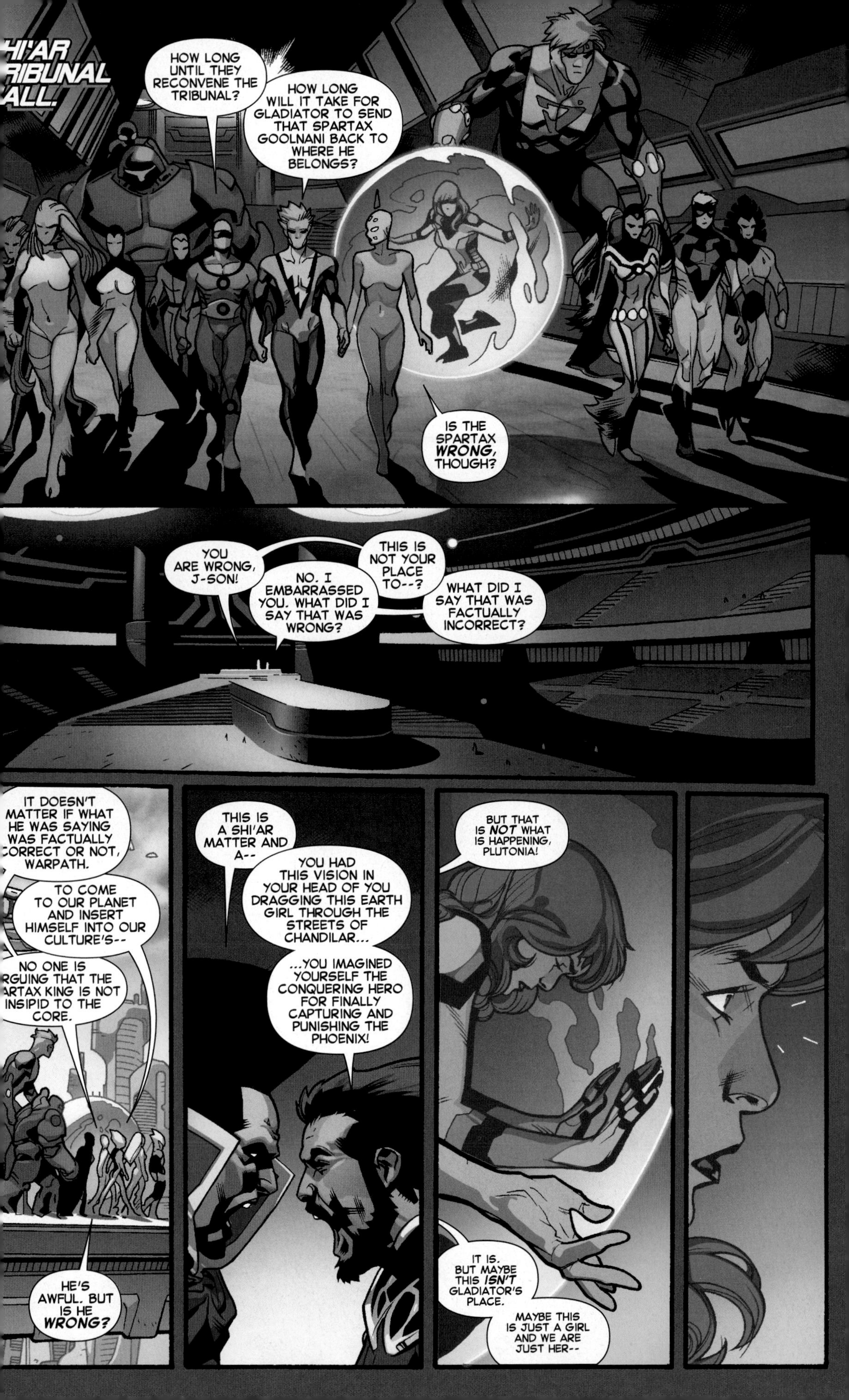
HI'AR TRIBUNAL ALL.
HOW LONG UNTIL THEY RECONVENE THE TRIBUNAL?
HOW LONG WILL IT TAKE FOR GLADIATOR TO SEND THAT SPARTAX GOOLNANI BACK TO WHERE HE BELONGS?
IS THE SPARTAX WRONG, THOUGH?
YOU ARE WRONG, J-SON!
THIS IS NOT YOUR PLACE TO--?
NO. I EMBARRASSED YOU. WHAT DID I SAY THAT WAS WRONG?
WHAT DID I SAY THAT WAS FACTUALLY INCORRECT?
IT DOESN'T MATTER IF WHAT HE WAS SAYING WAS FACTUALLY CORRECT OR NOT, WARPATH.
TO COME TO OUR PLANET AND INSERT HIMSELF INTO OUR CULTURE'S--
NO ONE IS RGUING THAT THE ARTAX KING IS NOT INSIPID TO THE CORE.
HE'S AWFUL. BUT IS HE WRONG?
THIS IS A SHI'AR MATTER AND A--
YOU HAD THIS VISION IN YOUR HEAD OF YOU DRAGGING THIS EARTH GIRL THROUGH THE STREETS OF CHANDILAR...
...YOU IMAGINED YOURSELF THE CONQUERING HERO FOR FINALLY CAPTURING AND PUNISHING THE PHOENIX!
BUT THAT IS NOT WHAT IS HAPPENING, PLUTONIA!
IT IS. BUT MAYBE THIS ISN'T GLADIATOR'S PLACE.
MAYBE THIS IS JUST A GIRL AND WE ARE JUST HER--

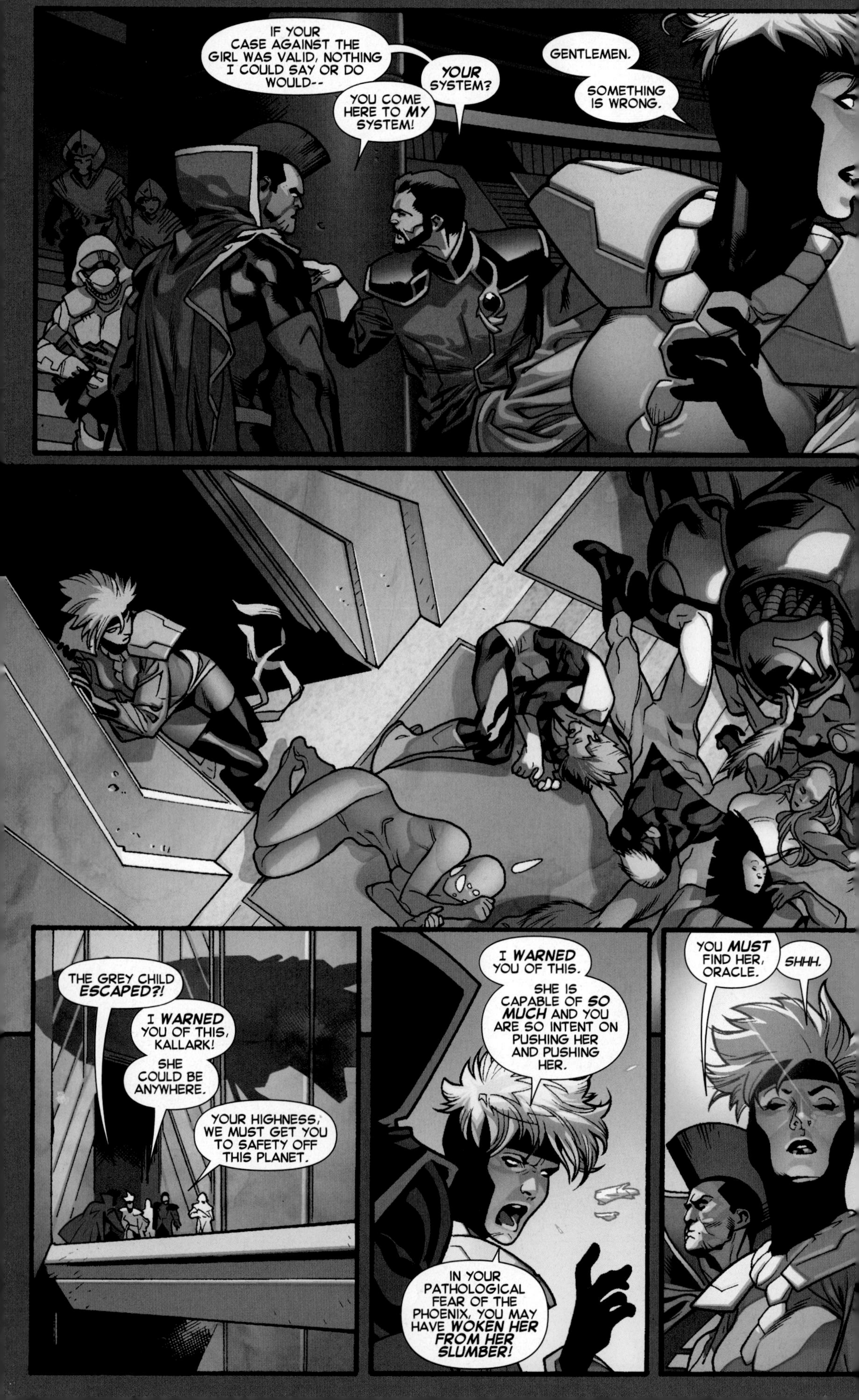
IF YOUR CASE AGAINST THE GIRL WAS VALID, NOTHING I COULD SAY OR DO WOULD--
YOU COME HERE TO *MY* SYSTEM!
YOUR SYSTEM?
GENTLEMEN.
SOMETHING IS WRONG.
THE GREY CHILD *ESCAPED?!*
I *WARNED* YOU OF THIS, KALLARK!
SHE COULD BE ANYWHERE.
YOUR HIGHNESS, WE MUST GET YOU TO SAFETY OFF THIS PLANET.
I *WARNED* YOU OF THIS.
SHE IS CAPABLE OF *SO MUCH* AND YOU ARE SO INTENT ON PUSHING HER AND PUSHING HER.
IN YOUR PATHOLOGICAL FEAR OF THE PHOENIX, YOU MAY HAVE *WOKEN HER FROM HER SLUMBER!*
YOU *MUST* FIND HER, ORACLE.
SHHH.

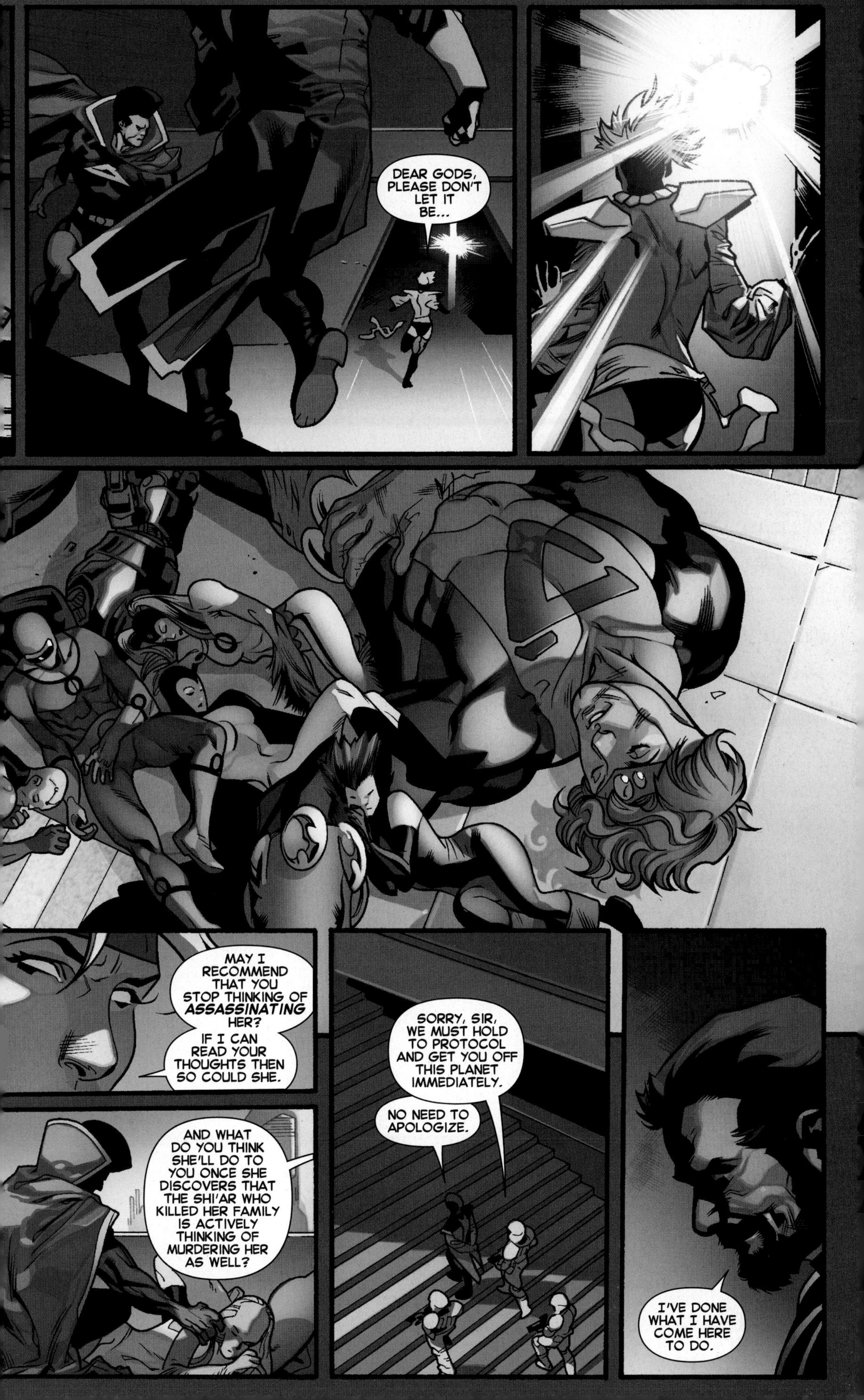
DEAR GODS, PLEASE DON'T LET IT BE...
MAY I RECOMMEND THAT YOU STOP THINKING OF *ASSASSINATING* HER?
IF I CAN READ YOUR THOUGHTS THEN SO COULD SHE.
AND WHAT DO YOU THINK SHE'LL DO TO YOU ONCE SHE DISCOVERS THAT THE SHI'AR WHO KILLED HER FAMILY IS ACTIVELY THINKING OF MURDERING HER AS WELL?
SORRY, SIR, WE MUST HOLD TO PROTOCOL AND GET YOU OFF THIS PLANET IMMEDIATELY.
NO NEED TO APOLOGIZE.
I'VE DONE WHAT I HAVE COME HERE TO DO.

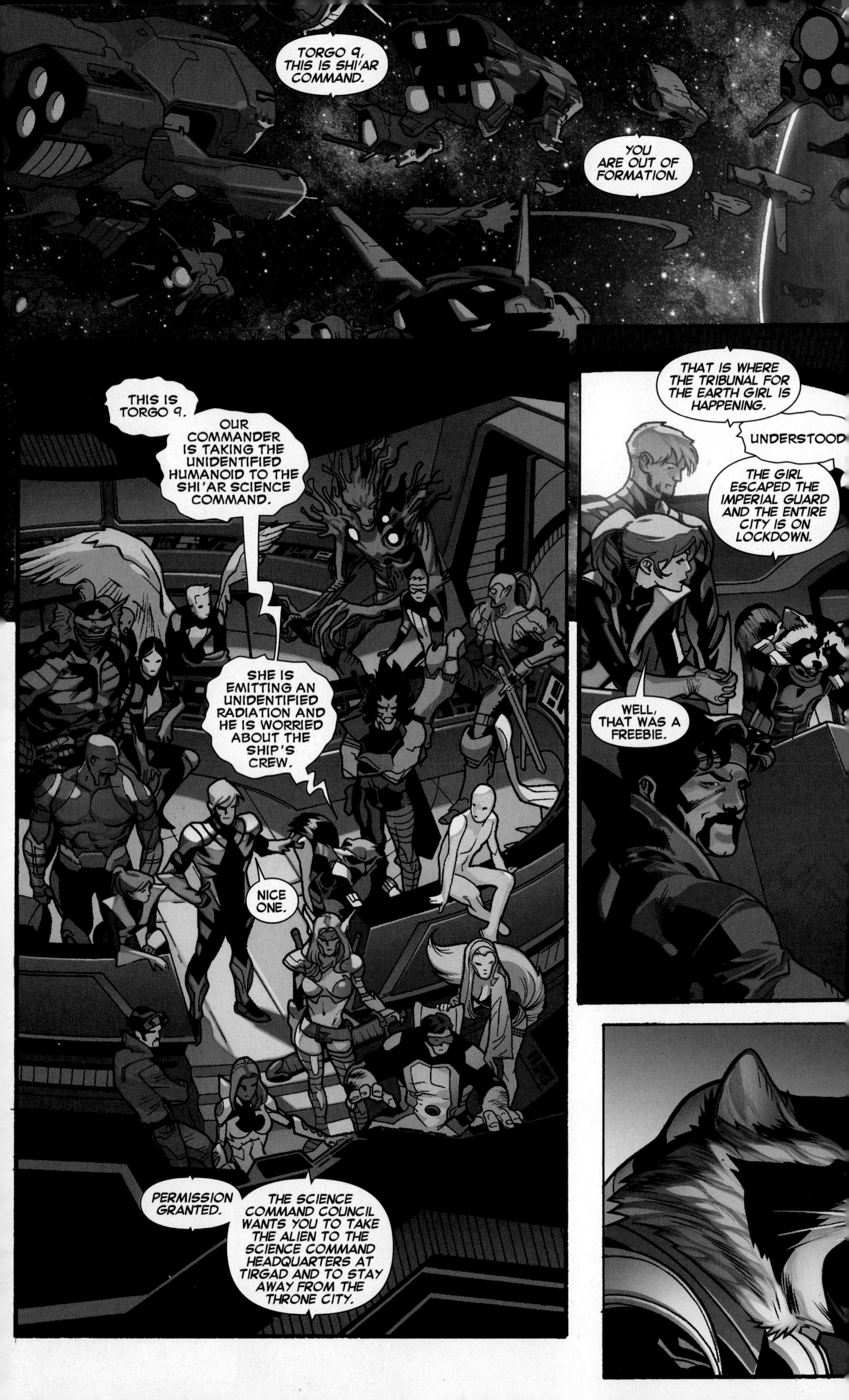
TORGO 9, THIS IS SHI'AR COMMAND.
YOU ARE OUT OF FORMATION.
THIS IS TORGO 9.
OUR COMMANDER IS TAKING THE UNIDENTIFIED HUMANOID TO THE SHI'AR SCIENCE COMMAND.
SHE IS EMITTING AN UNIDENTIFIED RADIATION AND HE IS WORRIED ABOUT THE SHIP'S CREW.
NICE ONE.
PERMISSION GRANTED.
THE SCIENCE COMMAND COUNCIL WANTS YOU TO TAKE THE ALIEN TO THE SCIENCE COMMAND HEADQUARTERS AT TIRGAD AND TO STAY AWAY FROM THE THRONE CITY.
THAT IS WHERE THE TRIBUNAL FOR THE EARTH GIRL IS HAPPENING.
UNDERSTOOD
THE GIRL ESCAPED THE IMPERIAL GUARD AND THE ENTIRE CITY IS ON LOCKDOWN.
WELL, THAT WAS A FREEBIE.

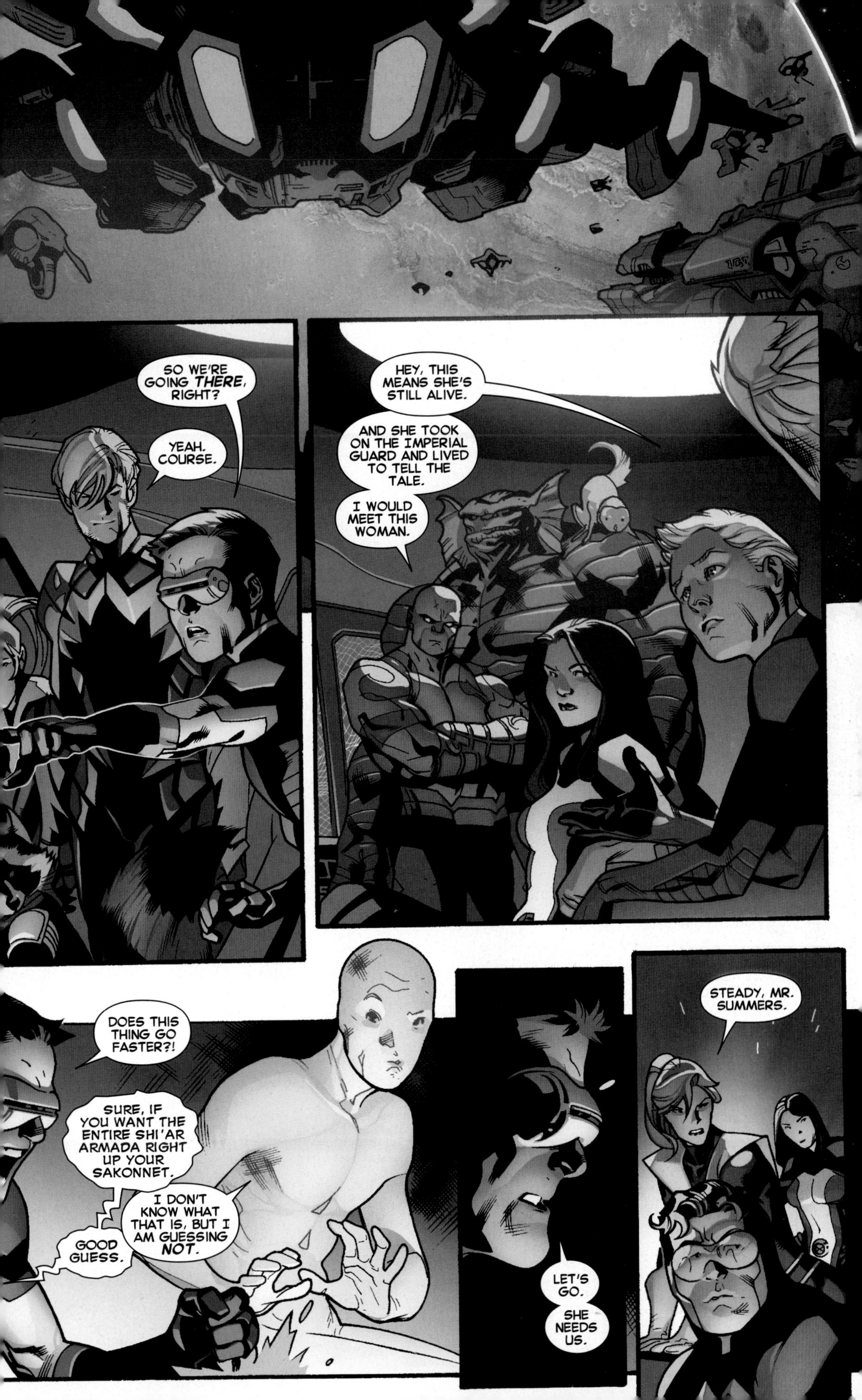
SO WE'RE GOING *THERE*, RIGHT?
YEAH. COURSE.
HEY, THIS MEANS SHE'S STILL ALIVE.
AND SHE TOOK ON THE IMPERIAL GUARD AND LIVED TO TELL THE TALE.
I WOULD MEET THIS WOMAN.
DOES THIS THING GO FASTER?!
SURE, IF YOU WANT THE ENTIRE SHI'AR ARMADA RIGHT UP YOUR SAKONNET.
I DON'T KNOW WHAT THAT IS, BUT I AM GUESSING *NOT*.
GOOD GUESS.
LET'S GO.
SHE NEEDS US.
STEADY, MR. SUMMERS.

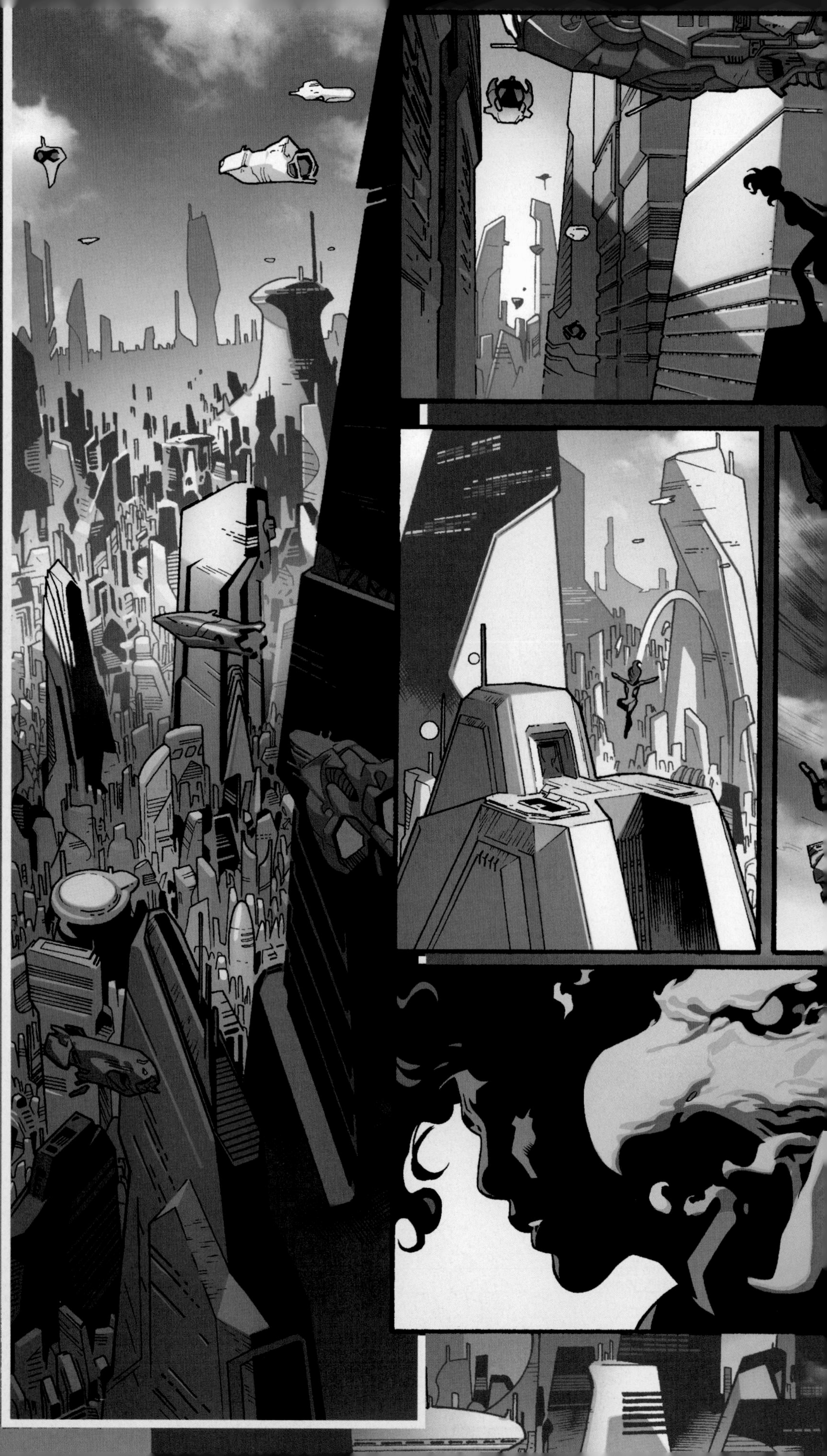

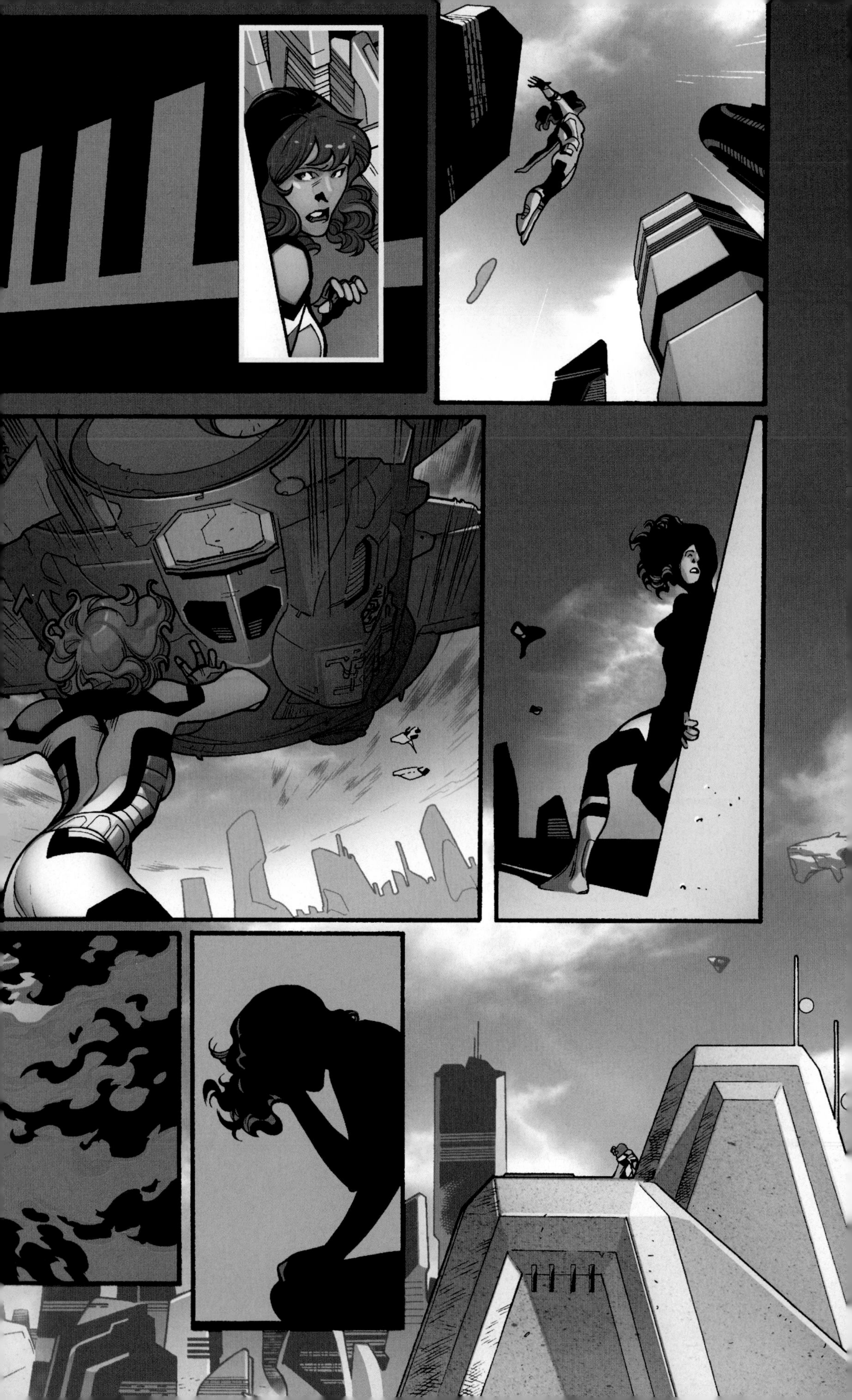

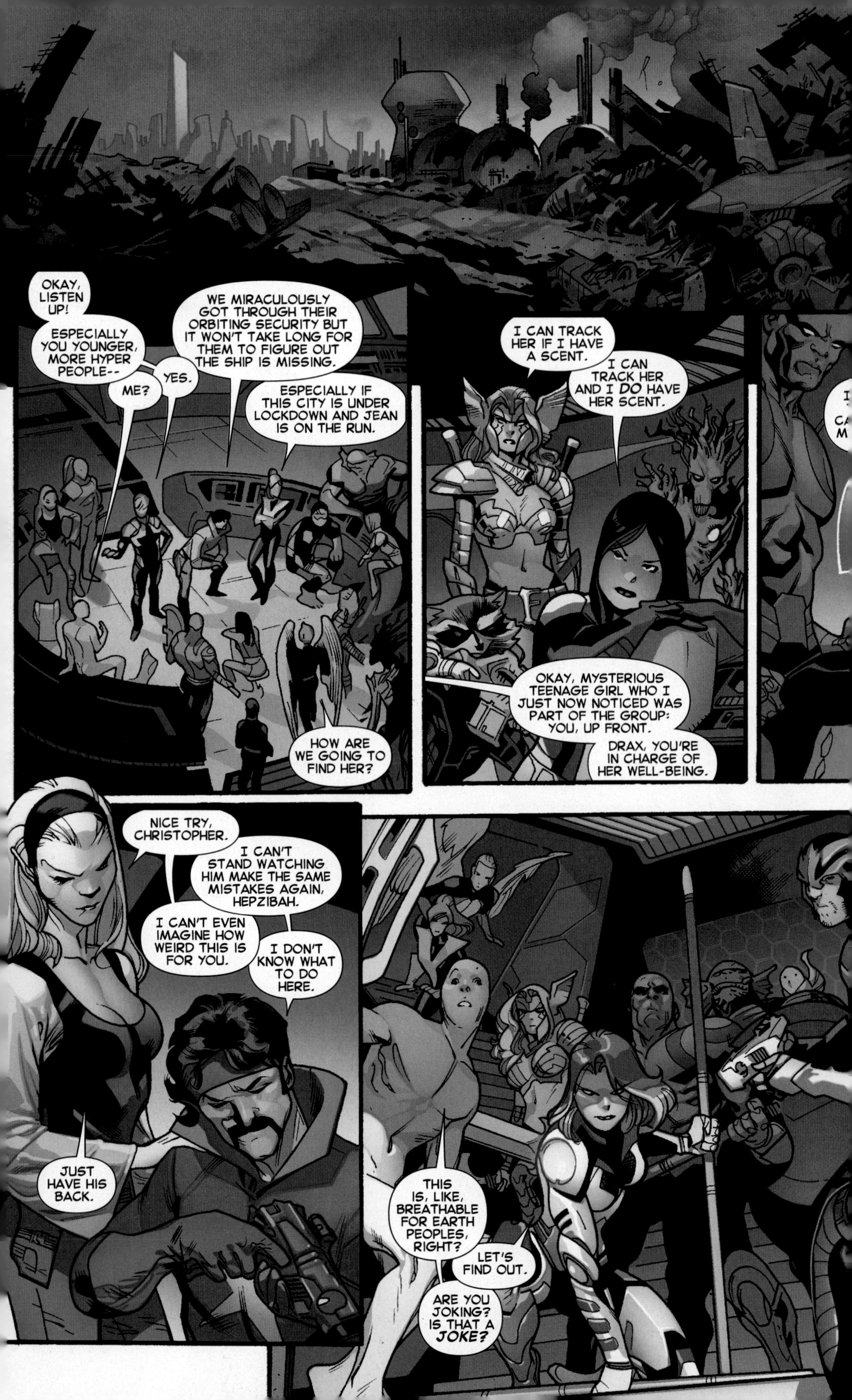
OKAY, LISTEN UP!
ESPECIALLY YOU YOUNGER, MORE HYPER PEOPLE--
ME?
YES.
WE MIRACULOUSLY GOT THROUGH THEIR ORBITING SECURITY BUT IT WON'T TAKE LONG FOR THEM TO FIGURE OUT THE SHIP IS MISSING.
ESPECIALLY IF THIS CITY IS UNDER LOCKDOWN AND JEAN IS ON THE RUN.
HOW ARE WE GOING TO FIND HER?
I CAN TRACK HER IF I HAVE A SCENT.
I CAN TRACK HER AND I *DO* HAVE HER SCENT.
OKAY, MYSTERIOUS TEENAGE GIRL WHO I JUST NOW NOTICED WAS PART OF THE GROUP: YOU, UP FRONT.
DRAX, YOU'RE IN CHARGE OF HER WELL-BEING.
NICE TRY, CHRISTOPHER.
I CAN'T STAND WATCHING HIM MAKE THE SAME MISTAKES AGAIN, HEPZIBAH.
I CAN'T EVEN IMAGINE HOW WEIRD THIS IS FOR YOU.
I DON'T KNOW WHAT TO DO HERE.
JUST HAVE HIS BACK.
THIS IS, LIKE, BREATHABLE FOR EARTH PEOPLES, RIGHT?
LET'S FIND OUT.
ARE YOU JOKING? IS THAT A ***JOKE?***

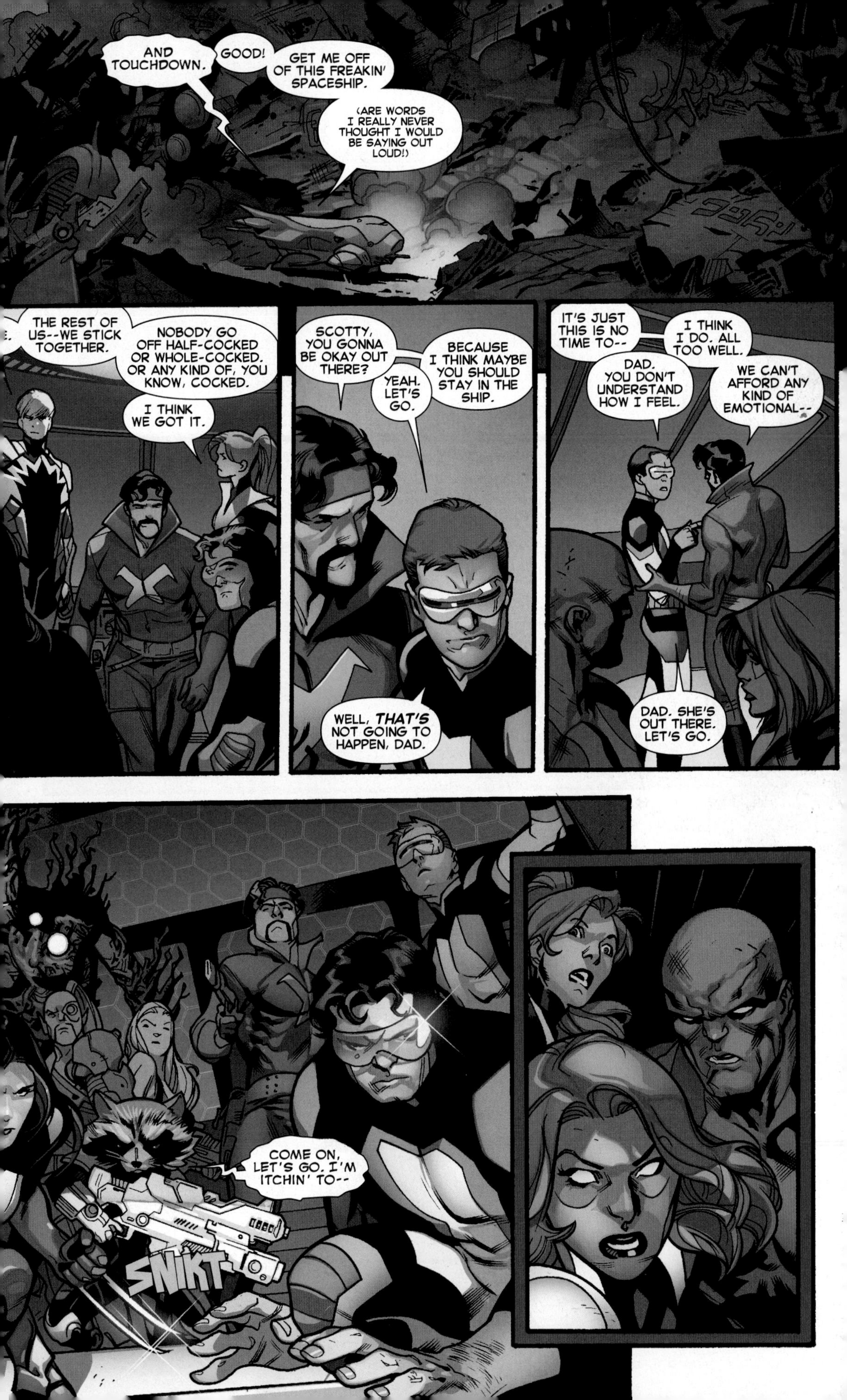
AND TOUCHDOWN.
GOOD!
GET ME OFF OF THIS FREAKIN' SPACESHIP.
(ARE WORDS I REALLY NEVER THOUGHT I WOULD BE SAYING OUT LOUD!)
THE REST OF US--WE STICK TOGETHER.
NOBODY GO OFF HALF-COCKED OR WHOLE-COCKED. OR ANY KIND OF, YOU KNOW, COCKED.
I THINK WE GOT IT.
SCOTTY, YOU GONNA BE OKAY OUT THERE?
YEAH. LET'S GO.
BECAUSE I THINK MAYBE YOU SHOULD STAY IN THE SHIP.
WELL, THAT'S NOT GOING TO HAPPEN, DAD.
IT'S JUST THIS IS NO TIME TO--
I THINK I DO. ALL TOO WELL.
DAD. YOU DON'T UNDERSTAND HOW I FEEL.
WE CAN'T AFFORD ANY KIND OF EMOTIONAL--
DAD. SHE'S OUT THERE. LET'S GO.
COME ON, LET'S GO. I'M ITCHIN' TO--
SNIKT

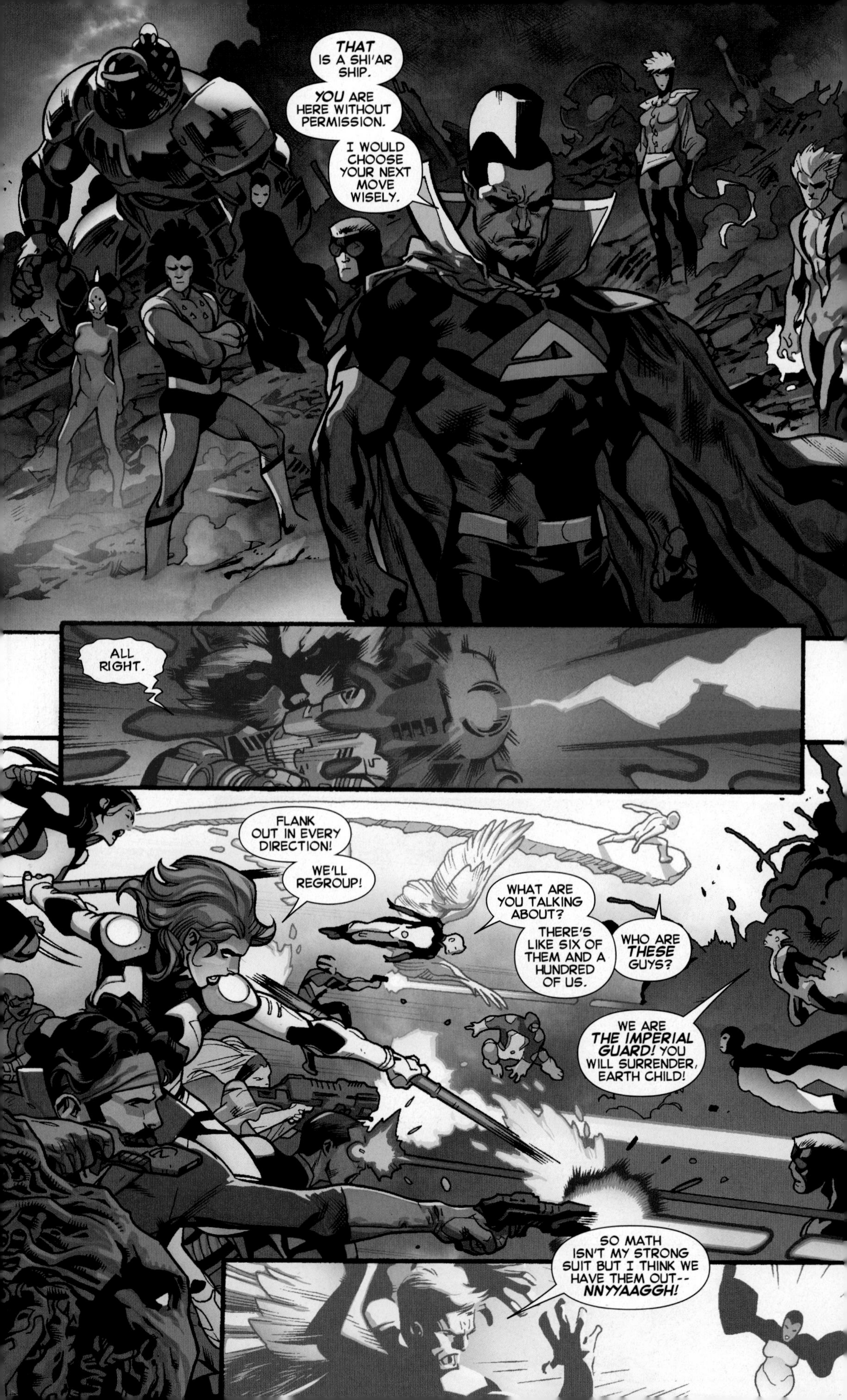
THAT IS A SHI'AR SHIP.
YOU ARE HERE WITHOUT PERMISSION.
I WOULD CHOOSE YOUR NEXT MOVE WISELY.
ALL RIGHT.
FLANK OUT IN EVERY DIRECTION!
WE'LL REGROUP!
WHAT ARE YOU TALKING ABOUT?
THERE'S LIKE SIX OF THEM AND A HUNDRED OF US.
WHO ARE THESE GUYS?
WE ARE THE IMPERIAL GUARD! YOU WILL SURRENDER, EARTH CHILD!
SO MATH ISN'T MY STRONG SUIT BUT I THINK WE HAVE THEM OUT-- NNYYAAGGH!

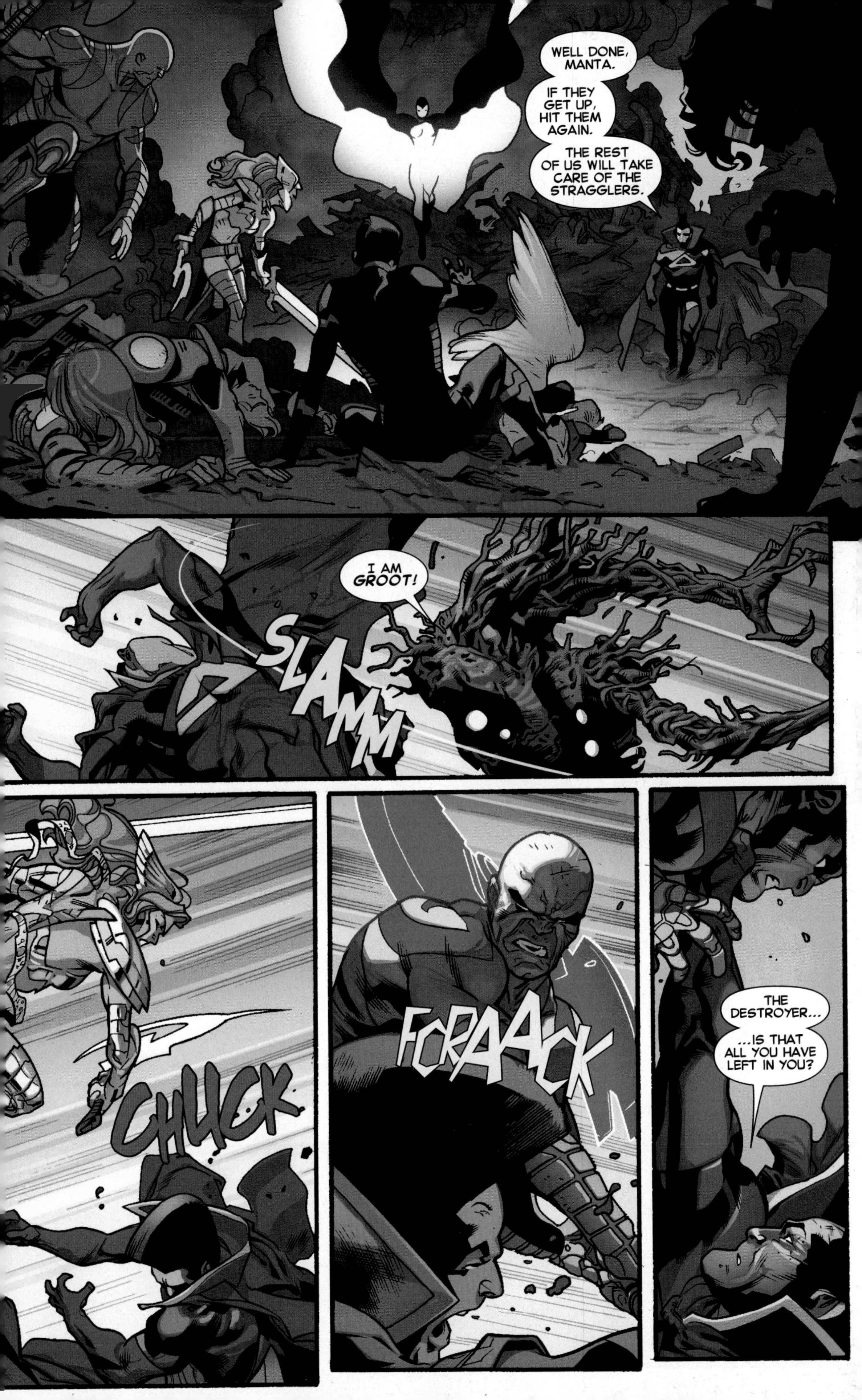
WELL DONE, MANTA.
IF THEY GET UP, HIT THEM AGAIN.
THE REST OF US WILL TAKE CARE OF THE STRAGGLERS.
I AM GROOT!
SLAMM
CHUCK
FCRAACK
THE DESTROYER...
...IS THAT ALL YOU HAVE LEFT IN YOU?

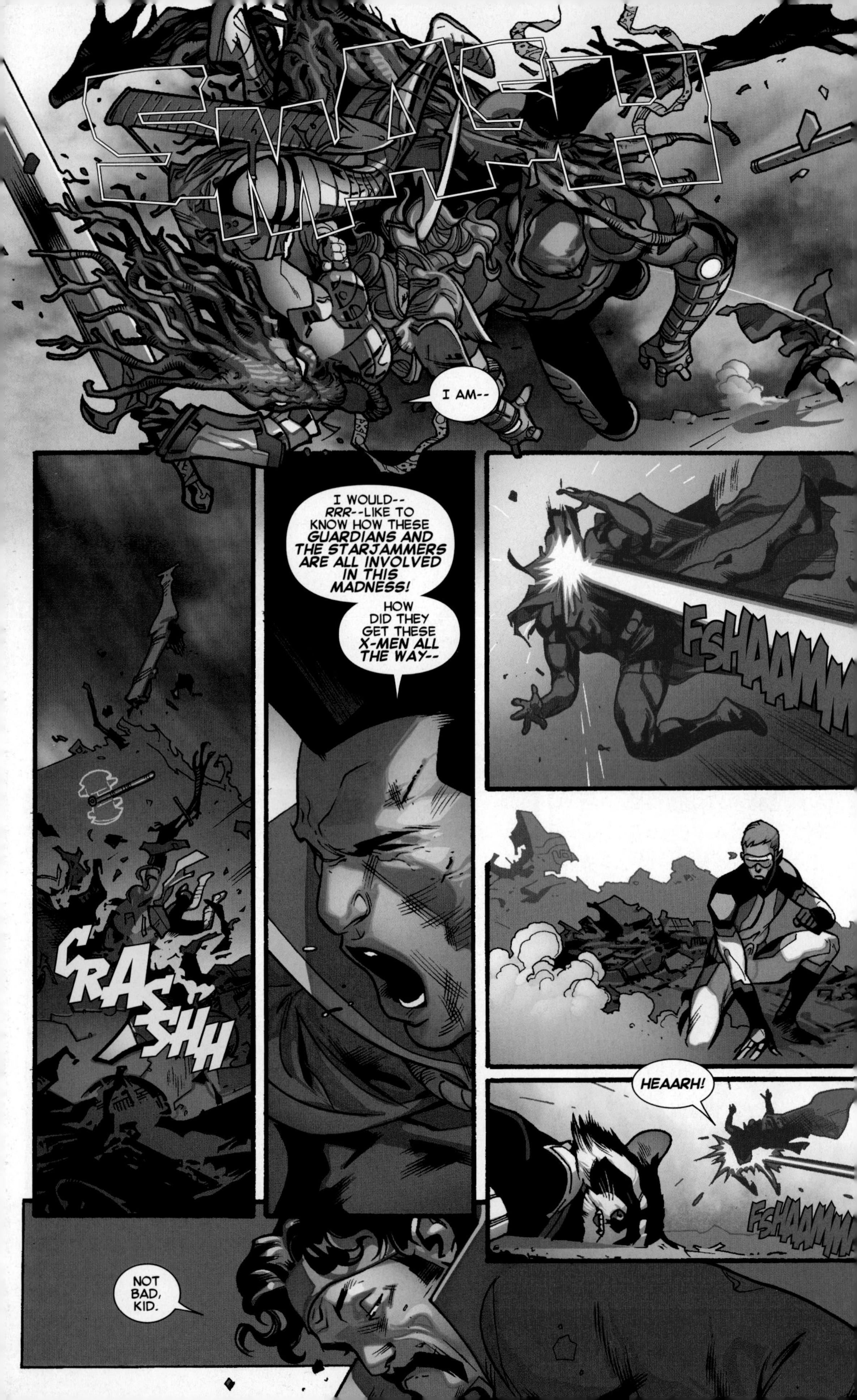

SMASH
I AM--
CRASHH
I WOULD-- RRR--LIKE TO KNOW HOW THESE GUARDIANS AND THE STARJAMMERS ARE ALL INVOLVED IN THIS MADNESS!
HOW DID THEY GET THESE X-MEN ALL THE WAY--
FSHAAMM
HEAARH!
FSHAAMM
NOT BAD, KID.

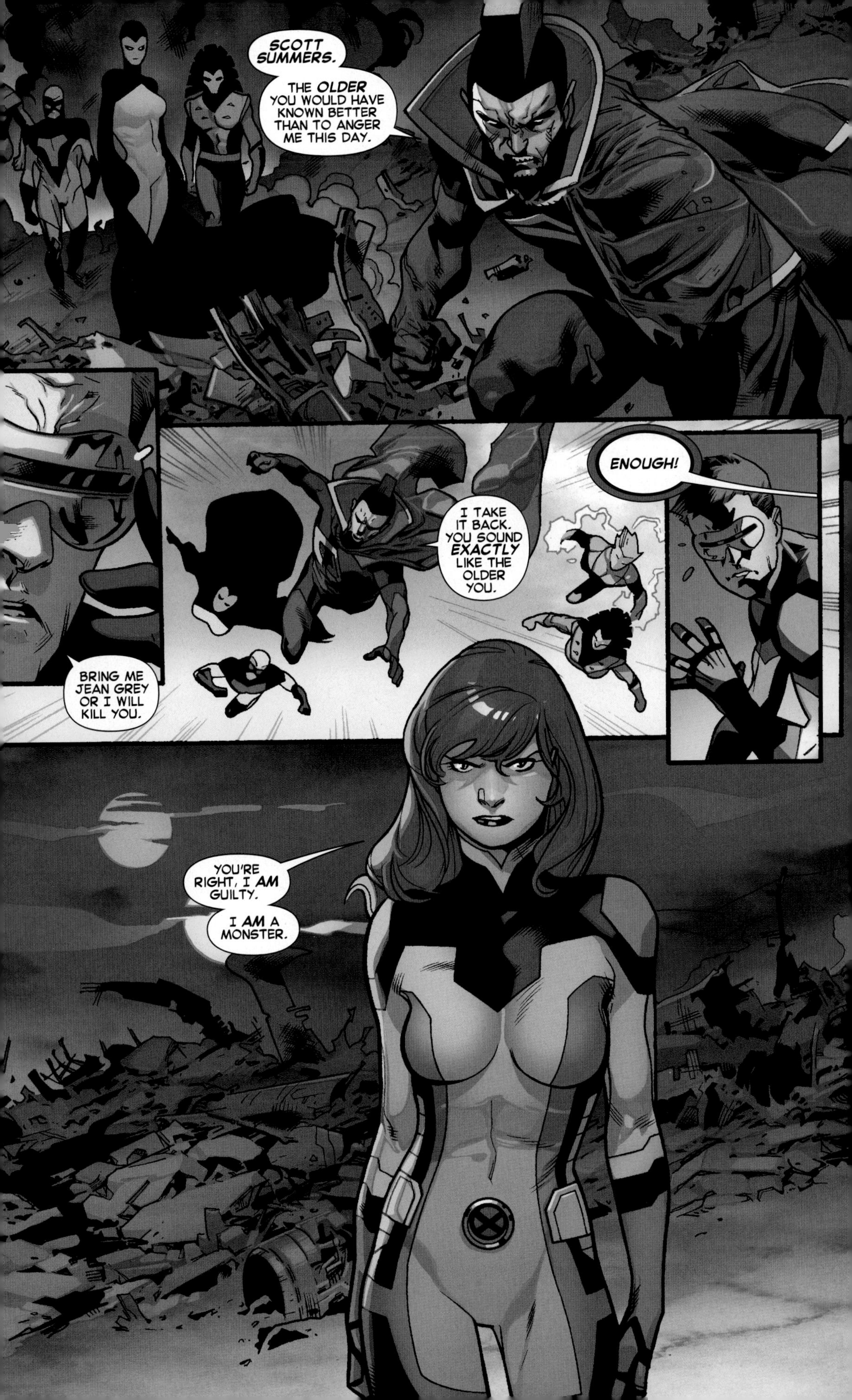
SCOTT SUMMERS.
THE OLDER YOU WOULD HAVE KNOWN BETTER THAN TO ANGER ME THIS DAY.
BRING ME JEAN GREY OR I WILL KILL YOU.
I TAKE IT BACK. YOU SOUND EXACTLY LIKE THE OLDER YOU.
ENOUGH!
YOU'RE RIGHT, I AM GUILTY.
I AM A MONSTER.

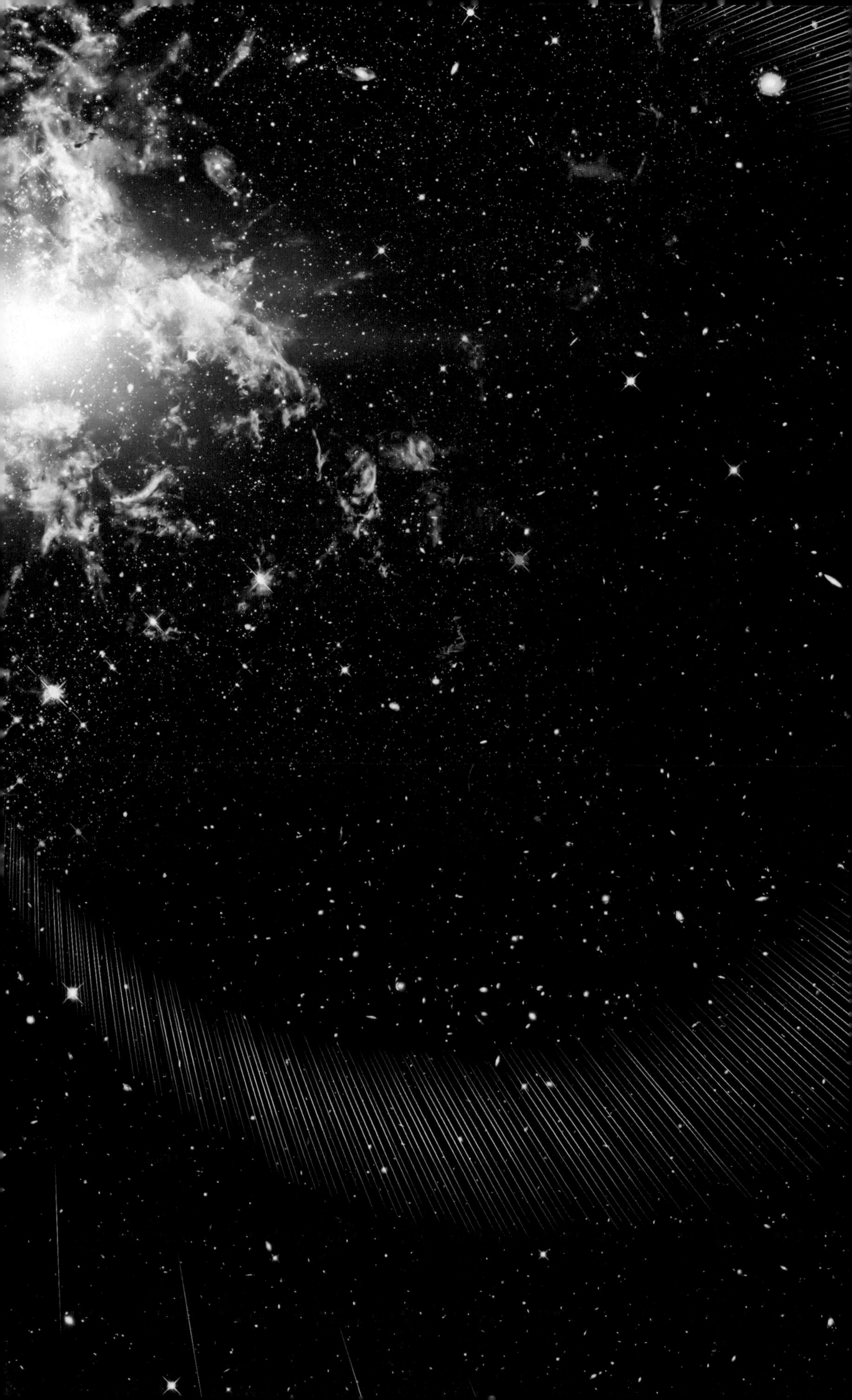

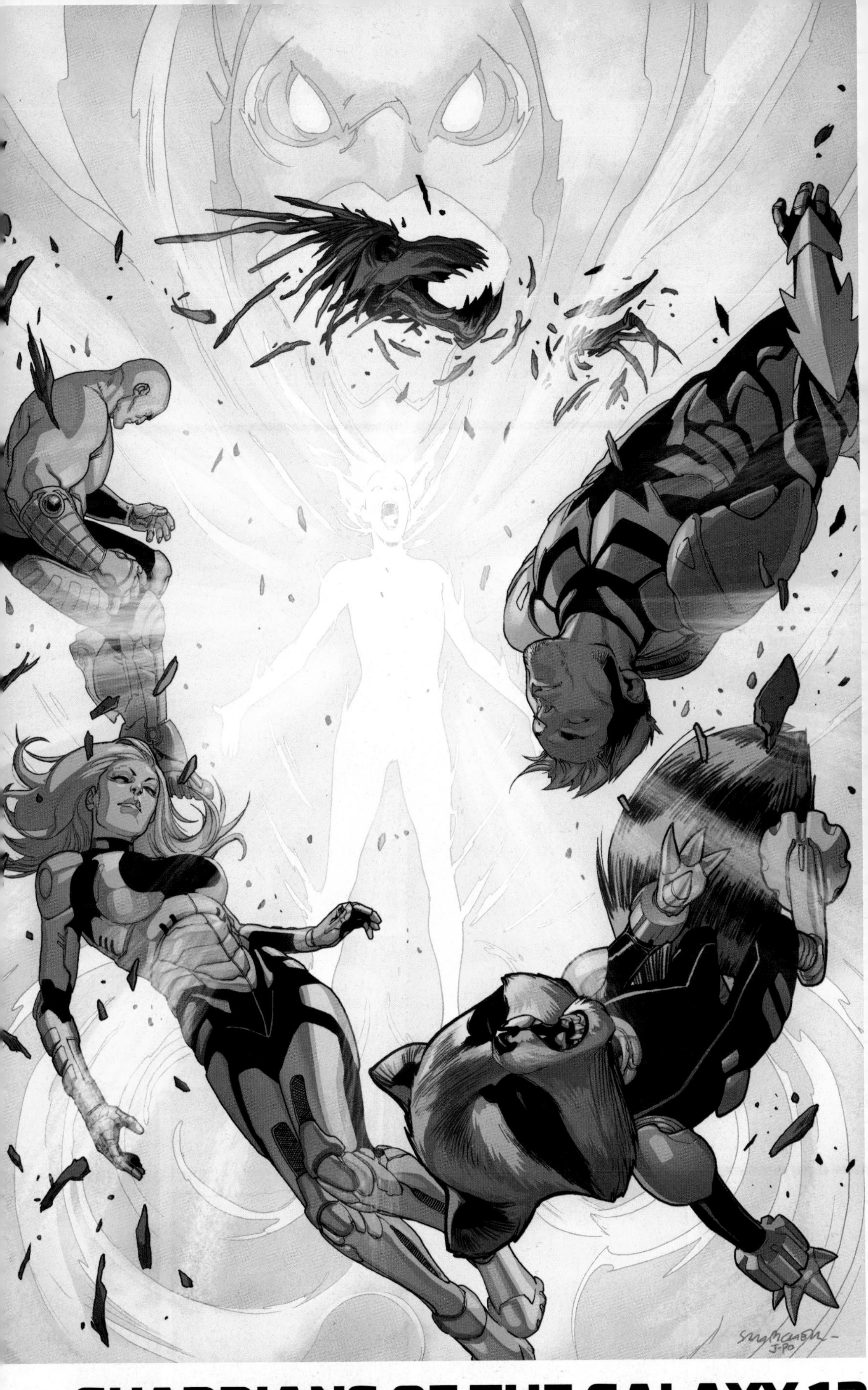

GUARDIANS OF THE GALAXY 13

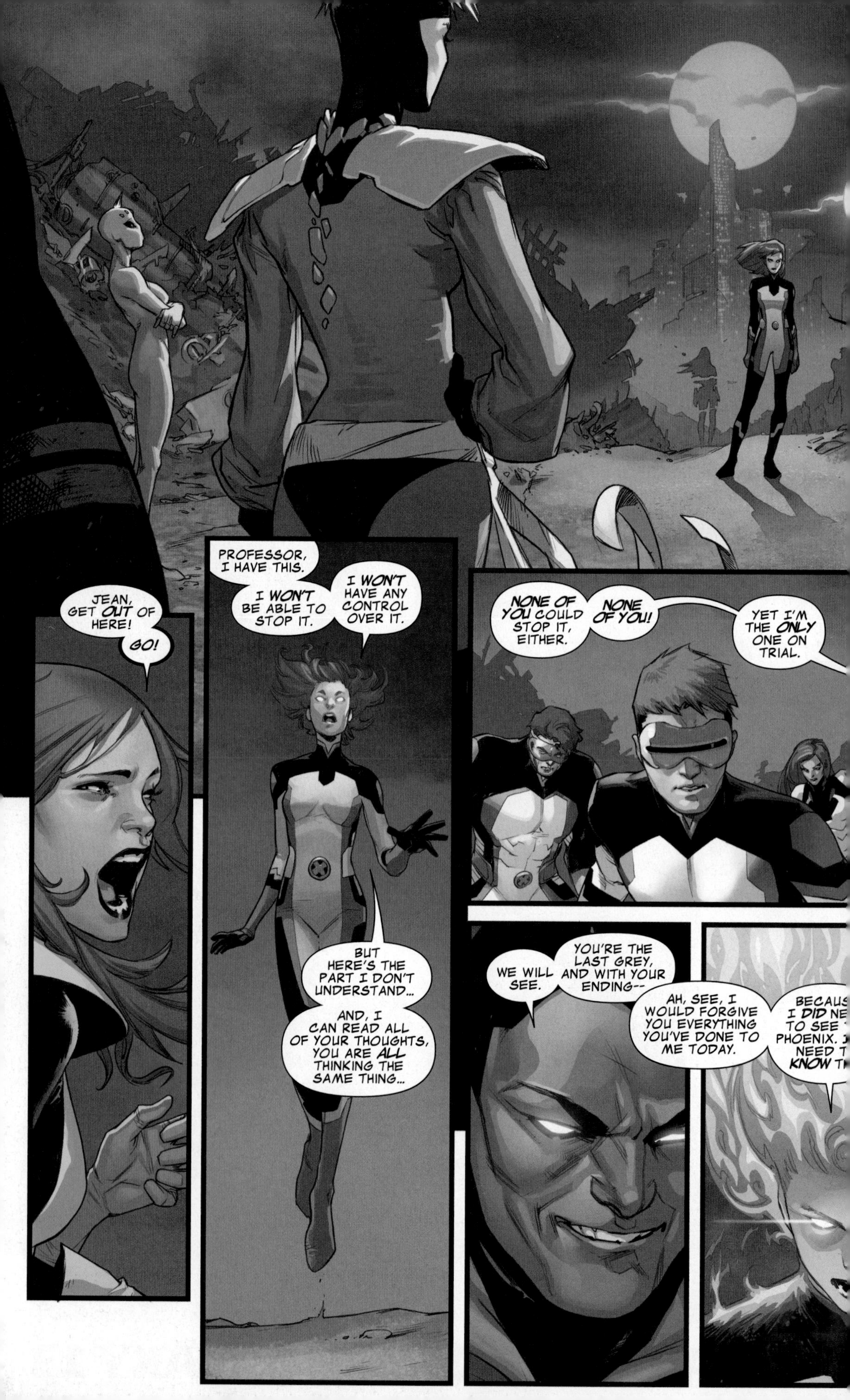
JEAN, GET OUT OF HERE!
GO!
PROFESSOR, I HAVE THIS.
I WON'T BE ABLE TO STOP IT.
I WON'T HAVE ANY CONTROL OVER IT.
BUT HERE'S THE PART I DON'T UNDERSTAND...
AND, I CAN READ ALL OF YOUR THOUGHTS, YOU ARE ALL THINKING THE SAME THING...
NONE OF YOU COULD STOP IT, EITHER.
NONE OF YOU!
YET I'M THE ONLY ONE ON TRIAL.
YOU'RE THE LAST GREY, AND WITH YOUR ENDING--
WE WILL SEE.
AH, SEE, I WOULD FORGIVE YOU EVERYTHING YOU'VE DONE TO ME TODAY.
BECAUS I DID NE TO SEE PHOENIX. NEED T KNOW T

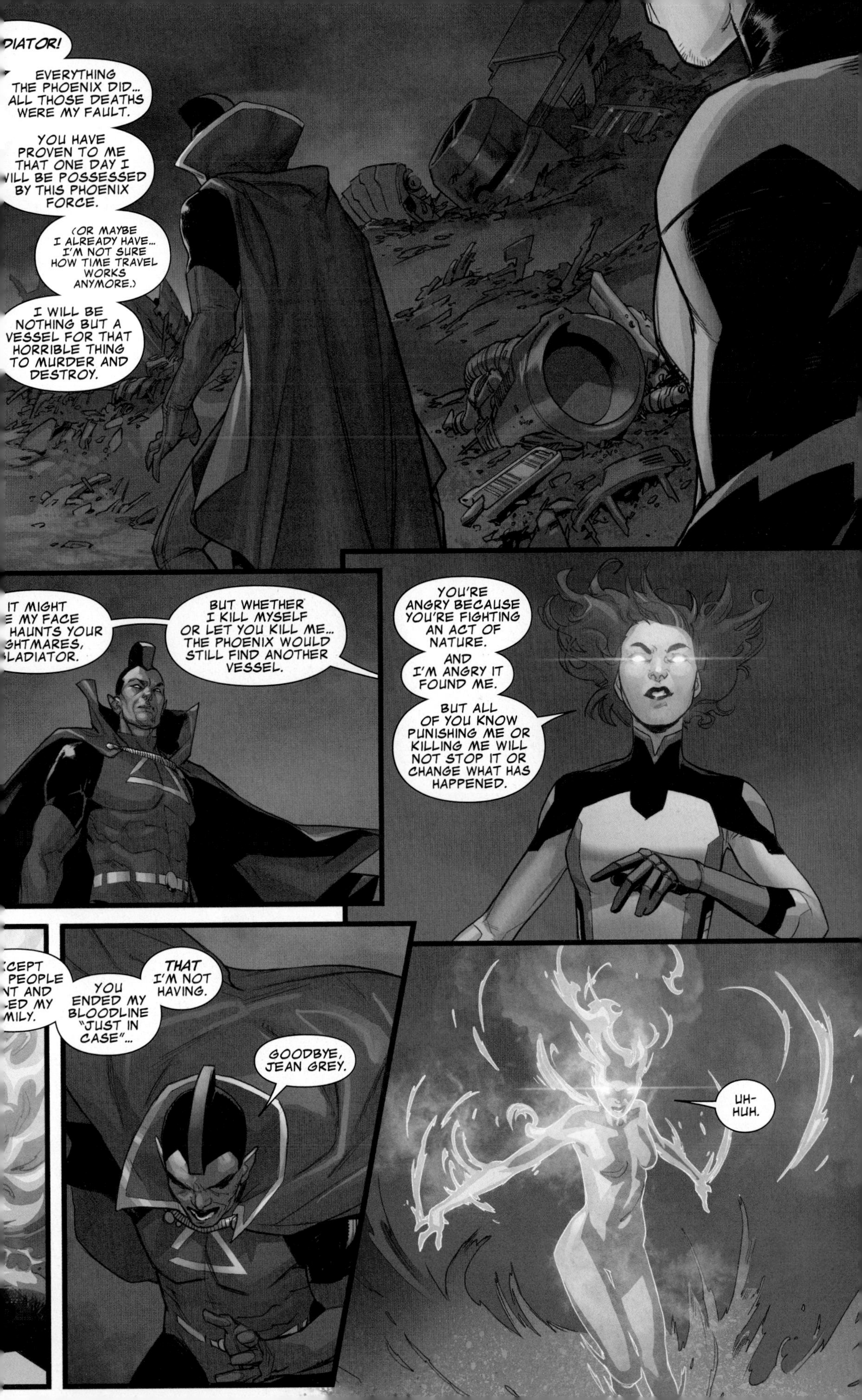

DIATOR!
EVERYTHING THE PHOENIX DID... ALL THOSE DEATHS WERE MY FAULT.
YOU HAVE PROVEN TO ME THAT ONE DAY I VILL BE POSSESSED BY THIS PHOENIX FORCE.
(OR MAYBE I ALREADY HAVE... I'M NOT SURE HOW TIME TRAVEL WORKS ANYMORE.)
I WILL BE NOTHING BUT A VESSEL FOR THAT HORRIBLE THING TO MURDER AND DESTROY.
IT MIGHT E MY FACE HAUNTS YOUR GHTMARES, LADIATOR.
BUT WHETHER I KILL MYSELF OR LET YOU KILL ME... THE PHOENIX WOULD STILL FIND ANOTHER VESSEL.
YOU'RE ANGRY BECAUSE YOU'RE FIGHTING AN ACT OF NATURE.
AND I'M ANGRY IT FOUND ME.
BUT ALL OF YOU KNOW PUNISHING ME OR KILLING ME WILL NOT STOP IT OR CHANGE WHAT HAS HAPPENED.
CEPT PEOPLE NT AND ED MY MILY.
YOU ENDED MY BLOODLINE "JUST IN CASE"...
THAT I'M NOT HAVING.
GOODBYE, JEAN GREY.
UH-HUH.

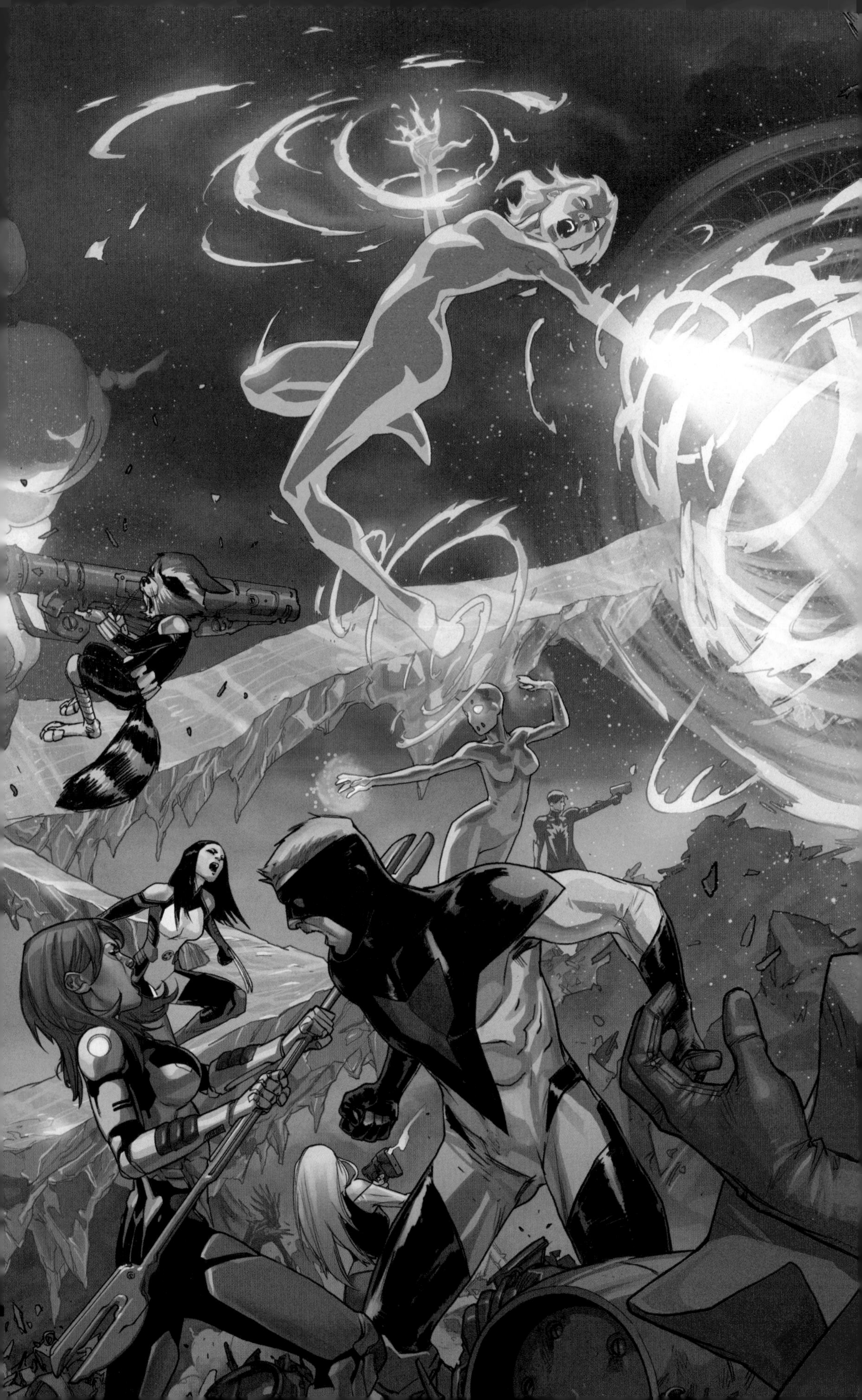

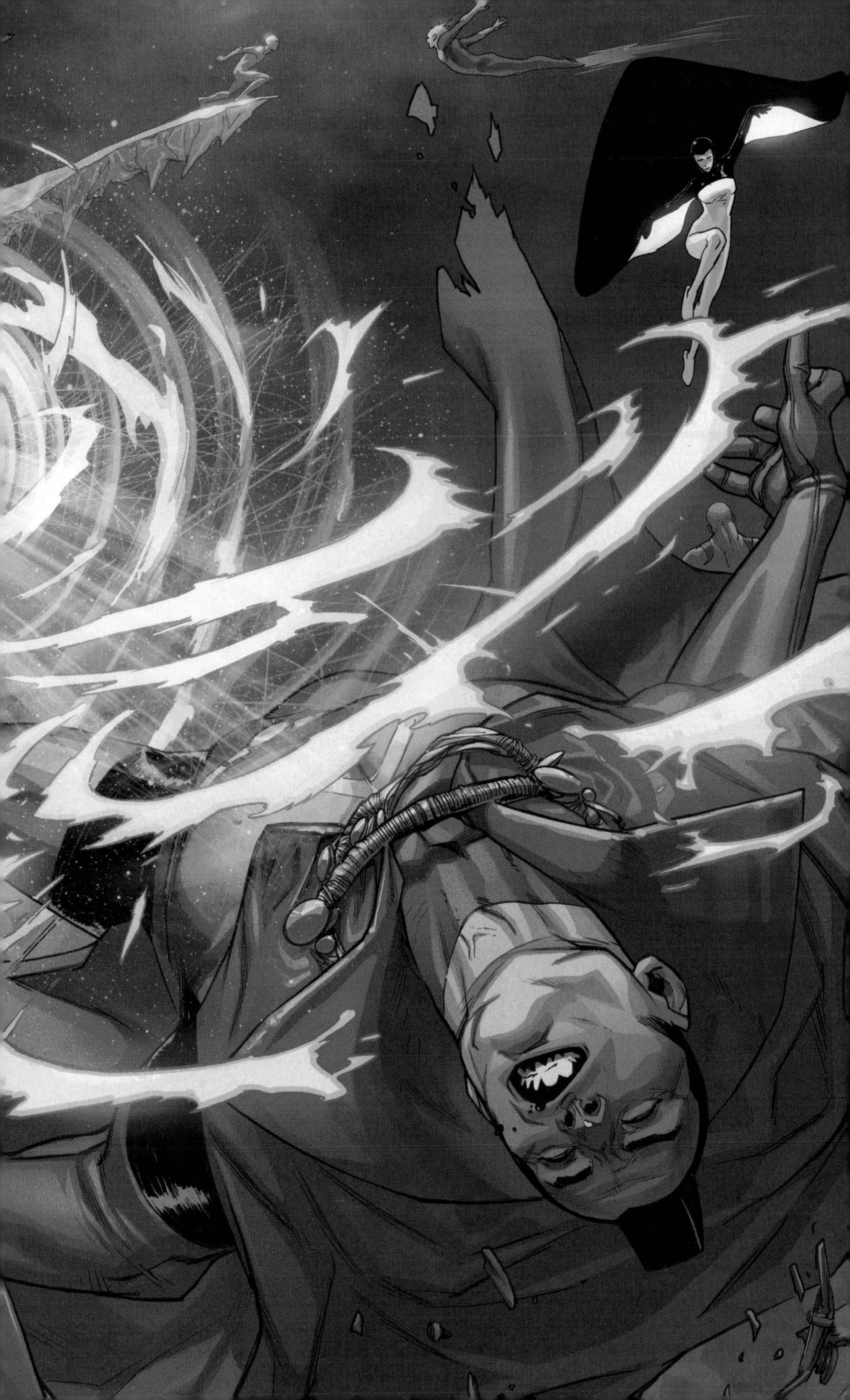

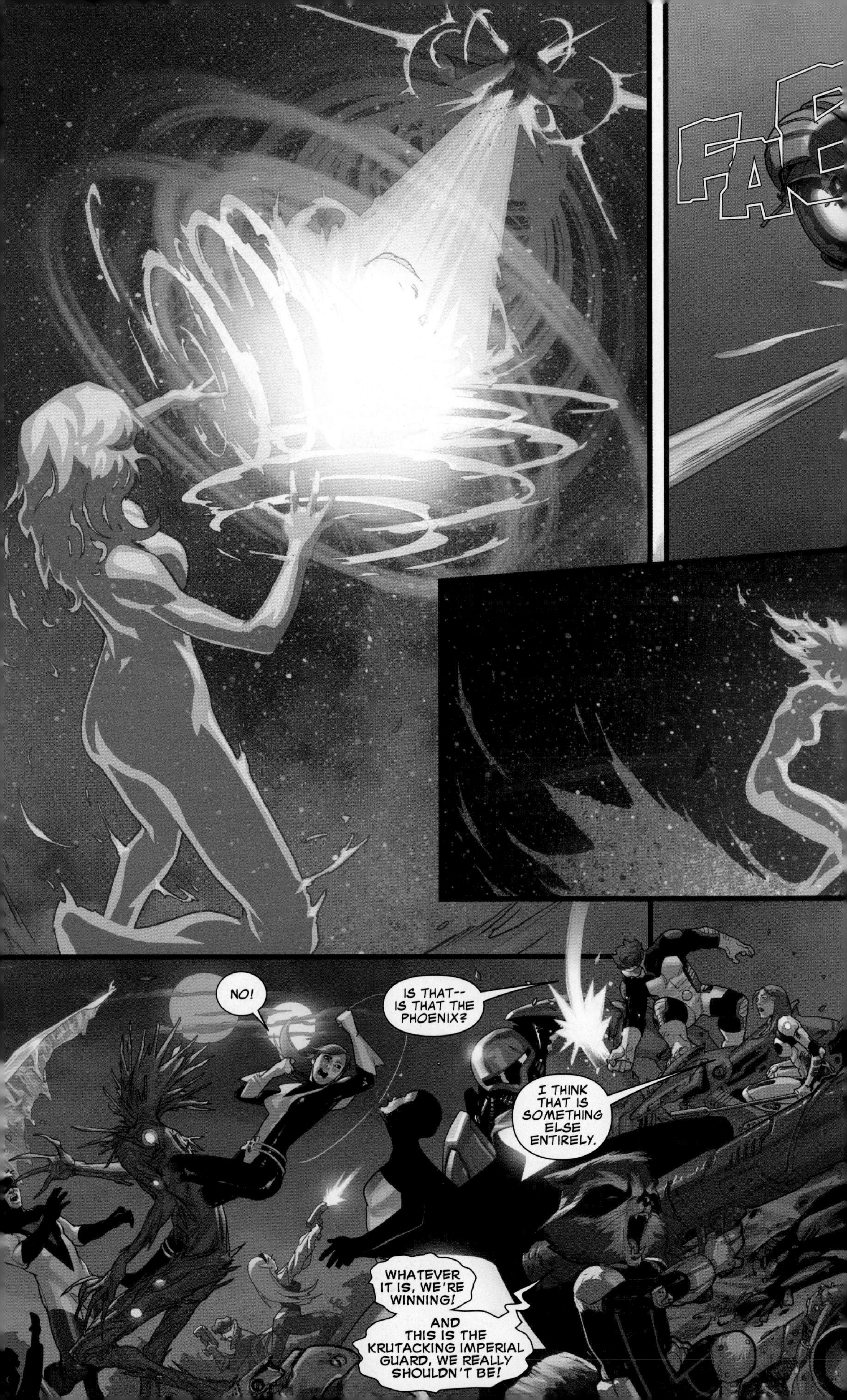
NO!
IS THAT-- IS THAT THE PHOENIX?
I THINK THAT IS SOMETHING ELSE ENTIRELY.
WHATEVER IT IS, WE'RE WINNING!
AND THIS IS THE KRUTACKING IMPERIAL GUARD, WE REALLY SHOULDN'T BE!

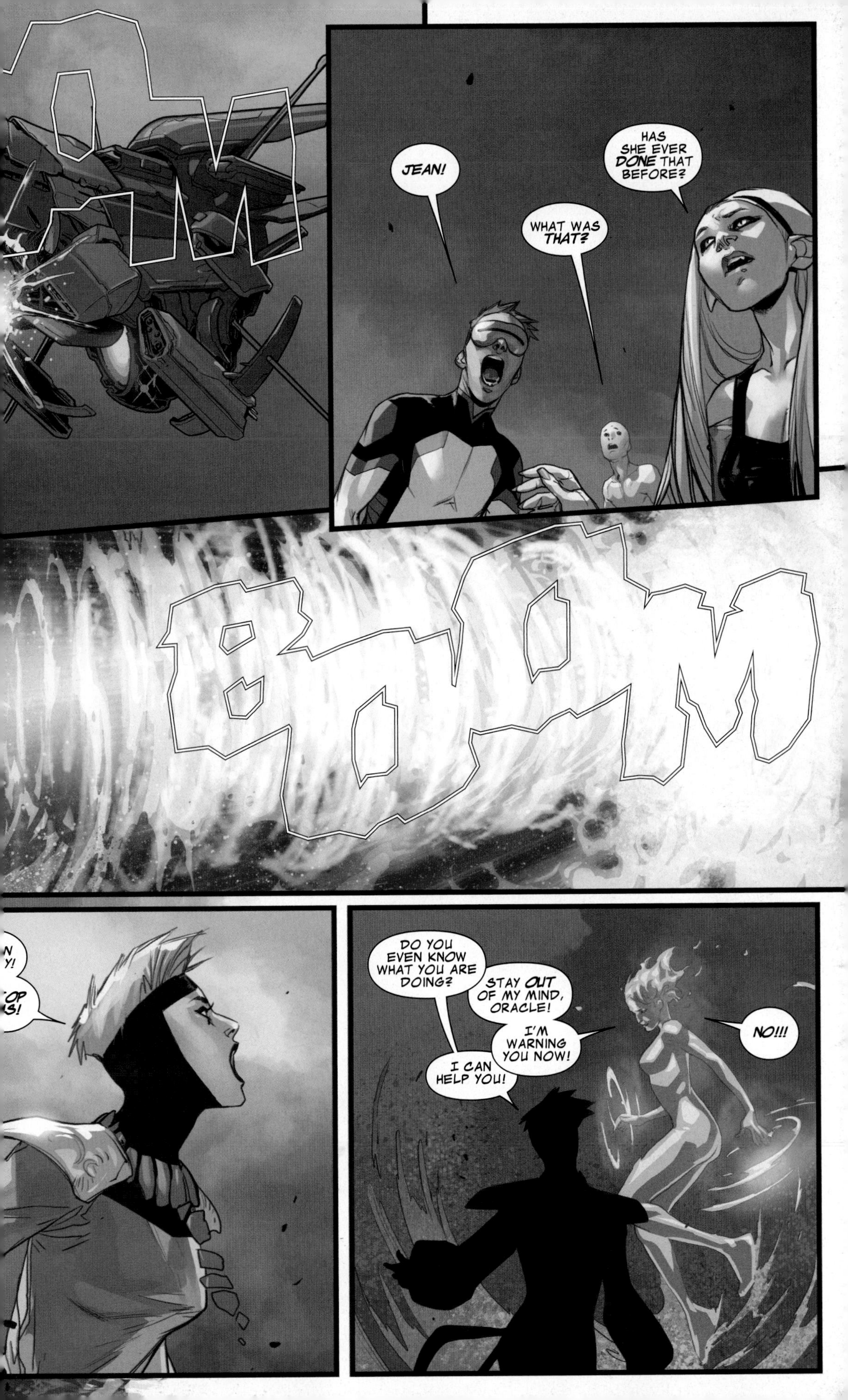
JEAN!
HAS SHE EVER DONE THAT BEFORE?
WHAT WAS THAT?
BOOM
DO YOU EVEN KNOW WHAT YOU ARE DOING?
STAY OUT OF MY MIND, ORACLE!
I'M WARNING YOU NOW!
I CAN HELP YOU!
NO!!!

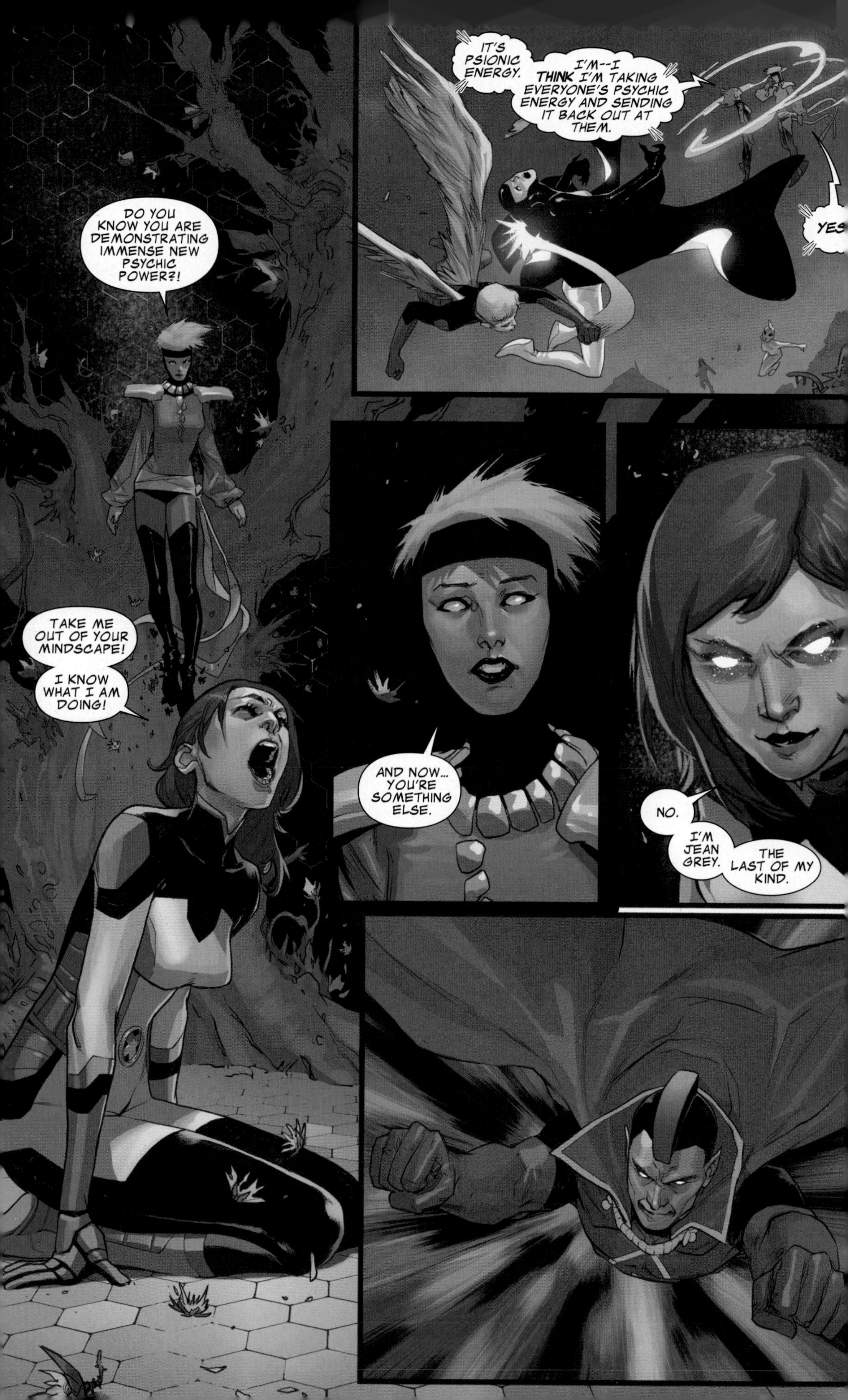
DO YOU KNOW YOU ARE DEMONSTRATING IMMENSE NEW PSYCHIC POWER?!
IT'S PSIONIC ENERGY.
I'M--I THINK I'M TAKING EVERYONE'S PSYCHIC ENERGY AND SENDING IT BACK OUT AT THEM.
YES
TAKE ME OUT OF YOUR MINDSCAPE!
I KNOW WHAT I AM DOING!
AND NOW... YOU'RE SOMETHING ELSE.
NO.
I'M JEAN GREY.
THE LAST OF MY KIND.

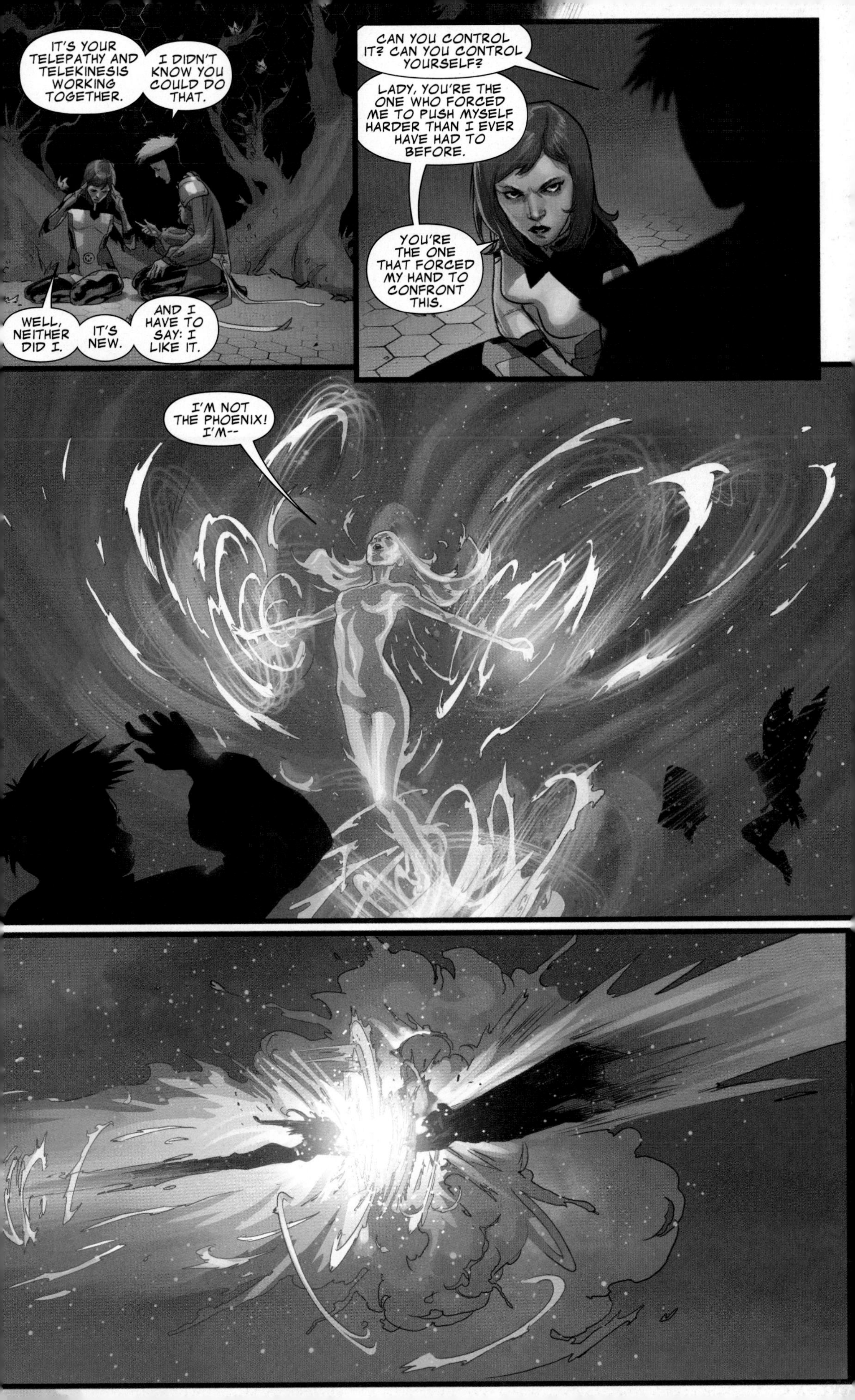
IT'S YOUR TELEPATHY AND TELEKINESIS WORKING TOGETHER.
I DIDN'T KNOW YOU COULD DO THAT.
WELL, NEITHER DID I.
IT'S NEW.
AND I HAVE TO SAY: I LIKE IT.
CAN YOU CONTROL IT? CAN YOU CONTROL YOURSELF?
LADY, YOU'RE THE ONE WHO FORCED ME TO PUSH MYSELF HARDER THAN I EVER HAVE HAD TO BEFORE.
YOU'RE THE ONE THAT FORCED MY HAND TO CONFRONT THIS.
I'M NOT THE PHOENIX! I'M--

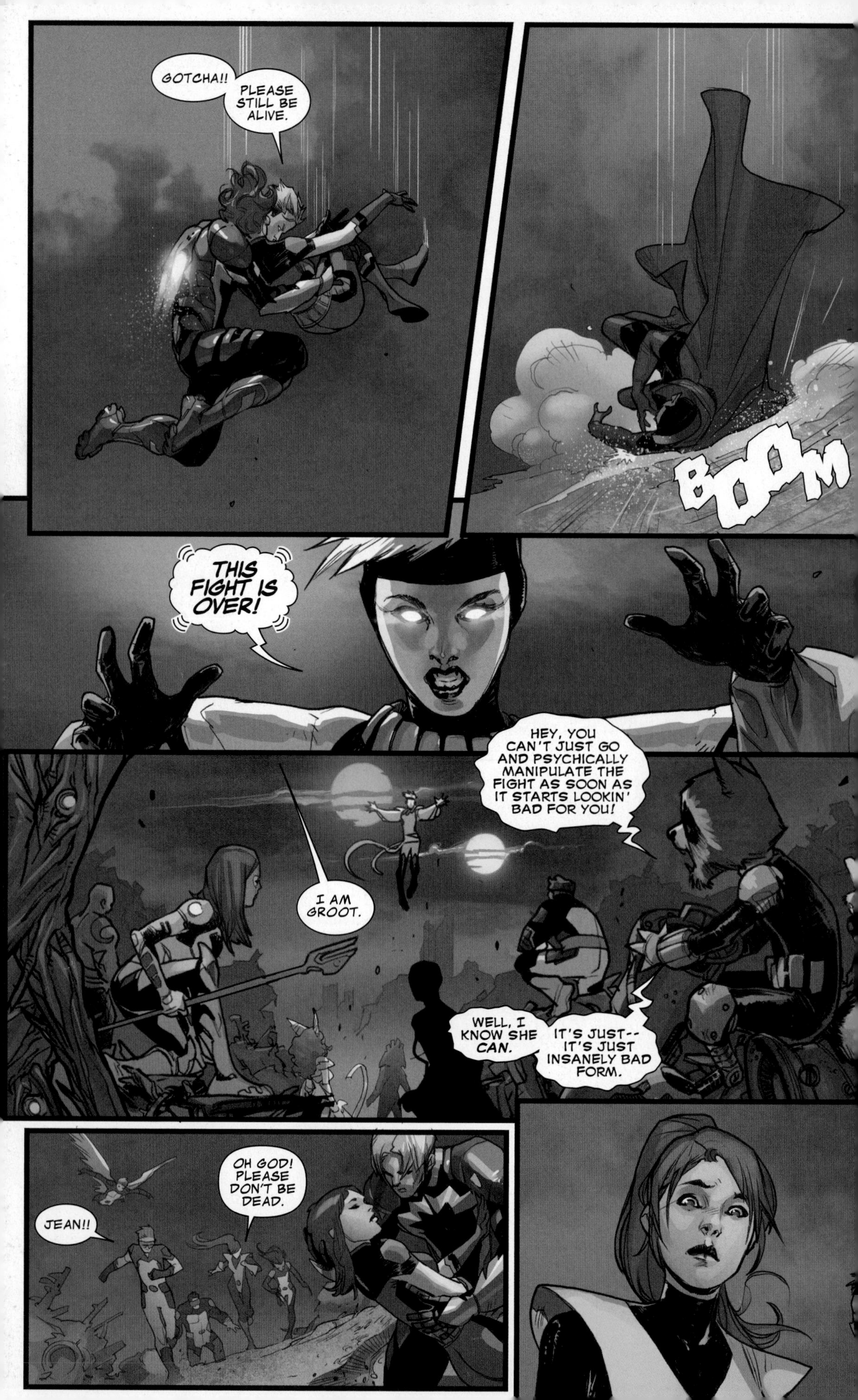

GOTCHA!!
PLEASE STILL BE ALIVE.
BOOM
THIS FIGHT IS OVER!
HEY, YOU CAN'T JUST GO AND PSYCHICALLY MANIPULATE THE FIGHT AS SOON AS IT STARTS LOOKIN' BAD FOR YOU!
I AM GROOT.
WELL, I KNOW SHE CAN.
IT'S JUST-- IT'S JUST INSANELY BAD FORM.
JEAN!!
OH GOD! PLEASE DON'T BE DEAD.

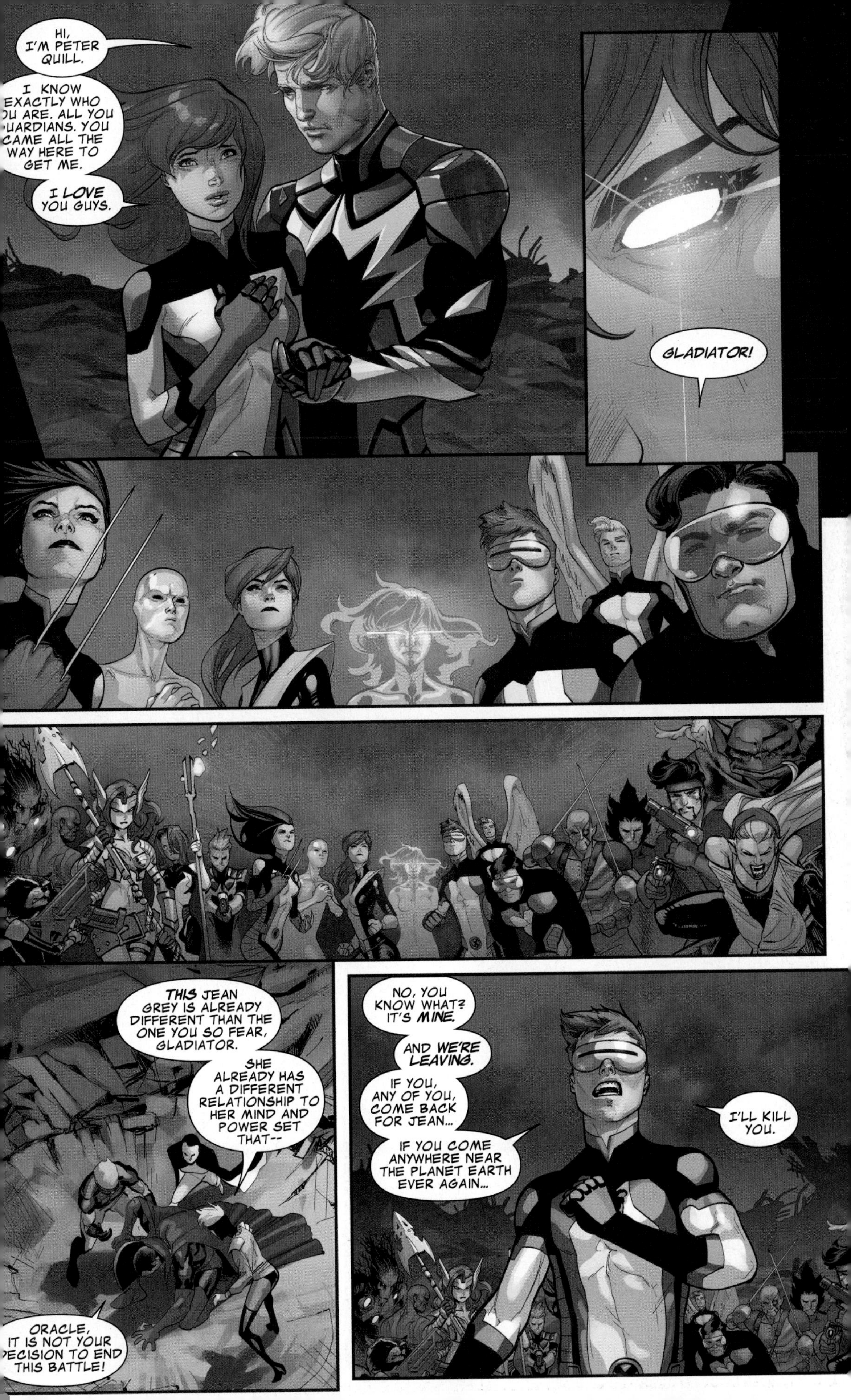
HI, I'M PETER QUILL.
I KNOW EXACTLY WHO YOU ARE. ALL YOU GUARDIANS. YOU CAME ALL THE WAY HERE TO GET ME.
I LOVE YOU GUYS.
GLADIATOR!
THIS JEAN GREY IS ALREADY DIFFERENT THAN THE ONE YOU SO FEAR, GLADIATOR.
SHE ALREADY HAS A DIFFERENT RELATIONSHIP TO HER MIND AND POWER SET THAT--
ORACLE, IT IS NOT YOUR DECISION TO END THIS BATTLE!
NO, YOU KNOW WHAT? IT'S MINE.
AND WE'RE LEAVING.
IF YOU, ANY OF YOU, COME BACK FOR JEAN...
IF YOU COME ANYWHERE NEAR THE PLANET EARTH EVER AGAIN...
I'LL KILL YOU.

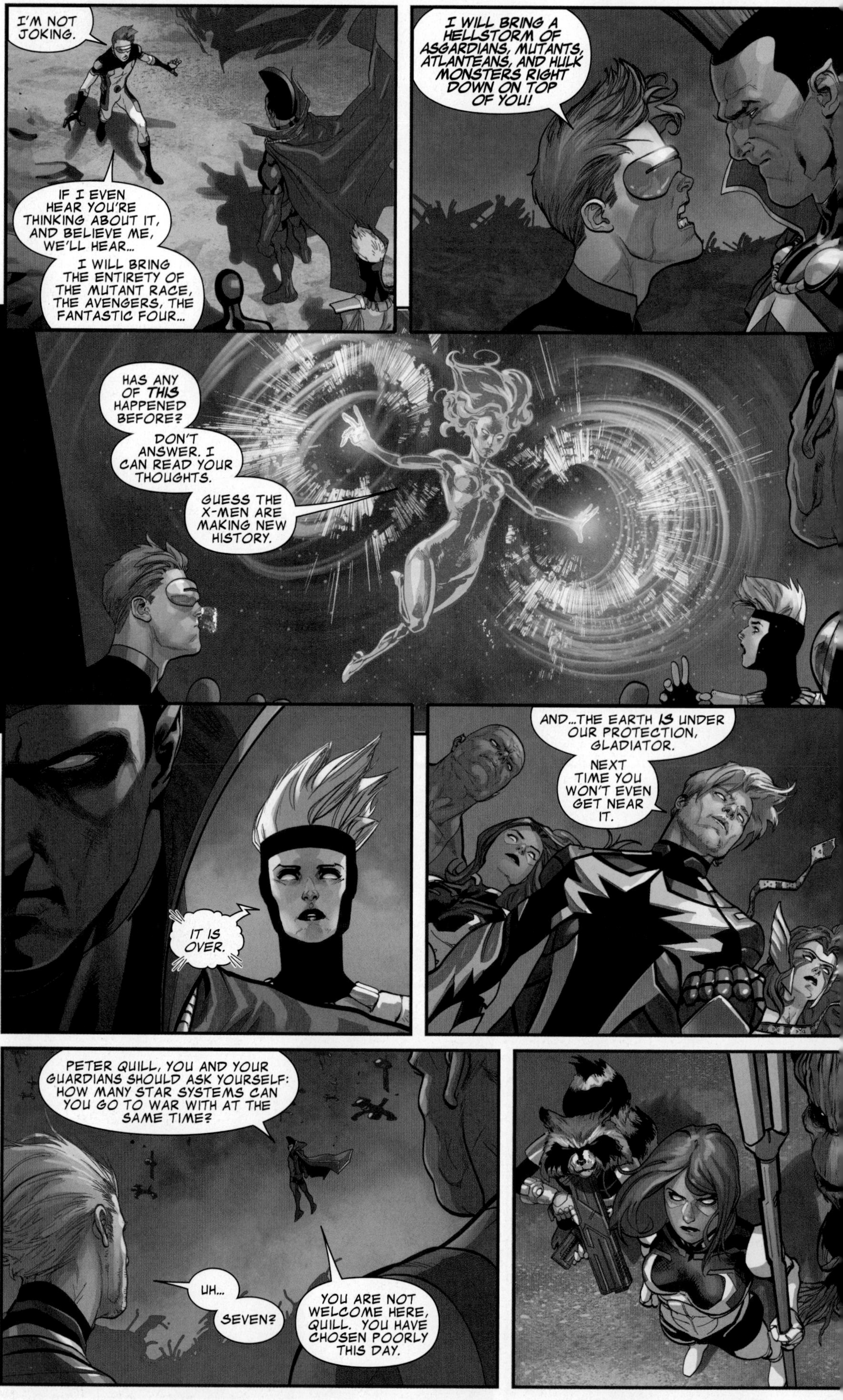
I'M NOT JOKING.
IF I EVEN HEAR YOU'RE THINKING ABOUT IT, AND BELIEVE ME, WE'LL HEAR...
I WILL BRING THE ENTIRETY OF THE MUTANT RACE, THE AVENGERS, THE FANTASTIC FOUR...
I WILL BRING A HELLSTORM OF ASGARDIANS, MUTANTS, ATLANTEANS, AND HULK MONSTERS RIGHT DOWN ON TOP OF YOU!
HAS ANY OF THIS HAPPENED BEFORE?
DON'T ANSWER. I CAN READ YOUR THOUGHTS.
GUESS THE X-MEN ARE MAKING NEW HISTORY.
IT IS OVER.
AND...THE EARTH IS UNDER OUR PROTECTION, GLADIATOR.
NEXT TIME YOU WON'T EVEN GET NEAR IT.
PETER QUILL, YOU AND YOUR GUARDIANS SHOULD ASK YOURSELF: HOW MANY STAR SYSTEMS CAN YOU GO TO WAR WITH AT THE SAME TIME?
UH...
SEVEN?
YOU ARE NOT WELCOME HERE, QUILL. YOU HAVE CHOSEN POORLY THIS DAY.

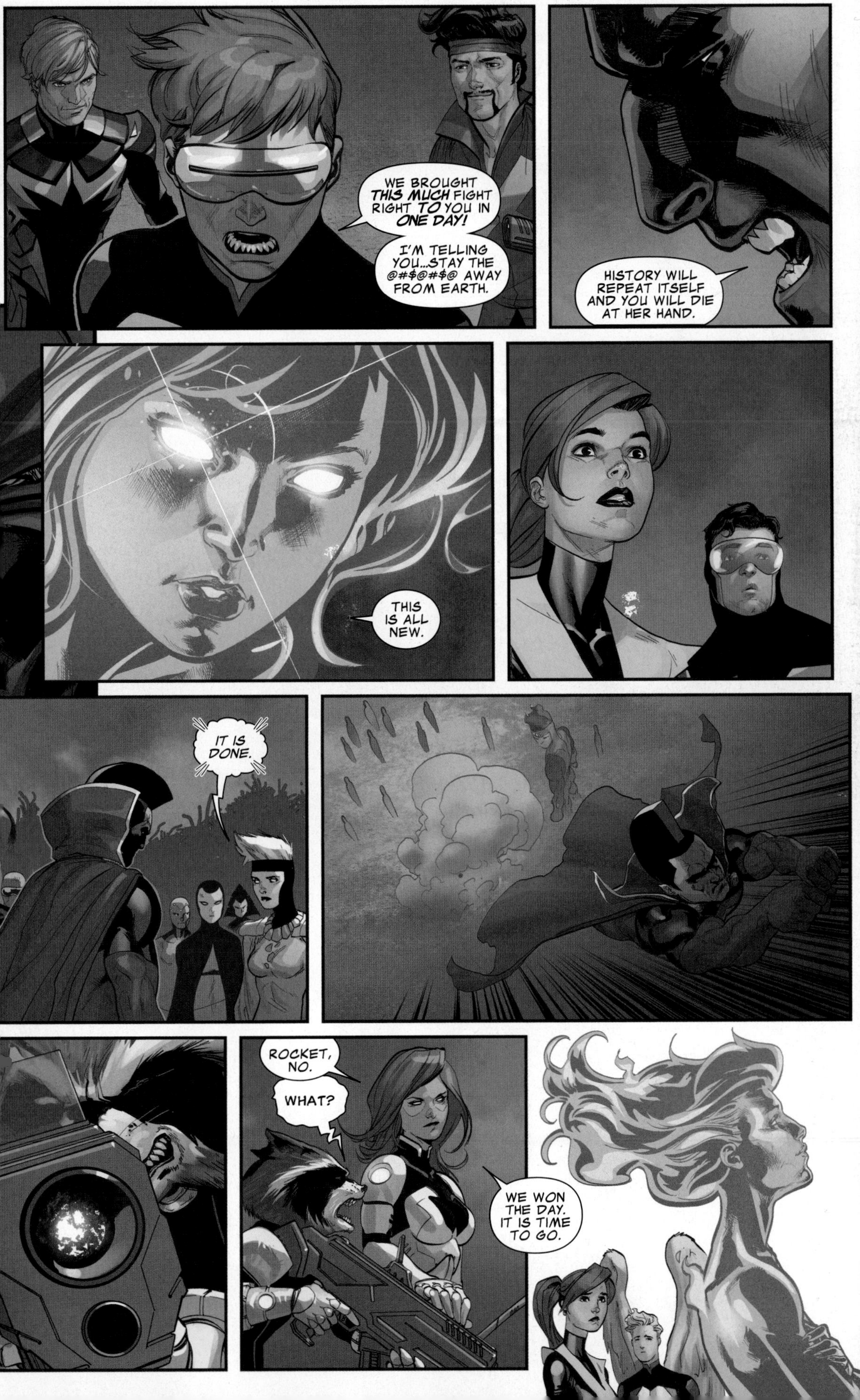
WE BROUGHT THIS MUCH FIGHT RIGHT TO YOU IN ONE DAY!
I'M TELLING YOU...STAY THE @#$@#$@ AWAY FROM EARTH.
HISTORY WILL REPEAT ITSELF AND YOU WILL DIE AT HER HAND.
THIS IS ALL NEW.
IT IS DONE.
ROCKET, NO.
WHAT?
WE WON THE DAY. IT IS TIME TO GO.

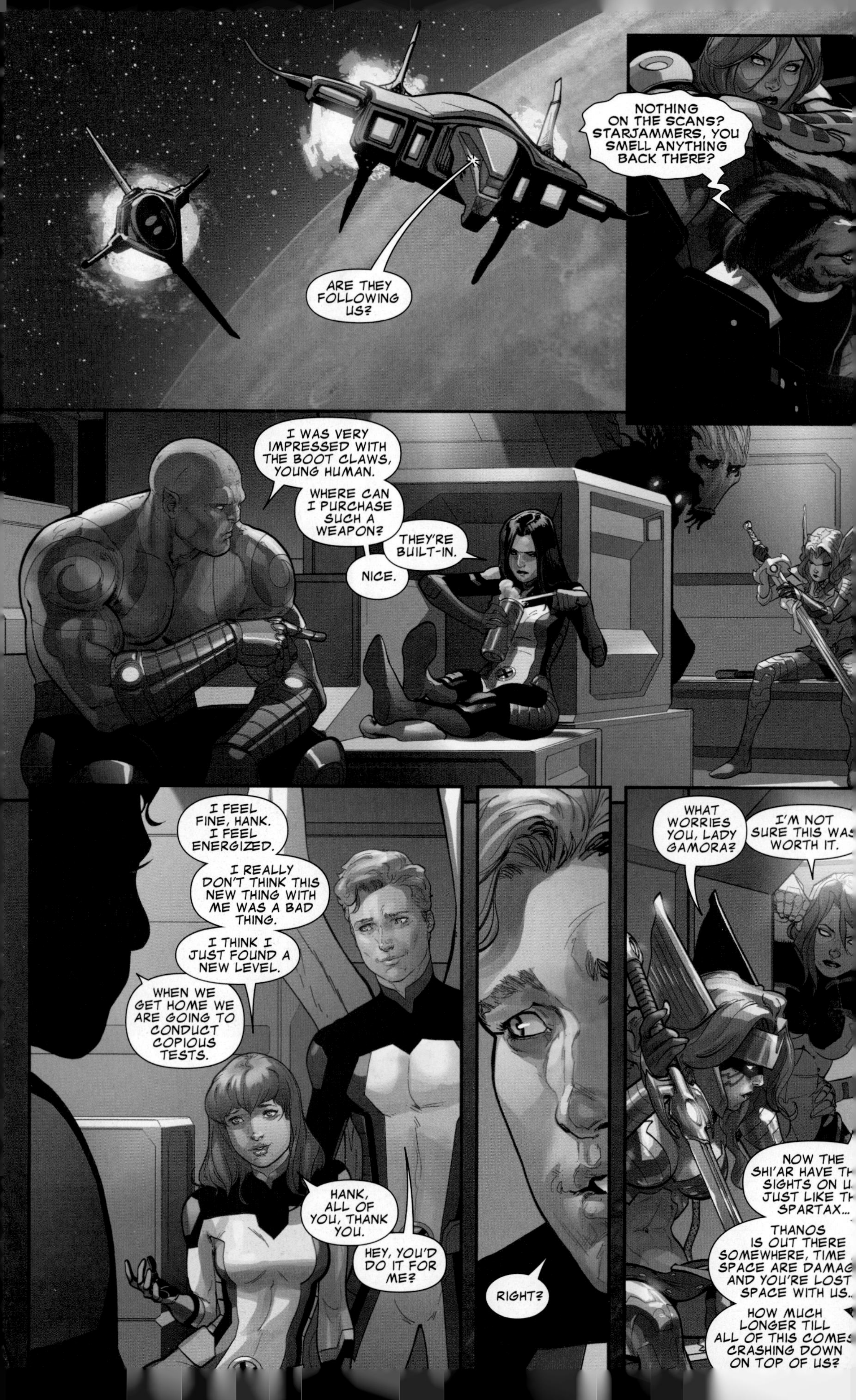
ARE THEY FOLLOWING US?
NOTHING ON THE SCANS? STARJAMMERS, YOU SMELL ANYTHING BACK THERE?
I WAS VERY IMPRESSED WITH THE BOOT CLAWS, YOUNG HUMAN.
WHERE CAN I PURCHASE SUCH A WEAPON?
THEY'RE BUILT-IN.
NICE.
I FEEL FINE, HANK. I FEEL ENERGIZED.
I REALLY DON'T THINK THIS NEW THING WITH ME WAS A BAD THING.
I THINK I JUST FOUND A NEW LEVEL.
WHEN WE GET HOME WE ARE GOING TO CONDUCT COPIOUS TESTS.
HANK, ALL OF YOU, THANK YOU.
HEY, YOU'D DO IT FOR ME?
RIGHT?
WHAT WORRIES YOU, LADY GAMORA?
I'M NOT SURE THIS WAS WORTH IT.
NOW THE SHI'AR HAVE TH SIGHTS ON U JUST LIKE TH SPARTAX...
THANOS IS OUT THERE SOMEWHERE, TIME SPACE ARE DAMAG AND YOU'RE LOST SPACE WITH US...
HOW MUCH LONGER TILL ALL OF THIS COMES CRASHING DOWN ON TOP OF US?

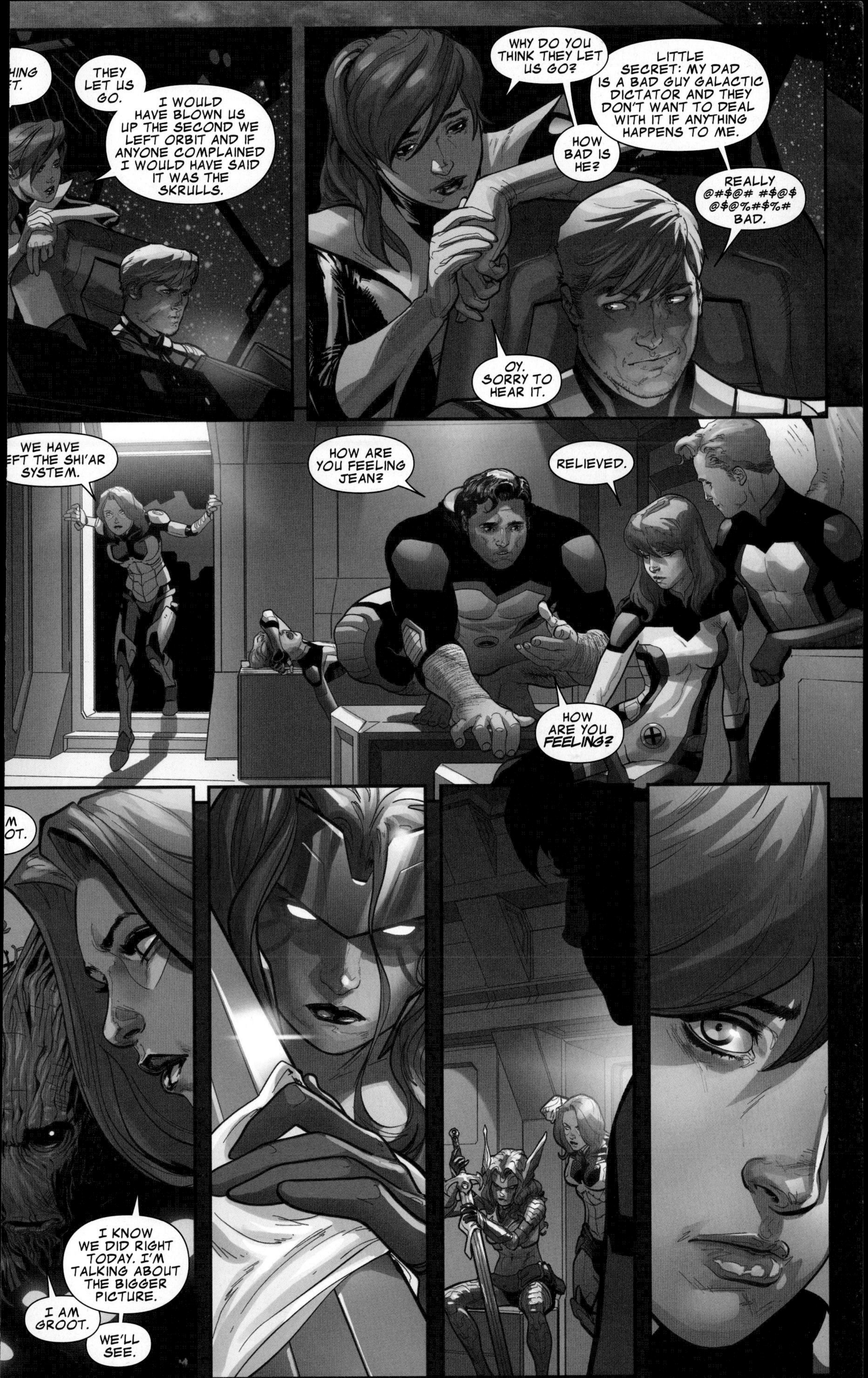

HING
FT.
THEY LET US GO.
I WOULD HAVE BLOWN US UP THE SECOND WE LEFT ORBIT AND IF ANYONE COMPLAINED I WOULD HAVE SAID IT WAS THE SKRULLS.
WHY DO YOU THINK THEY LET US GO?
LITTLE SECRET: MY DAD IS A BAD GUY GALACTIC DICTATOR AND THEY DON'T WANT TO DEAL WITH IT IF ANYTHING HAPPENS TO ME.
HOW BAD IS HE?
REALLY @#$@# #$@$ @$@%#$%# BAD.
OY. SORRY TO HEAR IT.
WE HAVE EFT THE SHI'AR SYSTEM.
HOW ARE YOU FEELING JEAN?
RELIEVED.
HOW ARE YOU FEELING?
M
OT.
I KNOW WE DID RIGHT TODAY. I'M TALKING ABOUT THE BIGGER PICTURE.
I AM GROOT.
WE'LL SEE.

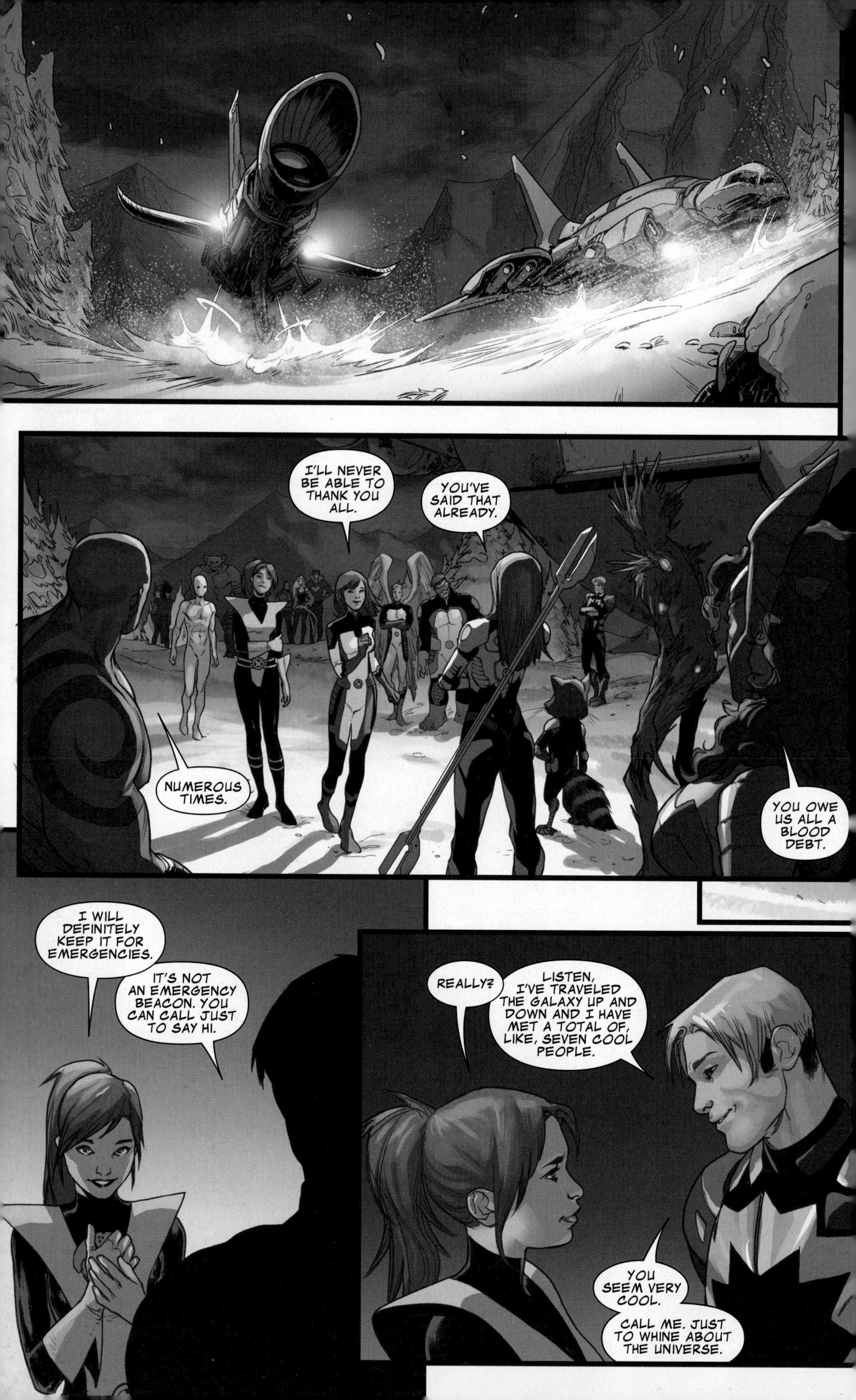
I'LL NEVER BE ABLE TO THANK YOU ALL.
YOU'VE SAID THAT ALREADY.
NUMEROUS TIMES.
YOU OWE US ALL A BLOOD DEBT.
I WILL DEFINITELY KEEP IT FOR EMERGENCIES.
IT'S NOT AN EMERGENCY BEACON. YOU CAN CALL JUST TO SAY HI.
REALLY?
LISTEN, I'VE TRAVELED THE GALAXY UP AND DOWN AND I HAVE MET A TOTAL OF, LIKE, SEVEN COOL PEOPLE.
YOU SEEM VERY COOL.
CALL ME. JUST TO WHINE ABOUT THE UNIVERSE.

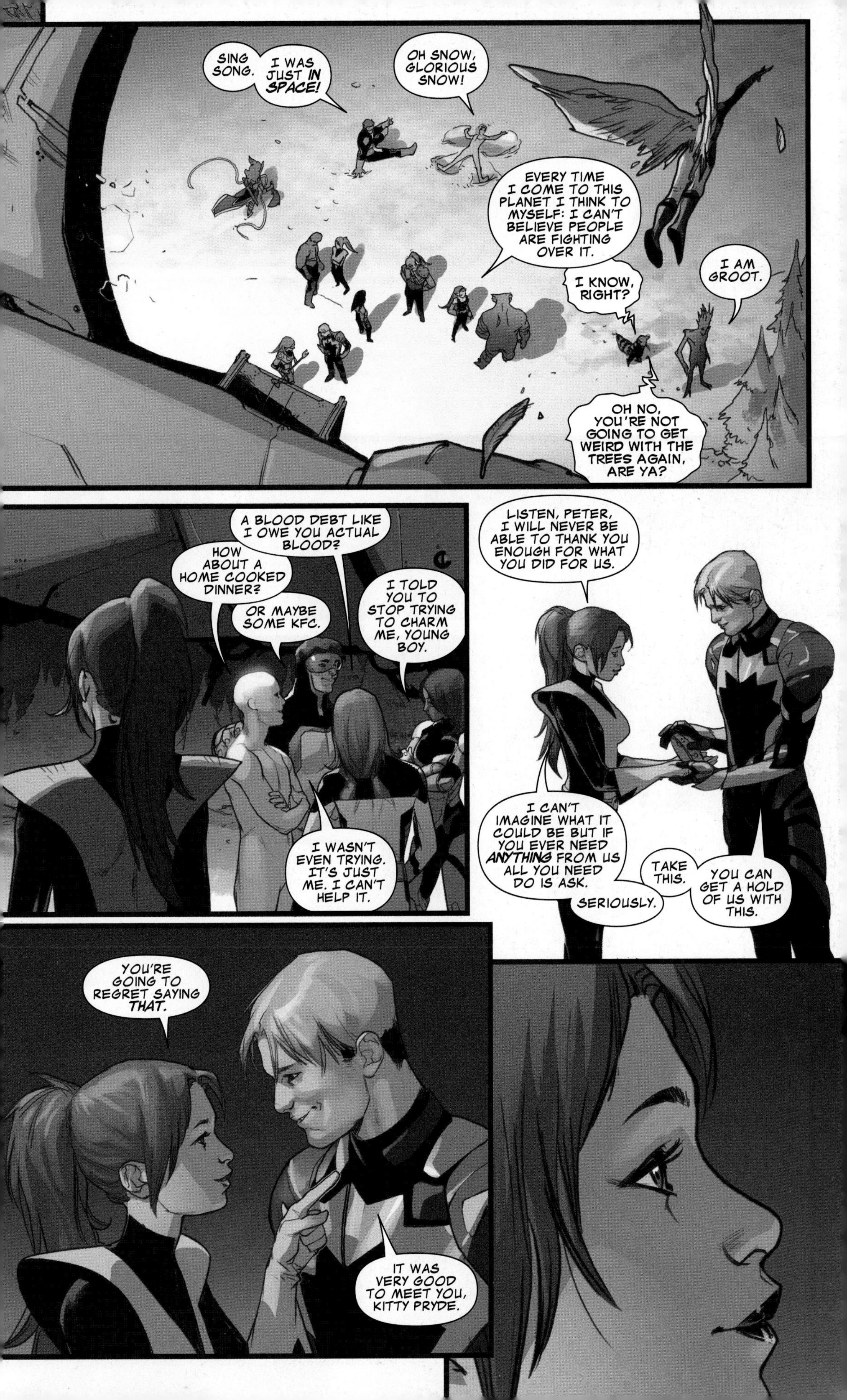
SING SONG.
I WAS JUST IN SPACE!
OH SNOW, GLORIOUS SNOW!
EVERY TIME I COME TO THIS PLANET I THINK TO MYSELF: I CAN'T BELIEVE PEOPLE ARE FIGHTING OVER IT.
I KNOW, RIGHT?
I AM GROOT.
OH NO, YOU'RE NOT GOING TO GET WEIRD WITH THE TREES AGAIN, ARE YA?
HOW ABOUT A HOME COOKED DINNER?
A BLOOD DEBT LIKE I OWE YOU ACTUAL BLOOD?
OR MAYBE SOME KFC.
I TOLD YOU TO STOP TRYING TO CHARM ME, YOUNG BOY.
I WASN'T EVEN TRYING. IT'S JUST ME. I CAN'T HELP IT.
LISTEN, PETER, I WILL NEVER BE ABLE TO THANK YOU ENOUGH FOR WHAT YOU DID FOR US.
I CAN'T IMAGINE WHAT IT COULD BE BUT IF YOU EVER NEED ANYTHING FROM US ALL YOU NEED DO IS ASK.
SERIOUSLY.
TAKE THIS.
YOU CAN GET A HOLD OF US WITH THIS.
YOU'RE GOING TO REGRET SAYING THAT.
IT WAS VERY GOOD TO MEET YOU, KITTY PRYDE.

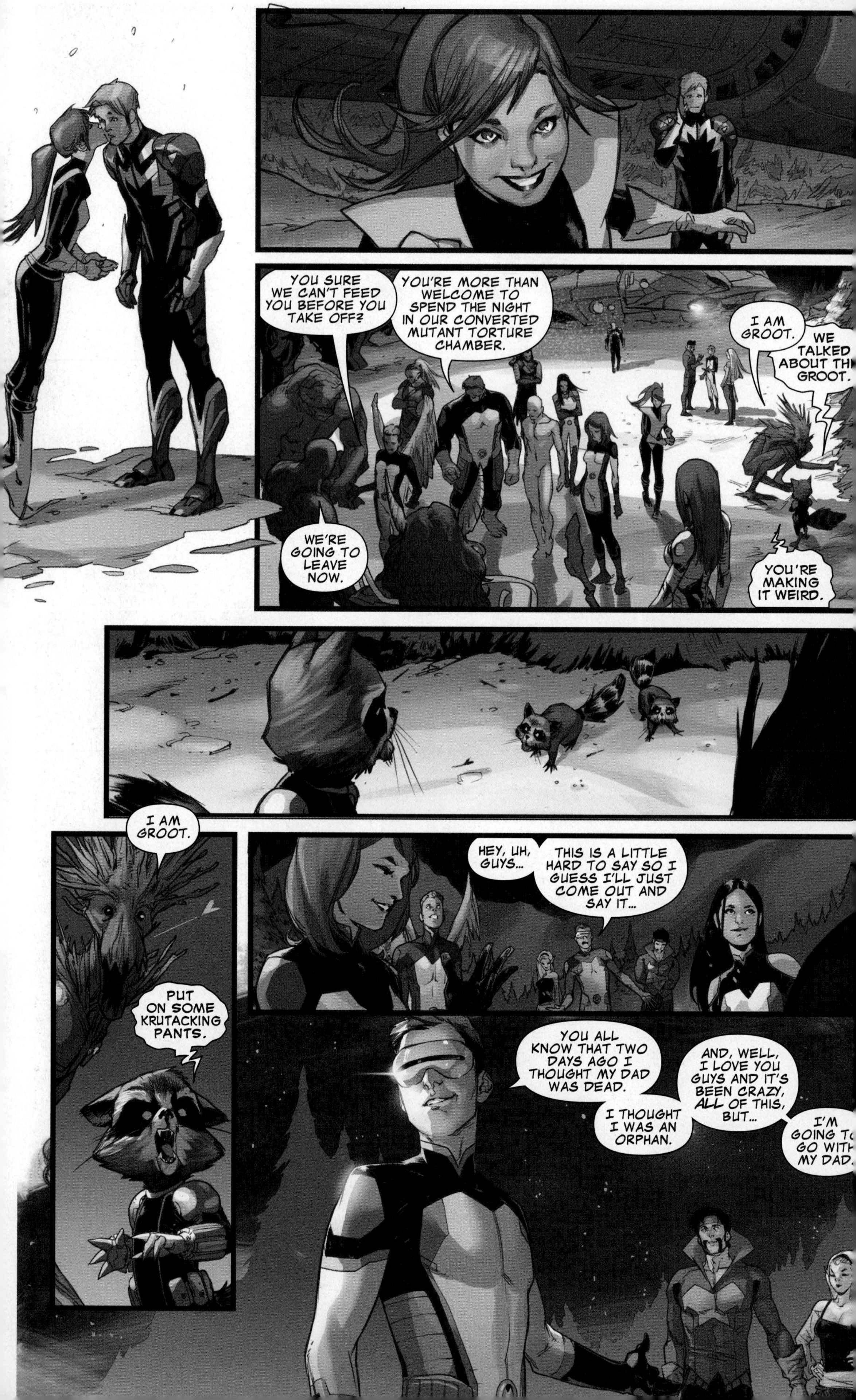
YOU SURE WE CAN'T FEED YOU BEFORE YOU TAKE OFF?
YOU'RE MORE THAN WELCOME TO SPEND THE NIGHT IN OUR CONVERTED MUTANT TORTURE CHAMBER.
WE'RE GOING TO LEAVE NOW.
I AM GROOT.
WE TALKED ABOUT TH GROOT.
YOU'RE MAKING IT WEIRD.
I AM GROOT.
PUT ON SOME KRUTACKING PANTS.
HEY, UH, GUYS...
THIS IS A LITTLE HARD TO SAY SO I GUESS I'LL JUST COME OUT AND SAY IT...
YOU ALL KNOW THAT TWO DAYS AGO I THOUGHT MY DAD WAS DEAD.
I THOUGHT I WAS AN ORPHAN.
AND, WELL, I LOVE YOU GUYS AND IT'S BEEN CRAZY, ALL OF THIS, BUT...
I'M GOING T GO WITH MY DAD.

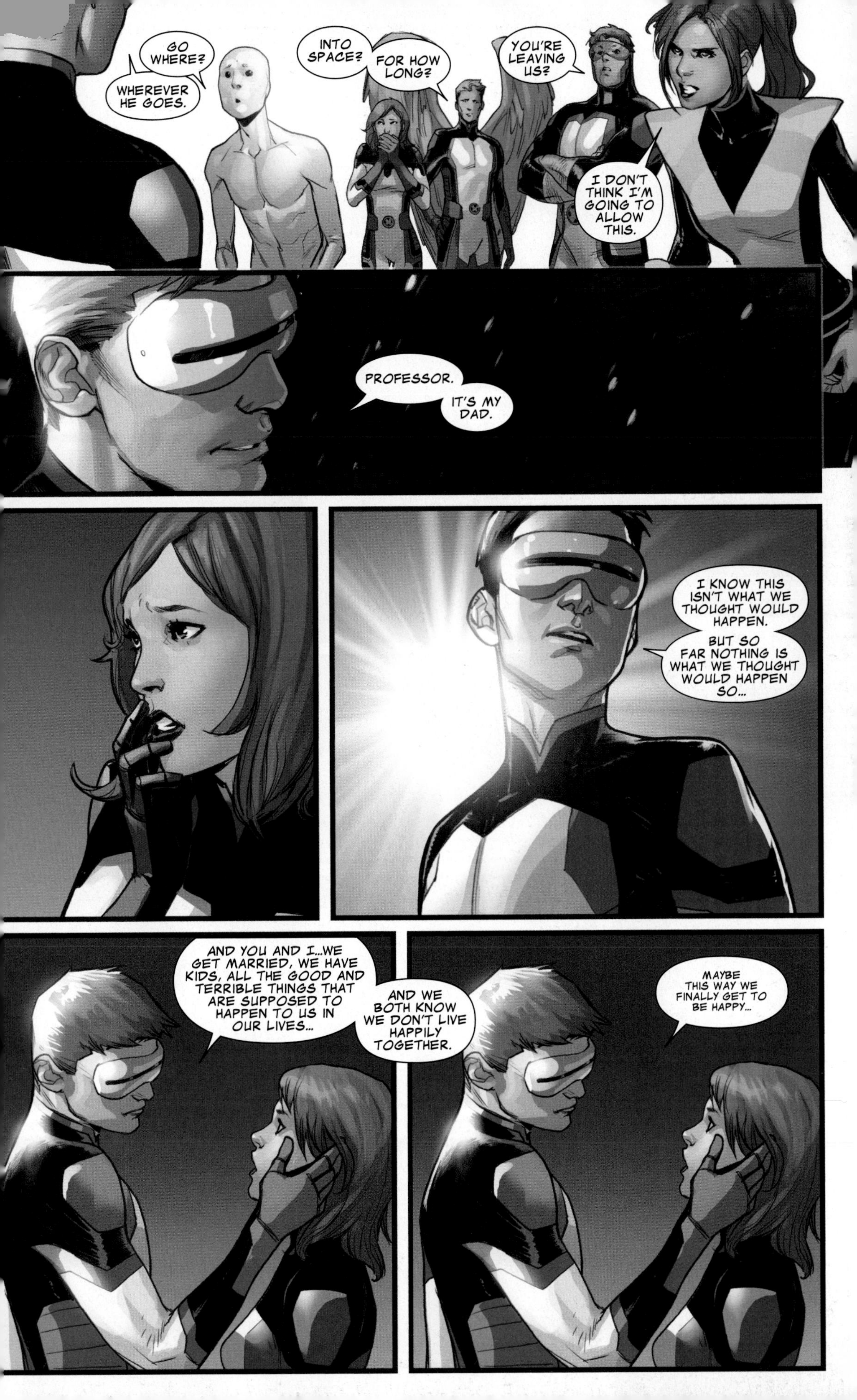
GO WHERE?
WHEREVER HE GOES.
INTO SPACE?
FOR HOW LONG?
YOU'RE LEAVING US?
I DON'T THINK I'M GOING TO ALLOW THIS.
PROFESSOR.
IT'S MY DAD.
I KNOW THIS ISN'T WHAT WE THOUGHT WOULD HAPPEN.
BUT SO FAR NOTHING IS WHAT WE THOUGHT WOULD HAPPEN SO...
AND YOU AND I...WE GET MARRIED, WE HAVE KIDS, ALL THE GOOD AND TERRIBLE THINGS THAT ARE SUPPOSED TO HAPPEN TO US IN OUR LIVES...
AND WE BOTH KNOW WE DON'T LIVE HAPPILY TOGETHER.
MAYBE THIS WAY WE FINALLY GET TO BE HAPPY...

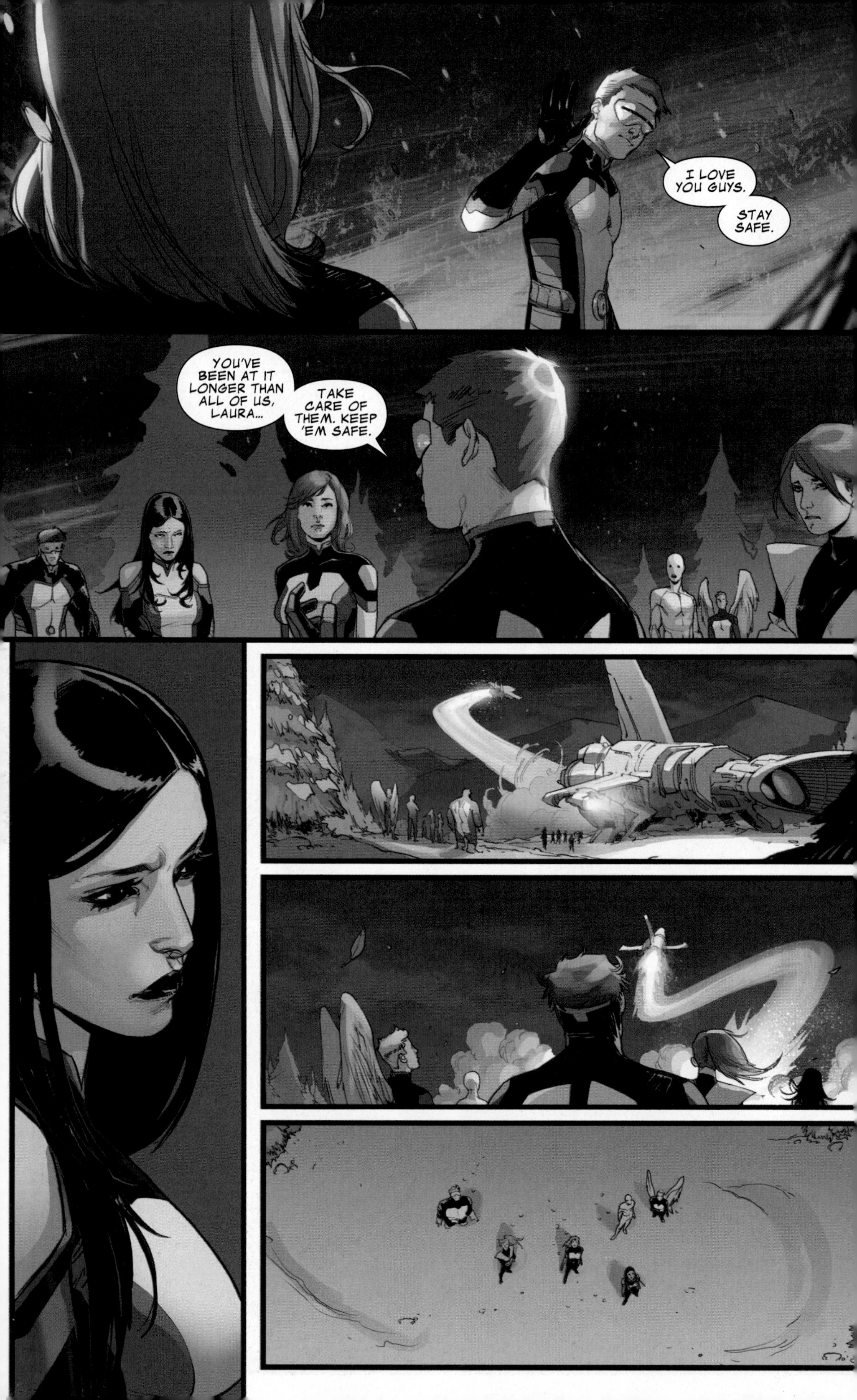
I LOVE YOU GUYS.
STAY SAFE.
YOU'VE BEEN AT IT LONGER THAN ALL OF US, LAURA...
TAKE CARE OF THEM. KEEP 'EM SAFE.

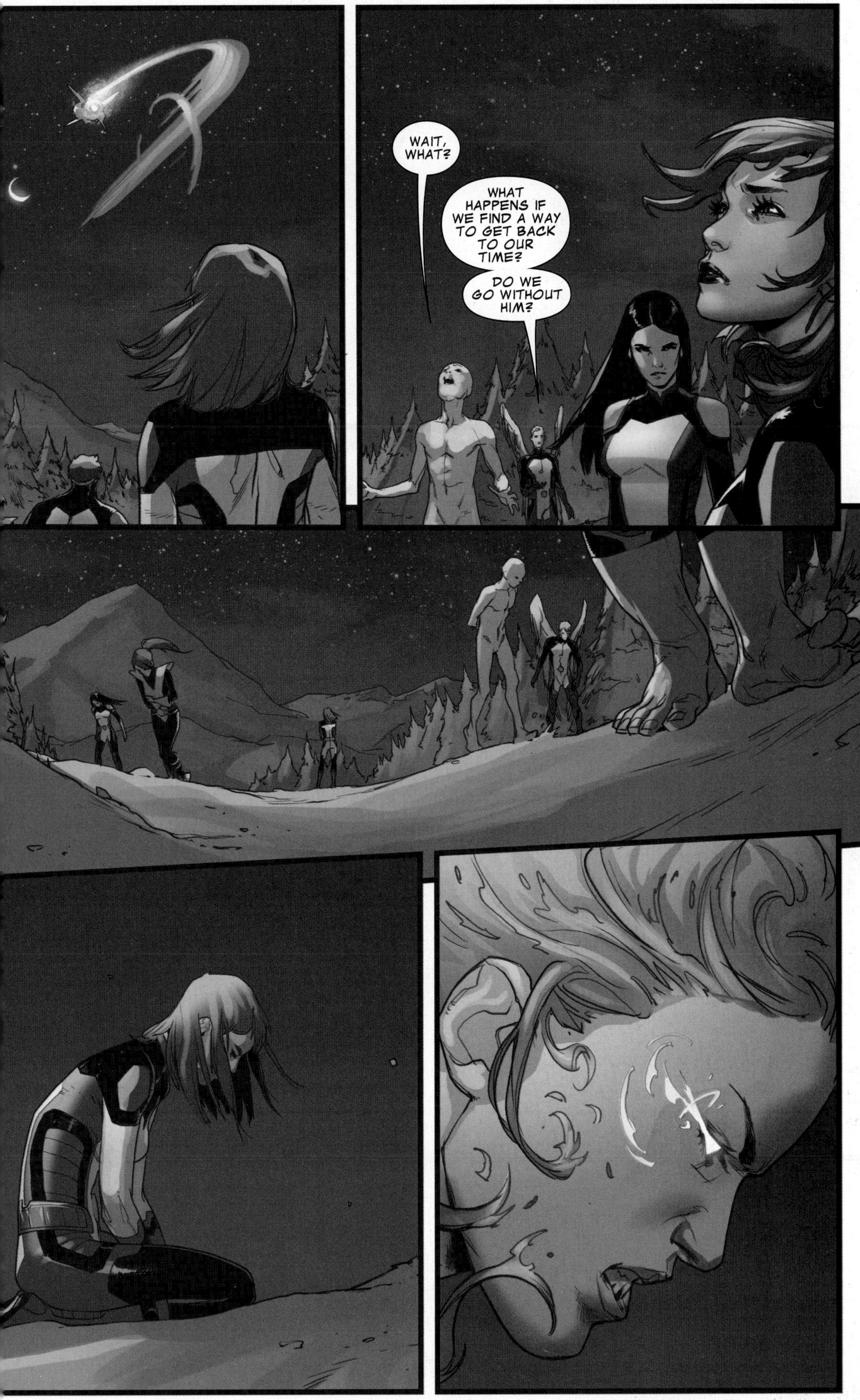
WAIT, WHAT?
WHAT HAPPENS IF WE FIND A WAY TO GET BACK TO OUR TIME?
DO WE GO WITHOUT HIM?

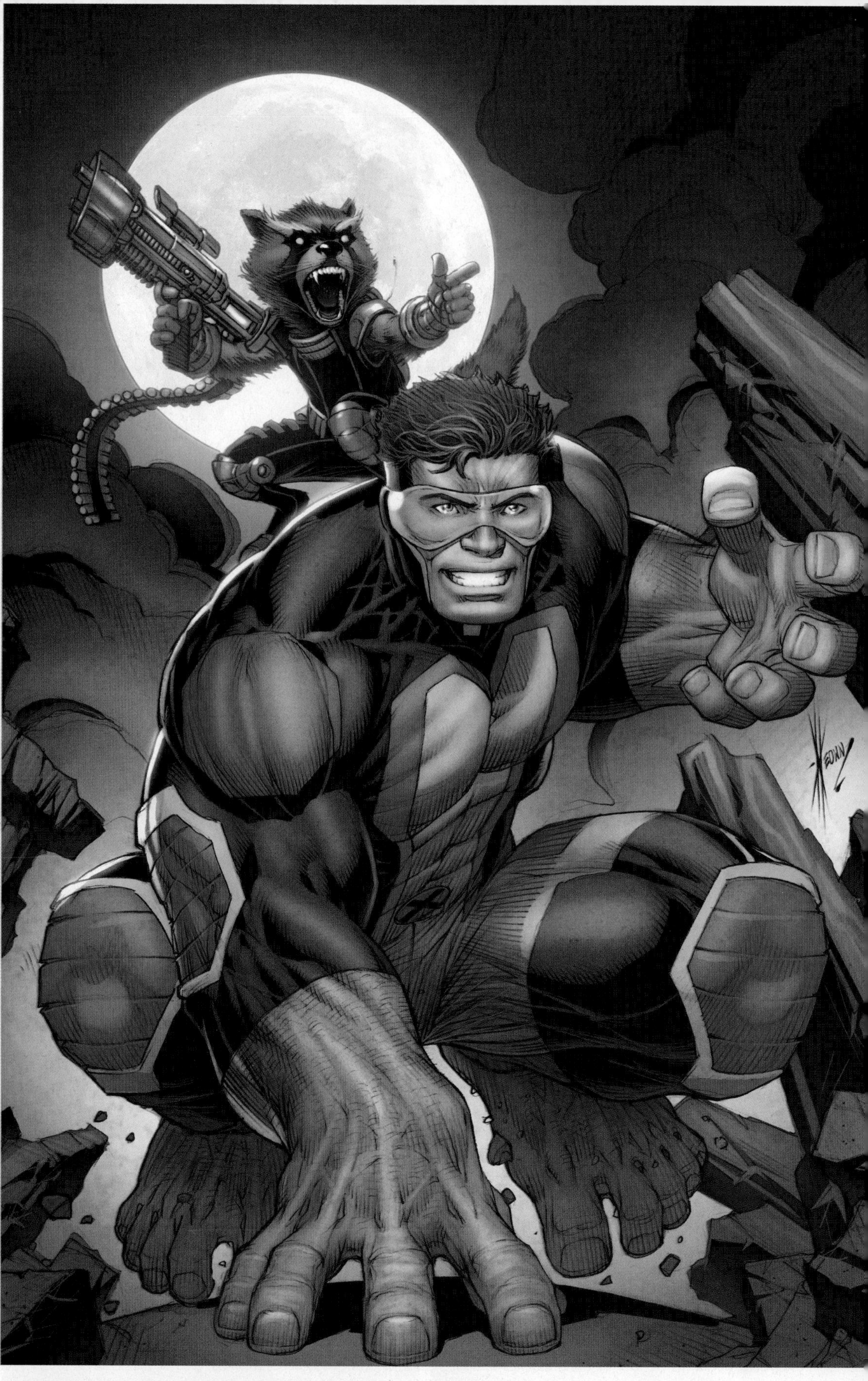

GUARDIANS OF THE GALAXY *#11* VARIANT
BY DALE KEOWN & JASON KEITH

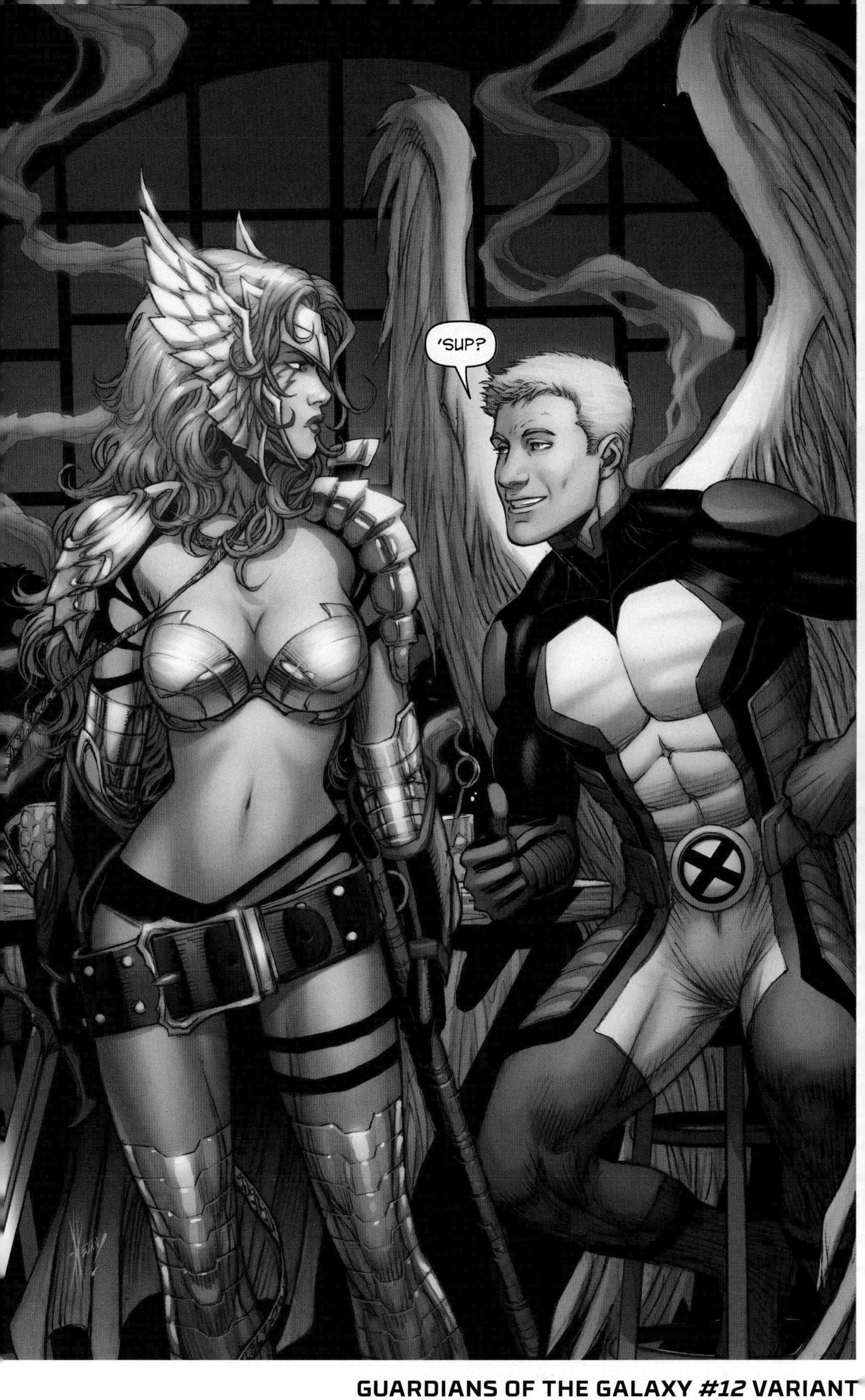
'SUP?

GUARDIANS OF THE GALAXY *#12* VARIANT
BY DALE KEOWN & JASON KEITH

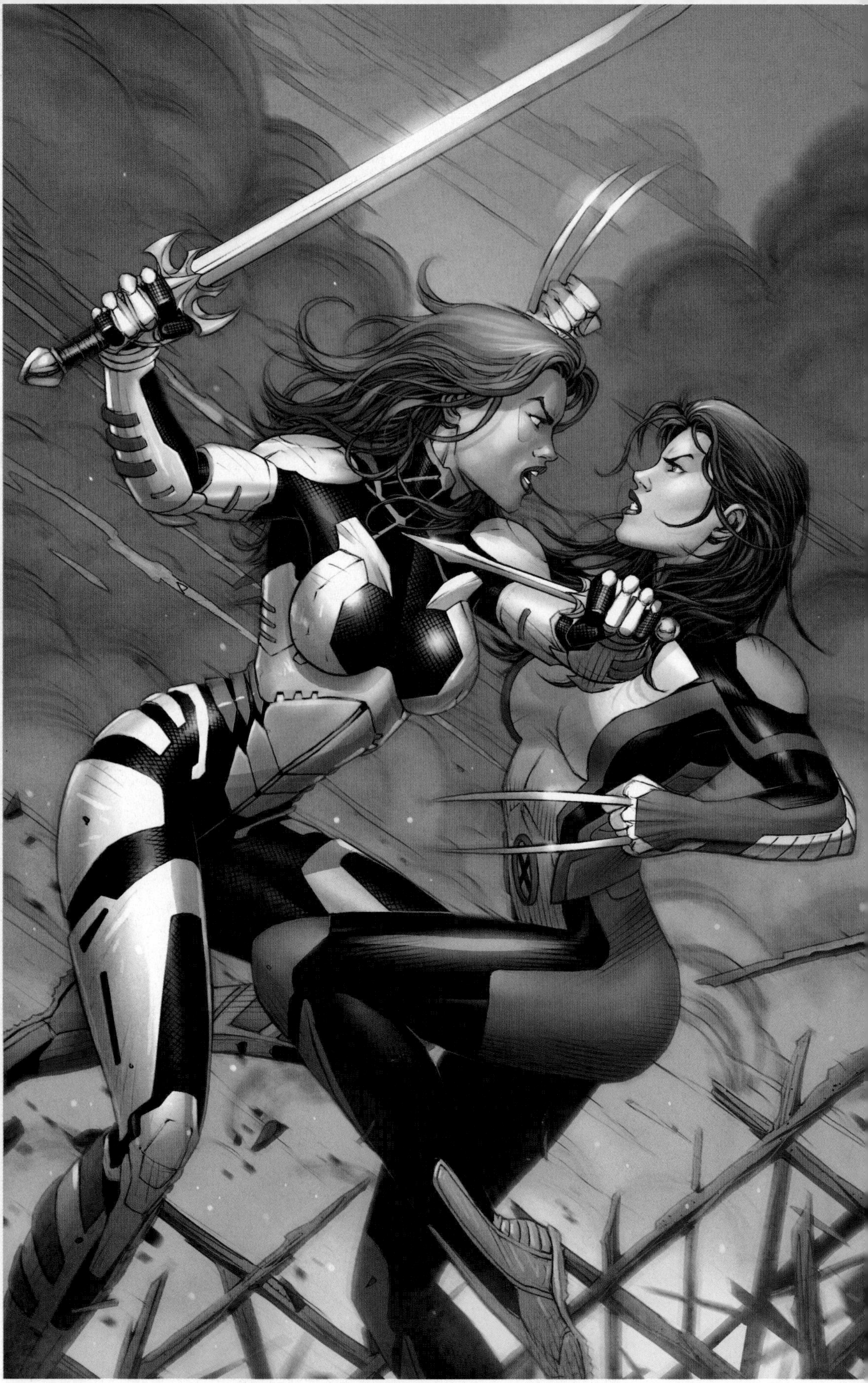

GUARDIANS OF THE GALAXY *#13* VARIANT
BY DALE KEOWN & JASON KEITH

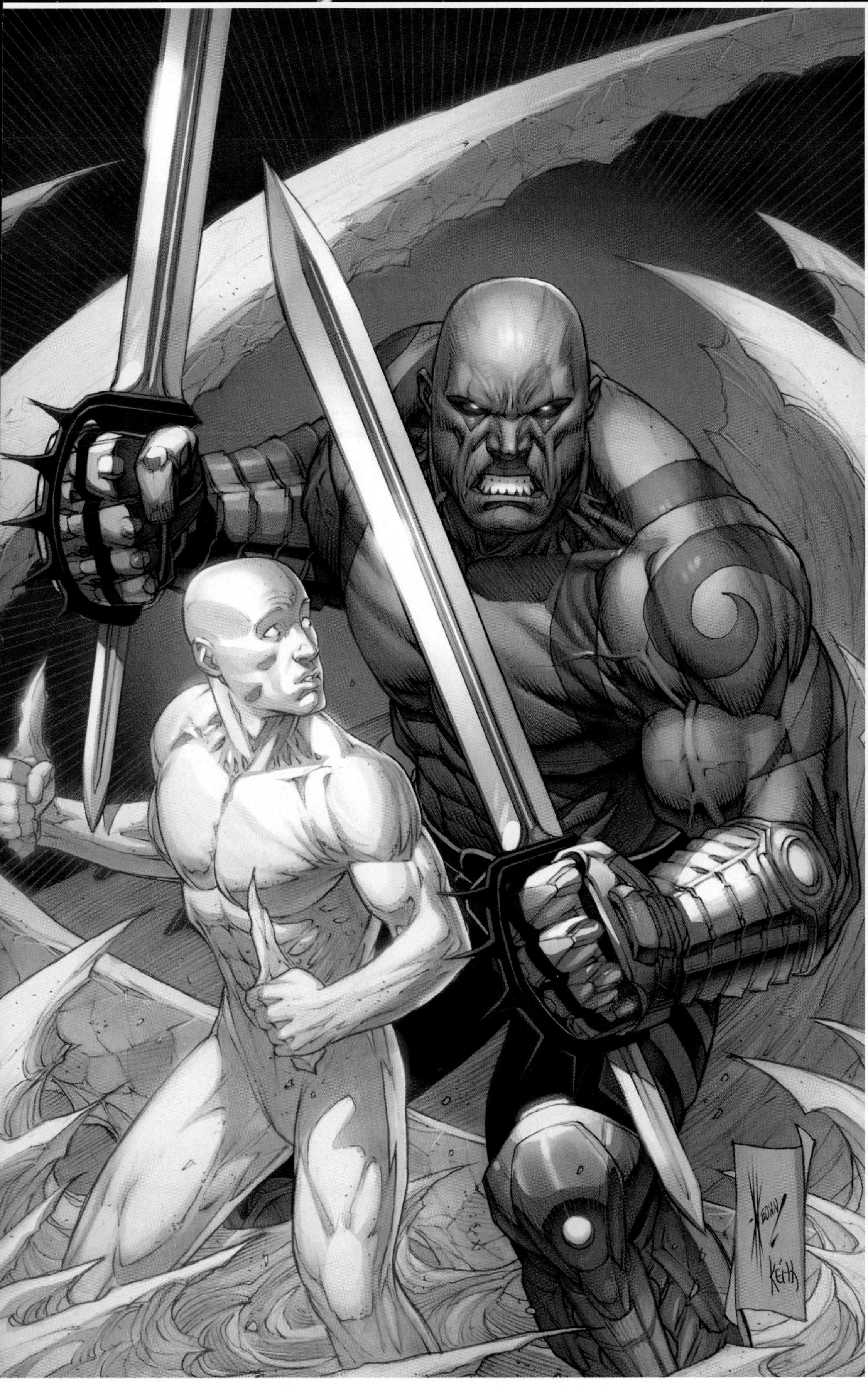

ALL-NEW X-MEN *#22* VARIANT
BY DALE KEOWN & JASON KEITH

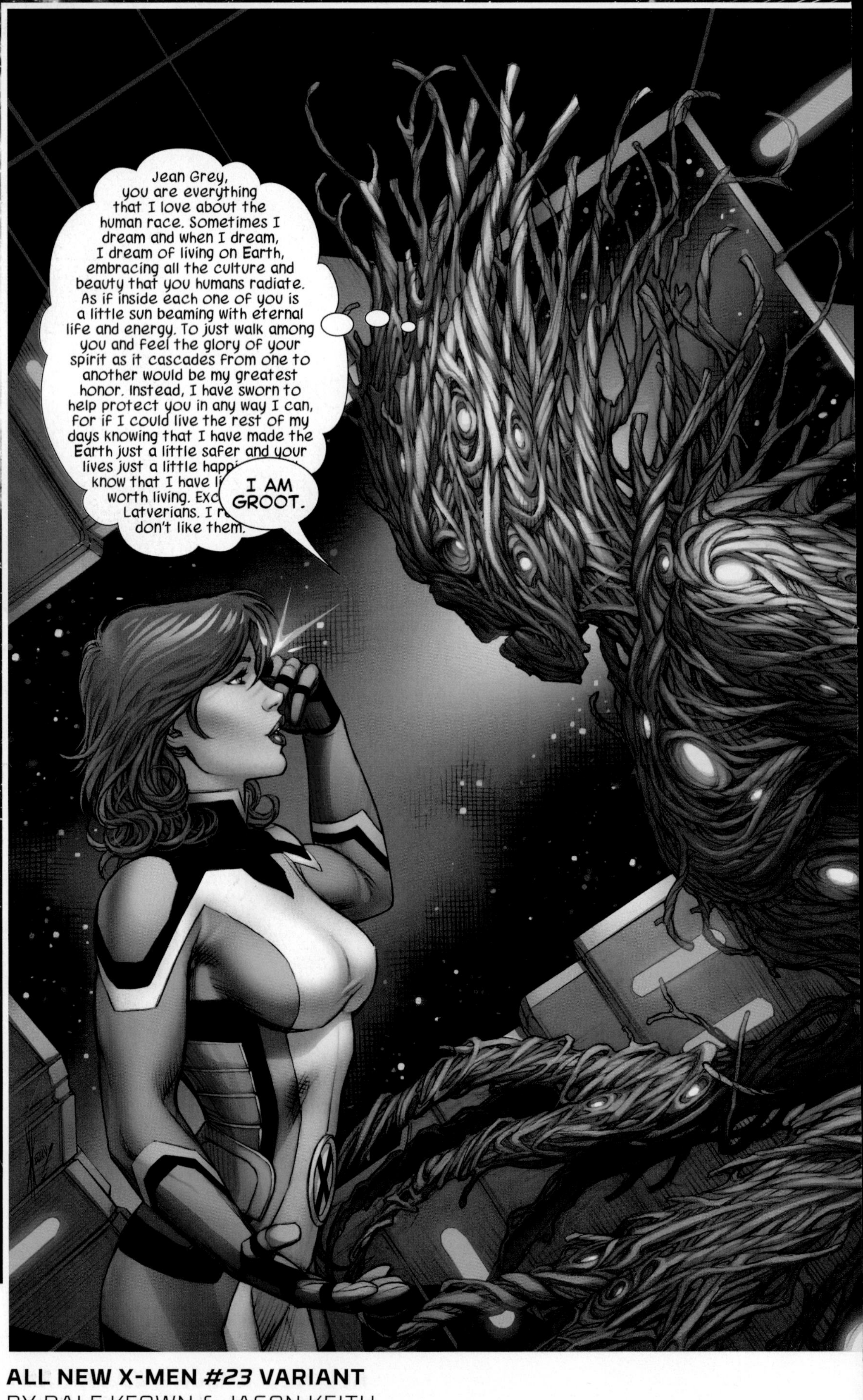
Jean Grey, you are everything that I love about the human race. Sometimes I dream and when I dream, I dream of living on Earth, embracing all the culture and beauty that you humans radiate. As if inside each one of you is a little sun beaming with eternal life and energy. To just walk among you and feel the glory of your spirit as it cascades from one to another would be my greatest honor. Instead, I have sworn to help protect you in any way I can, for if I could live the rest of my days knowing that I have made the Earth just a little safer and your lives just a little happi
know that I have li
worth living. Exc
Latverians. I r
don't like them.
I AM GROOT.

ALL NEW X-MEN *#23* VARIANT
BY DALE KEOWN & JASON KEITH

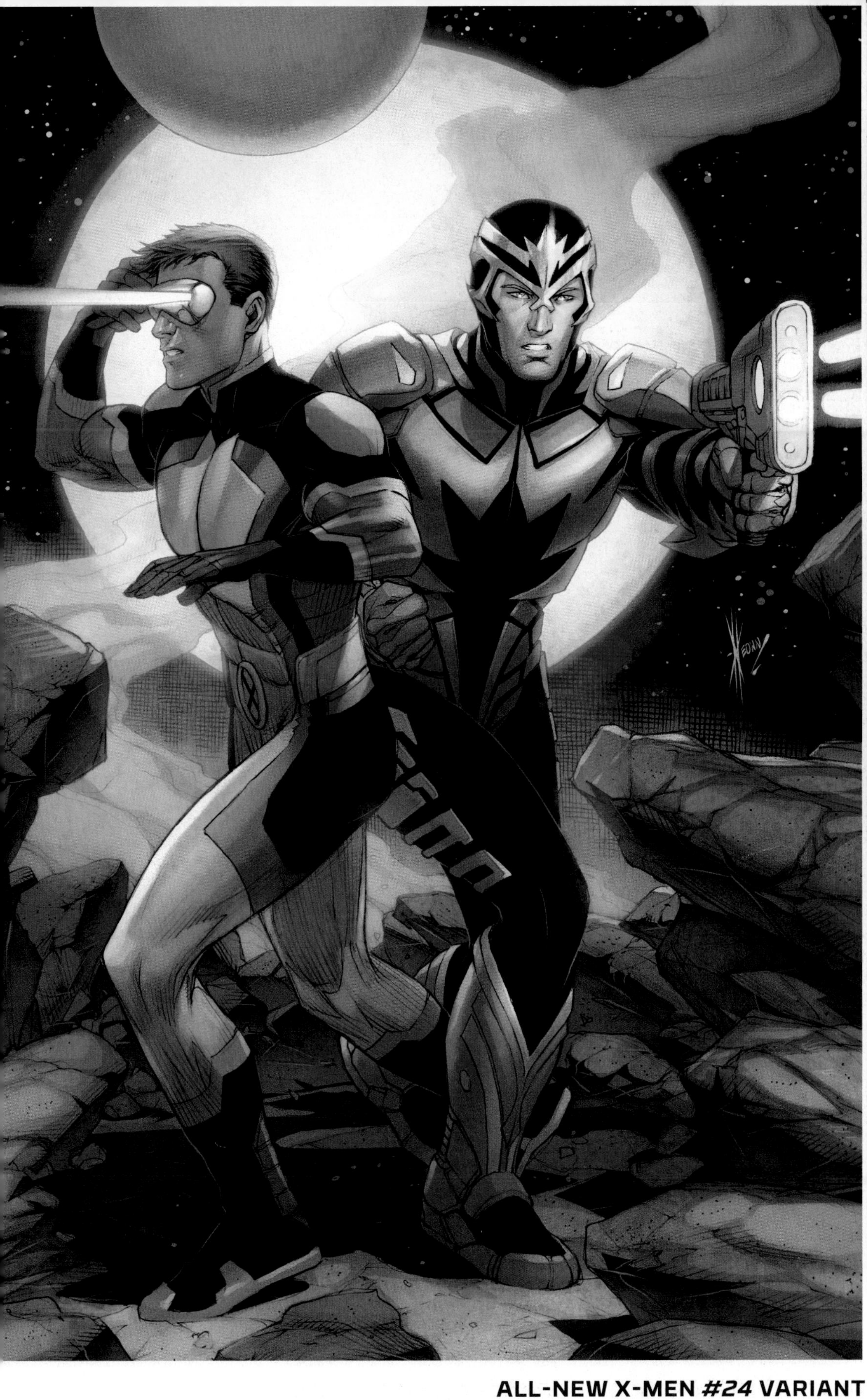

ALL-NEW X-MEN #24 VARIANT
BY DALE KEOWN & JASON KEITH

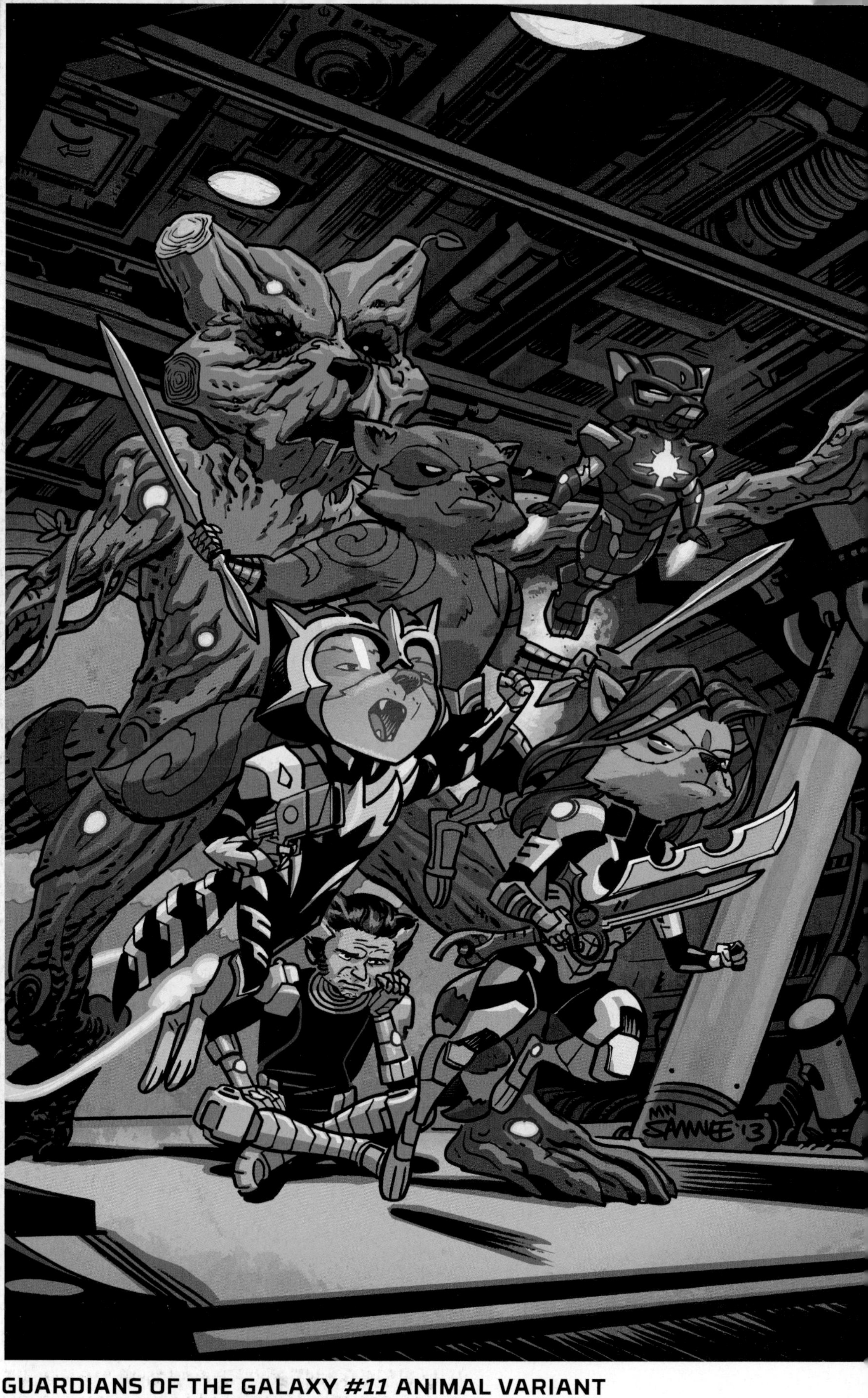
MW SAMNEE '13

GUARDIANS OF THE GALAXY *#11* ANIMAL VARIANT
BY CHRIS SAMNEE & MATTHEW WILSON

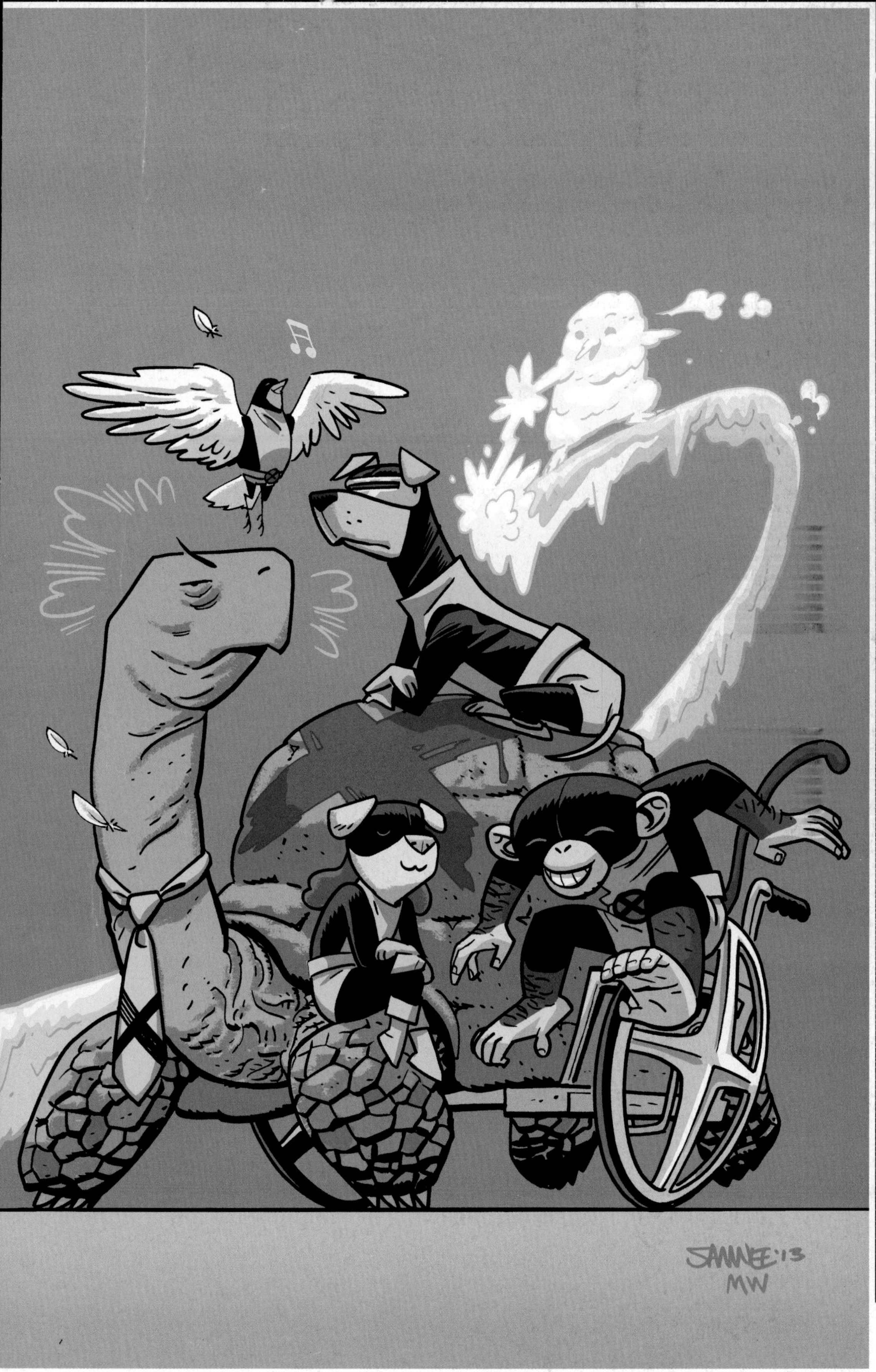
SAMNEE '13
MW

ALL-NEW X-MEN *#22* ANIMAL VARIANT
BY CHRIS SAMNEE & MATTHEW WILSON

MARVEL AR AUGMENTED REALITY

MARVEL AUGMENTED REALITY (AR) ENHANCES AND CHANGES THE WAY YOU EXPERIENCE COMICS!

TO ACCESS THE FREE MARVEL AR CONTENT IN THIS BOOK*:

1. Locate the AR logo within the comic.
2. Go to Marvel.com/AR in your web browser.
3. Search by series title to find the corresponding AR.
4. Enjoy Marvel AR!

*All AR content that appears in this book has been archived and will be available only at Marvel.com/AR – no longer in the Marvel AR App. Content subject to change and availability.